REASSESSING JEWISH LIFE IN MEDIEVAL EUROPE

This book reevaluates the prevailing notion that Jews in medieval Christian Europe lived under an appalling regime of ecclesiastical limitation, governmental exploitation and expropriation, and unceasing popular violence. Robert Chazan argues that, because Jewish life in medieval Western Christendom was indeed beset with grave difficulties, it was nevertheless an environment rich in opportunities; the Jews of medieval Europe overcame obstacles, grew in number, explored innovative economic options, and fashioned enduring new forms of Jewish living. His research also provides a reconsideration of the legacy of medieval Jewish life, which is often depicted as wholly destructive and projected as the underpinning of the twentieth-century catastrophes of antisemitism and the Holocaust. Dr. Chazan's research proves that, although Jewish life in the medieval West laid the foundation for much Jewish suffering in the post-medieval world, it also stimulated considerable Jewish ingenuity, which lies at the root of impressive Jewish successes in the modern West.

Robert Chazan is S. H. and Helen R. Scheuer Professor of Jewish History in the Skirball Department of Hebrew and Judaic Studies at New York University. His most recent books are *God, Humanity, and History: The Hebrew First Crusade Narratives* (2000), *Fashioning Jewish Identity in Medieval Western Christendom* (Cambridge, 2004), and *The Jews of Medieval Western Christendom* (Cambridge, 2006).

Reassessing Jewish Life in Medieval Europe

ROBERT CHAZAN

CAMBRIDGE
UNIVERSITY PRESS

CAMBRIDGE
UNIVERSITY PRESS

32 Avenue of the Americas, New York NY 10013-2473, USA

Cambridge University Press is part of the University of Cambridge.

It furthers the University's mission by disseminating knowledge in the pursuit of
education, learning and research at the highest international levels of excellence.

www.cambridge.org
Information on this title: www.cambridge.org/9780521145435

© Robert Chazan 2010

First published 2010

A catalogue record for this publication is available from the British Library

Library of Congress Cataloguing in Publication data

Chazan, Robert.
Reassessing Jewish life in Medieval Europe / Robert Chazan.
p.   cm.
Includes bibliographical references and index.
ISBN 978-0-521-76304-2 (hardback) – ISBN 978-0-521-14543-5 (pbk.)
1. Jews – Europe, Western – History – To 1500.   2. Christianity and other religions – Judaism –
History.   3. Judaism – Relations – Christianity – History.   4. Europe, Western – Ethnic
relations.   I. Title.
DS135.E81C54   2010
305.892´4040902–dc22   2010026604

ISBN 978-0-521-76304-2 Hardback
ISBN 978-0-521-14543-5 Paperback

Contents

Acknowledgments

This project has taken me well beyond my normal range of research and writing. Thus, I have been more deeply dependent than usual on colleagues and friends for their input in areas that I do not command. Happily, a number of such colleagues and friends have responded generously to my entreaties for aid. I would like to thank Professor Michael Toch for reading Chapters 5 and 6 and for sharing his rich knowledge of medieval Jewish demography and economic life. Professor David Engel, my Skirball Department colleague for many years, and Professor Steven Fine have read and commented upon Chapter 4, making available to me their rich knowledge of modern Jewish historiography. For many reasons, the Epilogue was especially difficult for me to write, and I am thus indebted to Professor Steven Cohen, Professor Hasia Diner, and Professor Marion Kaplan for their reading of the Epilogue and for sharing their diverse perspectives with me. Clearly, all these fine scholars bear no responsibility for the shortcomings that remain, despite their best efforts.

Once again, the settings from which this book has emerged have been stimulating and supportive. I have found a remarkable academic home in NYU's Skirball Department of Hebrew and Judaic Studies for nearly a quarter century. In the Skirball Department, I find myself surrounded by brilliant and productive colleagues, ever ready to stop and chat about mutual scholarly interests, and gifted students deeply committed to their study of the Jewish past. My immediate home environment remains what is has been for many decades now – warm and supportive to the utmost. My wife, Dr. Saralea Chazan, immersed in her practice, her research, and her writing, has once more encouraged this project throughout. Without her ongoing encouragement, this book could not have been completed. Our grown children and their spouses – all involved in creative academic and professional careers of their own – have nonetheless found the time to listen and lend their backing. Their children have simply been a wellspring of enjoyment to their grandparents.

Prologue: Group Narratives: Their Tenacity and Their Accuracy

Human beings require meaningful personal narratives, which may or may not correspond to the realities of the individual's actual life trajectory. The same is true on the group level as well. Societies of all kinds construct meaningful group narratives that may or may not correspond to the realities of the group's experience. These narratives constitute coping devices, enabling the group to assimilate its past into a coherent and positive pattern and thus to engage the future constructively and creatively. Once well established, these narratives tend to be resistant to change, because their usefulness convinces group members of their truth.[1]

Group narratives do on occasion break down for some members of society, normally because they are challenged by an alternative and more useful narrative. Two examples we shall encounter regularly in this study are the replacement for many Europeans of the traditional Christian historical narrative by a Greco-Roman–centered narrative highly critical of Christianity and the replacement for many Jews of the nineteenth-century, emancipation-oriented Jewish narrative by a nationalist alternative. In both cases, the new narratives enabled those embracing them to pursue alternative objectives and ideals, while asserting the roots of these objectives and ideals in the group past. Rarely, however, do group narratives succumb simply to the accumulation of conflicting empirical

---

[1] Yosef Hayim Yerushalmi's *Zakhor: Jewish History and Jewish Memory* opened a vigorous and fruitful discussion of what I am here calling group narrative. I have decided to use the term "group narrative" out of a sense that "Jewish memory" is somewhat too passive and fails to capture the sense of usefulness that "group narrative" suggests. Note the important observations of Amos Funkenstein, "Collective Memory and Historical Consciousness," 5–26.

evidence. These narratives tend to be quite flexible and regularly prove capable of accommodating problematic data successfully.

Challenging a well-established narrative about Jewish life in medieval Europe by engagement with empirical evidence is the objective of the current book, and it is in all likelihood an objective doomed to failure. The well-established narrative of Jewish life in medieval Europe as a vale of tears, an unending sequence of majority (Christian) persecution and minority (Jewish) suffering, finds powerful support in many and diverse quarters. These include traditional Jewish thinking; traditional Christian thinking; innovative early modern and modern thinking about the overall horrors of medieval western Christendom, with persecution of Jews constituting a salient example; modern emancipationist Jewish thinking; and modern nationalist Jewish thinking. For all these different groups, the narrative of medieval Jewish suffering served usefully. This impressive array of supports makes the traditional narrative of Jewish life in medieval Europe virtually impregnable. Yet the realities of Jewish life in medieval Europe do not actually square with the narrative. Thus, despite the obstacles to confronting this powerful narrative with the realities, the effort to do so seems worth undertaking.[2]

For traditional Jewish historical thinking, God promised early on in Israelite/Jewish history that his chosen people would sin, would endure the harsh punishment of exile from the land promised to them, and would suffer incessant pain and degradation. Jews traditionally interpreted defeat at the hands of Rome and destruction of the Second Temple in the year 70 as the onset of this divine punishment, destined to stretch out over many long centuries. This sense of exile was undifferentiated as to time and place. The paradigm was crucial. As Jewish population grew remarkably in medieval Christian Europe (a reality to which the traditional Jewish narrative was inattentive), Jewish suffering in Latin Christendom became the exemplar of exilic existence and suffering everywhere and at all times.

For Christians, a group narrative of Jewish history was critical. Because Christianity claimed that Jewish sinfulness had ruptured the bond

---

[2] I suspect that I am influenced by the traditional Jewish maxim that it is not one's obligation to complete a worthwhile task, but that one may not desist from undertaking it.

between God and the Israelite/Jewish people and resulted in replacement of the Jews with the Christian community as God's elected people, a narrative of Jewish history that would support these convictions had to be created, and it was. The Christian narrative of Jewish history went beyond the Jewish narrative in two ways. First, it identified precisely the Jewish sin that set exile and suffering in motion. For Christian thinkers, this sin was rejection of the divinely dispatched Messiah and – more shocking yet – culpability for the condemnation and crucifixion of that Messiah. In the Christian view, Jewish rejection of the Messiah led God to reject reciprocally the errant Jews and to replace them with a new and more loyal covenant community. In the process of specifying the Jewish sin and its ramifications, Christians also concluded that the exile depicted in the biblical corpus was to be permanent. God was not to redeem his former people as such; redemption would eventually come, but only at the point when Jews abandoned Judaism and accepted the Christian alternative. This reformulation of the earlier Jewish narrative of sin and punishment embedded itself deeply within Christian thinking, serving as the explanation in fact for the rise of Christianity. This harsher Christian version of Jewish sin and punishment was – like the Jewish version – uninterested in nuances of time and place. Jewish life post-Jesus at all times and everywhere exemplified the paradigm so crucial to Christianity's narrative of its own emergence. Ultimately, the traditional Jewish and traditional Christian narratives – crucial differences notwithstanding – strongly reinforced one another.

Toward the end of the Middle Ages, new European/Christian group narratives began to emerge, reflecting accelerating dissatisfaction with the structures of life in medieval Europe. Reformation thinkers vilified the Roman Catholic Church for its distance from the original Christian vision, for its repression of innovative and creative Christian thinking, and for more wide-ranging shortcomings, including persecution of Jews. Renaissance and Enlightenment thinkers were yet broader and harsher in their criticisms, targeting not only the medieval Roman Catholic Church, but Christianity in its entirety. For these thinkers, the propensity of Christian authorities to seek political power and to use that power to suppress free thought was reprehensible and required all-out battle against Christianity and its failures. Among the egregious shortcomings of

Christianity – these thinkers insisted – was persecution of Jews. For the Reformation leaders and the proponents of Renaissance and Enlightenment views, all of whom were European, medieval Christendom was the essential target of criticism. A third wave of reformist thinking has emerged during the second half of the twentieth century, occasioned by the horrors of the Holocaust. As observers of all persuasions have pondered the factors that gave rise to the effort at eradication of European Jewry, considerable attention has focused on the backdrop of prior Christian thinking about Judaism and Jews. Once again, for many this has translated into close scrutiny of medieval Latin Christendom. The diverse early modern and modern condemnations of the Roman Catholic Church or Christianity in its entirety have focused almost exclusively on medieval Europe, including its treatment of Jews, thus highlighting once again the dolorous fate of medieval Europe's Jews as well.

As new ideals of tolerance and societal inclusiveness took hold in modern Europe, its Jews, who had been formally segregated during the medieval centuries, became increasingly absorbed into majority society and thus began to assimilate many of the convictions of their environment, including its condemnation of medieval Christian Europe and the Roman Catholic Church. More important yet, the new Jewish quest for political and social rights found the traditional view of Jewish suffering highly useful. As opposition mounted to the granting of Jewish rights on the grounds that Jews were unfit for citizenship, Jewish spokesmen and liberal allies pointed to medieval Christian persecution as the reason for Jewish deficiencies. This meant that denying Jewish rights would constitute a double injustice. In the first place, Jews suffered deeply at the hands of the medieval Christian majority, with resultant deformation of Jewish economic activity and cultural norms. To then disqualify Jews from citizenship on the basis of this deformation would be utterly unfair. Jews – it was argued – must be given the freedom to alter the problematic characteristics of Jewish life forced upon them by medieval Christian persecution.

Toward the end of the nineteenth century, difficulties associated with the process of Jewish emancipation moved some Jews to reconsider the effort. The signs of unyielding opposition to Jews in diverse quarters convinced many Jewish nationalist/Zionists that true equality in Europe was chimerical, that Europe's Christian majority would never grant such equality. Moreover, evidence of loss of Jewish identity convinced the nationalist/Zionists that the price of successful emancipation – were it in fact achievable – would be peaceful but total eradication of the Jewish people. For the nationalist/Zionist thinkers, Jewish diaspora circumstances were ultimately untenable. Like the traditional Jewish and Christian narratives, this sense of the ills of diaspora existence was all-encompassing. Nonetheless, since the nationalist/Zionist thinkers were all Europeans, they tended to draw their evidence and their examples of diaspora woes from European Jewish history, especially from the Jewish experience in medieval western Christendom.

The traditional Jewish and Christian narratives of Jewish suffering, with their focus on medieval Europe, powerfully reinforced one another. The fact that the innovative general and Jewish narratives, despite the diversity in programs and ideals they supported, agreed with one another with regard to medieval Jewish suffering meant yet further reinforcement of the broad traditional image. Challenging this consensus has been essayed in only limited fashion, with little or no impact on the consensus, at least on the popular level.[3]

ARGUABLY THE MOST SIGNIFICANT CHALLENGE TO THE REIGNING CONsensus was mounted by the young Salo Baron in 1928. Baron – only thirty-three years old at the time – wrote a brief, but pathbreaking essay in the *Menorah Journal*, in which he questioned the underpinnings of nineteenth-century emancipationist thinking. The essay – entitled "Ghetto and Emancipation: Shall We Revisit the Traditional View?" – set out to undermine the sense of emancipation as a dramatic turning point in Jewish fate, with pre-emancipation Jewish existence an unmitigated horror and post-emancipation Jewish life an unadulterated blessing.[4]

---

[3] Note the important effort of Jonathan Elukin, *Living Together, Living Apart*, to revise the consensus. Elukin indicates that the starting point for his study came in the classroom, where students regularly raised the simple but perceptive question as to how Jewish communities could "continue to survive despite facing what seemed to be endless persecution, violence, and expulsion" (p. 1).

[4] Salo Baron, "Ghetto and Emancipation," 515–26. In Chapter 3, we shall note the observations of Charles Homer Haskins on the emergence of much Renaissance thinking from the Middle Ages and his claim that historical change always involves absorption of much of the old into the new.

For our purposes, it is the first half of Baron's analysis, his observations on pre-emancipation Jewish existence, that is significant.

Early on in his essay, Baron negates the broad tendency to project the pre-emancipation Jewish experience in western Christendom onto the whole of pre-emancipation Jewish life. He begins by specifying the subperiod of the Jewish "Middle Ages" on which he intends to focus. Utilizing terminology that subsequently has been more or less discarded, Baron notes that:

the Jewish "Middle Ages"... are not identical with the "Middle Ages" of Europe. The "Dark Ages" of the Jew are roughly comprised by the centuries immediately preceding the French Revolution, the sixteenth, seventeenth, and eighteenth centuries; the "Dark Ages" of Europe [not defined precisely by Baron] were really a time of relative prosperity and high civilization for the Jew. Until the Crusades a majority of Jewry lived under Islamic rule in relatively good circumstances, while even Western Jewry was far superior to its Christian neighbors in culture and economic status. Only in the last centuries of the European Middle Ages did the Jewish Middle Ages set in.[5]

Baron has here accomplished a number of objectives simultaneously. First, he has rejected the traditional Jewish and Christian views of the period between 70 and the French Revolution as homogeneous, characterized by unmitigated Jewish suffering; rather, he insists upon the worldwide concentration of Jews in the early medieval Islamic sphere, their favorable fortunes there, and the positive circumstances of European Jewry through the early centuries of what he calls the European "Middle Ages." Next, he limits the pre-emancipation period on which he intends to focus to the sixteenth through eighteenth centuries. Having defined this fairly narrow period as the Jewish "Middle/Dark Ages," even here Baron proceeds to challenge the allegedly sharp contrast between these three centuries and Jewish fortunes subsequent to the French Revolution. For our purposes, this means that whatever mitigations Baron introduced into the portrait of Jewish life during the sixteenth, seventeenth, and eighteenth centuries would have been all the more appropriate to the eleventh through fifteenth centuries, which is the period on which we shall focus.

---

[5] Ibid., 516.

Baron challenges the regnant view of the pre-emancipation period by looking at both the theory and the reality of pre-emancipation Jewish existence, again for him specifically the sixteenth, seventeenth, and eighteenth centuries in Christian Europe. He begins his challenge on the level of theory by addressing the notion that, during the pre-emancipation period, Jews suffered from lack of equality. To this, Baron responds that equality was not a feature of this period at all. "The simple fact is that there was no such thing then as 'equal rights.'"[6] Given the broad lack of equal rights, the question then becomes one of relative Jewish status, and Baron argues that in fact – when compared to the rights of most other groups in pre-emancipation society – Jewish rights were rather generous.

Subsequently, Baron addresses the theoretical view of Jews as *servi camerae*, that is, serfs of the treasury; of Jews as legally confined to ghettos; and of Jews as living under the constant threat of the Inquisition. To all these negative elements in pre-emancipation Jewish fate, Baron responds by again mitigating the prevailing portrait. He argues that the status of *servi camerae* was regularly contested and involved in any case positives as well as negatives, that the ghetto was from many perspectives a boon as well as a liability, that the inquisitorial courts were not as threatening to Jews as they subsequently seemed, and that in any case professing Jews were immune from inquisitorial jurisdiction. Finally, Baron contends that pre-emancipation Jews enjoyed the substantial benefit of full internal autonomy, which – Baron claimed in 1928 and regularly thereafter – offered enormous advantages to Jewish life, which were in fact lost through the dynamics of emancipation.[7]

From these theoretical perspectives, Baron moves to the realities. "Legally and in theory, we have seen, the status of the Jew was by no means an inferior one. But did actual events – persecutions, riots, pogroms, monetary extortions – reduce their theoretical legal privileges to fictions in practice?" To this Baron concludes: "Even here the traditional answer of Jewish historians does not square with the facts."[8]

---

[6] Ibid.

[7] Baron emphasized the importance of the autonomous Jewish community in his *The Jewish Community* and throughout his magisterial *A Social and Religious History of the Jews*.

[8] Baron, "Ghetto and Emancipation," 521.

Baron, concerned all through his lengthy scholarly career with demography, begins this aspect of his case by arguing that the realities of Jewish life were obviously not dire enough to diminish European Jewish population during the sixteenth, seventeenth, and eighteenth centuries. To the contrary, "it is certainly significant that despite minor attacks, periodic pogroms, and organized campaigns of conversion, the numbers of Jewry increased much more rapidly than the Gentile population."[9] Baron provides extensive data. He notes that from 1650 to 1900, the Jewish population of Europe increased from 650,000 to 8.5 million, while the general population increased from 100 million to 400 million. Thus, the Jewish growth rate was three times that of the general growth rate, suggesting that the impact of the negative aspects of Jewish existence during the sixteenth, seventeenth, and eighteenth centuries can hardly have been as real and sustained as often depicted.

After arguing that Jews must have enjoyed considerable physical security, Baron proceeds to claim that "despite all the restrictions placed on his [the Jew's] activities, it is no exaggeration to say that the Jewish income much surpassed the average Christian income in pre-Revolutionary times."[10] Acknowledging that this claim is impossible to prove, Baron nonetheless points to the achievements of a number of major Jewish banking houses. In fact, he goes further, suggesting that paradoxically many of the restrictions imposed on Jewish economic activities ultimately had beneficial results for Jews, as they were forced into the money trade and thus became well equipped for the advent of early capitalism.

Baron closes this line of argumentation by turning once again to the segregation of the ghetto, arguing that the ghetto, often depicted as a crippling infringement on Jewish life, in fact regularly protected Jews from violence and offered a multitude of additional benefits. "There [in the ghetto] the Jews might live in comparative peace, interrupted less by pogroms than were peasants by wars, engaged in finance and trade at least as profitable as most urban occupations, free to worship, and subject to the Inquisition only in extreme situations."[11]

At the close of his essay, Baron makes some final observations on the balance sheet of emancipation. "While Emancipation has meant a

---

[9] Ibid.
[10] Ibid., 523.
[11] Ibid., 523–24.

reduction of ancient evils, and while its balance sheet for the world at large and as well as for the Jews is favorable, it is not completely free of debits." This even-handedness – projecting the positives and negatives of the emancipatory process – is vintage Baron. The closing sentence in the essay introduced a term and notion that was to be identified with Salo Baron ever after. "Surely it is time to break with the lachrymose theory of pre-Revolutionary woe, and to adopt a view more in accord with historic truth."[12] Although Baron spoke of the "lachrymose theory of pre-Revolutionary woe" in the context of his essay examining sixteenth-, seventeenth-, and eighteenth-century Jewish life and Jewish experience subsequent to the French Revolution, the notion of breaking with the lachrymose view of the entire premodern Jewish past was associated with Salo Baron all through his subsequent scholarly career.[13]

Viewed from the perspective of eighty years and massive new investigation of medieval Jewish life, the Baron arguments do not seem as bold, striking, and sophisticated as they did upon their first appearance. Nonetheless, their impact has been considerable, first of all setting the course of Baron's own subsequent magisterial efforts. In both the first and second editions of his *Social and Religious History of the Jews*, Salo Baron remained true to the conclusion he drew in his 1928 essay.[14] At no point did he revert to the traditional Jewish and Christian view of medieval Jewish life that lay at the core of early modern and modern syntheses of the Jewish past. Rather, the Baron volumes on Jewish life in medieval Europe show post-traditional and post-ideological qualities; throughout all his subsequent *oeuvre*, he insisted upon placing all the major medieval Jewish communities and all the major aspects of Jewish existence in medieval western Christendom within their appropriate context, scrupulously portraying the positives and negatives of Jewish experience in measured fashion.

More broadly, Salo Baron's 1928 essay and his subsequent research and writing deeply influenced the study of medieval Jewish life in much of twentieth-century American academia. During his long tenure at

---

[12] Ibid., 526.

[13] See the important essay by David Engel, "Crisis and Lachrymosity," 243–64.

[14] Baron, *A Social and Religious History of the Jews*; idem, rev. ed.; 18 vols.; New York: Columbia University Press, (1952–83). For observations on Baron's subsequent fidelity to the 1928 essay, see Chapter 4 of this book.

Columbia, Baron trained many students, who in turn trained their own students. He influenced his students and his students' students away from the traditional Jewish and Christian views of the Jewish past with their insistence on unmitigated Jewish suffering and from the early modern and modern programmatic perspectives that reinforced the monolithic focus on Jewish misfortunes; instead, he moved them toward the more detailed and sophisticated understanding of medieval Jewish circumstances that was his own hallmark.

At the same time, Baron's innovative thinking made little headway outside the groves of academia. The inherent power of the traditional sense of Jewish suffering and the broad societal equation of medieval Europe with barbarism and persecution combined to maintain the popular sense of incessant medieval persecution and unending Jewish pain. The reality of the Holocaust served to buttress this popular sense considerably. For many observers, the frightful effort to destroy European Jewry was an obvious aftermath of the medieval European assault on Judaism and Jews. Hostile and venomous medieval Christendom – it was regularly felt – laid the foundation for the modern assault on the Jews of that inhospitable continent.

MY CURRENT EFFORT TO ACHIEVE A MORE BALANCED SENSE OF JEWISH life in medieval Europe owes much to the thinking of Salo Baron. I was fortunate enough to study with Baron during the last years of his teaching at Columbia University. In his teaching as in his writing, Baron was dismissive of slogans. In all the courses I took with him, I cannot recall his ever using the term "lachrymose," so regularly associated with him as a catch phrase to capture a broad thesis. Baron never made a case for the lachrymose theory of premodern Jewish existence and for the errors of that view. Rather, he taught in a way that exemplified a more nuanced approach to Jewish history and insisted – as he already did in 1928 – on careful examination of key aspects of Jewish existence and the balance sheet of debits and credits. What deeply impressed me and influenced me was his scrupulous avoidance of the dramatic and monochromatic, his insistence on judging the multifaceted nature of all historical developments and phenomena, and his focus on bedrock issues such as demography and economics. To an extent, this thoughtfulness diminished drama and excitement in favor of the balanced and cerebral. As a result, however, students like me came away with a sure sense that we were being exposed to careful and judicious consideration of the available evidence and to reasoned and reasonable conclusions.

My work in general over the years has been greatly influenced by my direct exposure to Salo Baron and his thinking, and this is very much the case with the present book. At the same time, this book – however deep the impact of Salo Baron – departs in numerous ways from his 1928 essay. In the first place, this study is by no means comparative. Baron explored in 1928 the purportedly sharp contrasts between pre-revolutionary and post-revolutionary European Jewish life. This book is focused on an earlier period only, with no effort to draw comparisons or contrasts with what came later. Moreover, the period on which I focus is not Baron's sixteenth, seventeenth, and eighteenth centuries; the focus of this study is the eleventh through fifteen centuries, the period during which Christian Europe rose to its position of dominance in the Western world and the Jewish population it housed became an increasingly potent force on the world Jewish scene.

This book begins with a close look at the traditional and modern group narratives that have combined to create the widely shared sense of medieval European Jewish life as an unending sequence of persecution and suffering. This examination of a variety of group narratives will suggest the powerful hold the image of medieval Jewish suffering in Christian Europe has on Jews and non-Jews alike. The second part of the book will then examine five major aspects of medieval Jewish life and subject them to careful scrutiny. In each case, the scrutiny will begin by indicating the traditional perspective, proceed to the actuality of Jewish disabilities and pain, and conclude with countervailing evidence of positive aspects of Jewish life in medieval Europe.

In many ways, the most important piece of evidence for positive Jewish circumstances in medieval Europe comes from the same consideration with which Baron began his 1928 case, that is to say, demographic realities. In the year 1000, the number of Jews in European Christian territory was miniscule, dwarfed by the overwhelmingly larger number of Jews living in the sphere of Islam and – to a lesser extent – the significant number of Jews living in Byzantine lands. By the year 1500, Catholic Europe was home to increasingly large Jewish communities, fated to soon reach parity with the older Jewry of the Islamic world and subsequently to far exceed it. This growth in numbers alone raises serious questions about the traditional sense of Jewish suffering in medieval Europe. The view of medieval Jewish life in Europe as harsh limitation and incessant physical violence simply does not square with the reality of a continuously growing community. Human groups do not flourish numerically under such circumstances. Were the traditional perspective correct, too many Jews would have been killed to allow for population growth, and additionally those who survived would hardly have chosen to remain in such a lethal environment.

Our considerations of the realities of medieval Jewish life will begin with demography and then proceed to additional spheres of Jewish life – economic activities, status in both the ecclesiastical and secular systems, relations with the non-Jewish majority, and maintenance of Jewish identity. In all these chapters, I shall not deny the negative aspects of Jewish experience; I shall, however, continuously insist on the countervailing positive elements in Jewish experience as well.

At the close of this examination of key aspects of Jewish life in medieval Europe, I shall add an Epilogue addressed to the legacy bequeathed by medieval Europe and its Jews to the modern West and its Jews. Once more, the popular perspective highlights only the negative, the extent to which the Holocaust was rooted in medieval Christian Europe and its imagery and treatment of Jews. I shall acknowledge this reality, but argue again that this is not the whole of the story. I shall urge that many of the positive aspects of medieval Jewish experience examined in the body of the book equipped the Jews of the modern West very well for success in the new era.

I am hardly sanguine about the prospect for dismantling the widespread negative impressions of Jewish life in medieval Europe. The proposed perspective on medieval western Christendom and its Jews will encounter widespread opposition and dismissal. However, I am committed to making this alternative view available, in hopes that it might have at least some impact on Jewish and non-Jewish thinking about a difficult yet creative period in the history of Europe and its Jews.

Introduction: The Emergence of Medieval European Jewry

I N THE YEAR 1000, THE AREAS OF EUROPE LOYAL TO THE ROMAN Church were limited in size and population and were backward in economic achievement, military strength, political stability, and cultural creativity. They constituted the least of the three Western religio-political power blocs at the time, far inferior to the largest and strongest power bloc – the far-flung Islamic world – and considerably inferior to the Greek Orthodox Byzantine Empire. Some of the richest areas of southern Europe on the Iberian and Italian peninsulas were under the control of Islamic rulers, and additional areas of Italy were governed by the Byzantines. Northern Europe remained mired in its historic backwardness.

These weak sectors of Europe endured incursions from every direction by powerful external enemies. From the south, they faced constant danger from the Muslim forces that controlled North Africa and the Mediterranean Sea; from the east, they encountered the pressure of their Greek Orthodox rivals; from the west and the north, they suffered devastating raids by the seagoing Norsemen, who regularly wreaked havoc all across the northwestern coast of the continent. In a vicious cycle, the weakness of western Christendom opened it to these incessant pressures and dangers, while the external threats and incursions contributed to the ongoing weakness and backwardness. Only the most optimistic could have dreamed of better days to come, of a period when Latin Christendom might equal its more powerful neighbors or perhaps even surpass them.[1]

---

[1] Works that clarify this process include: William Chester Jordan, *Europe in the High Middle Ages*; Jacques Le Goff, *The Birth of Europe*; Christopher Brooke, *Europe in the*

1

The Jewish world of the year 1000 reflected the broad distribution of resources and power just now indicated. The overwhelming majority of the world's Jews – perhaps as much as 80 percent of world Jewry – lived in the realm of Islam. Major Jewish settlements stretched from Mesopotamia through the eastern shores of the Mediterranean, all across North Africa, and over onto the Iberian and Italian peninsulas. Within this vast territory, Mesopotamia housed the largest concentration of Jews, as had been the case since the third century. There remained a considerable set of Jewish communities in Palestine and adjacent areas. Important Jewish settlements dotted the coast of North Africa. On the European continent itself, the largest Jewish populations inhabited regions under Muslim control, especially in the extensive areas of the Iberian peninsula dominated by Islam and in Sicily. The Byzantine Empire continued to host venerable Jewish settlements, although it lagged far behind the Islamic world in its Jewish population.

The Jewish population of Catholic Europe was miniscule in comparison to that of the Islamic realm and the Byzantine Empire. Small Jewish populations lived in the weak Christian principalities of Spain that huddled in the northern sectors of the peninsula, in the Christian territories of southern France, and in the Christian sectors of Italy. None of these sets of Jewish communities was large, powerful, or noteworthy from a cultural perspective. The backward areas of northern Europe hosted almost no discernible Jewish population, as had been the case from time immemorial. Once more, no observer in the year 1000 could have predicted radical change, with the Jewish population of Roman Catholic Europe eventually equaling or even surpassing that of the Islamic and Byzantine spheres.

The kind of change that could not possibly have been envisioned in the year 1000 in fact took place. By the year 1500, the distribution of population, wealth, and power in the Western world had changed dramatically. Western Christendom had come to dominate its rivals in every way. Christian forces had by 1500 driven the Muslim enclaves of 1000 off the European continent entirely. The Mediterranean coastline from Spain to the westernmost borders of Byzantine rule in Asia Minor lay entirely in

Central Middle Ages; John H. Mundy, *Europe in the High Middle Ages*; Denys Hay, *Europe in the Fourteenth and Fifteenth Centuries*.

the hands of Catholic rulers. Northern Europe was no longer backward. It harbored some of the most powerful and successful principalities of western Christendom, indeed of the Western world. The remarkable voyages undertaken at the end of the fifteenth century by explorers based in Catholic Europe opened a new chapter in its dominance, as vast new territories were colonized and subsequently contributed markedly to the accelerating strength of Latin Christendom.

The process of change was slow and steady, stretching over the five centuries between 1000 and 1500, and was distinguished by no dramatic events or obvious turning points.[2] During the latter decades of the tenth century and on into the eleventh century, western Christendom began to rouse itself and to expand on every possible level. The population grew; the economy developed; political stability was achieved; military strength was augmented; the beginnings of impressive cultural creativity appeared. Progress on each of these planes reinforced positive developments on the others. Over the course of the eleventh century already, Latin Christendom was no longer protecting itself from outside incursion, but had begun to attack its enemies, first on the European continent itself and then beyond.

The aggression began on the Iberian peninsula, where Islamic control of major territories was challenged and in many areas successfully supplanted. Christian forces reconquered territories long held by the Muslims. The process would not be complete until almost the year 1500, but by the end of the eleventh century it was well under way. The same is true on the Italian peninsula, where Norman forces from the north made their way southward during the eleventh century and broke Muslim control over key areas of Italy. By the end of the eleventh century, western Christendom had become strong enough to launch an assault on Muslim holdings in the Near East, beyond the perimeter of the European continent. While the successes of the First Crusade proved evanescent, the audacious assault is a measure of the remarkable progress of this rapidly developing society.

Progress was by no means limited to military achievement. Population increased steadily; forests were cut down and arable land expanded;

---

[2] The slowness of change was emphasized by R. W. Southern in his valuable *The Making of the Middle Ages*, which sketches the centrality of the twelfth century in this process of change.

the economy of western Christendom matured; increasingly effective political and religious organization evolved; innovative intellectual and cultural directions coalesced; new intellectual and spiritual institutions were fashioned. The modern West is replete with the impressive legacy of medieval Latin Christendom, including such disparate elements as the English monarchy and political system, the powerful papacy, the university system of the West, the Gothic cathedrals, and a host of innovative forms of intellectual and spiritual creativity.

To a significant extent, the impact of medieval Catholic Europe can also be seen in the recoiling from some of its features in the Reformation and the Enlightenment. For not all aspects of this rapidly developing society were salutary. Medieval western Christendom exhibited a remarkable commitment to cohesion and uniformity. This drive expressed itself in an unusual level of integration of church and state. The medieval Church led the way in organizational sophistication and, as a result, exerted enormous influence on society at large. This influence led regularly to the suppression of new and creative thinking and spirituality, culminating in the creation of the inquisition, which did untold harm to many in western Christendom who were seekers of truth and new religious insight. The commitment to cohesion and uniformity also expressed itself in aggressive negativity toward "others," meaning in the first place non-Christians and extending to alternative groupings within Christian society itself, such as gay people, persons with physical limitations, and women. This aggressiveness toward "others" eventuated in the proliferation of destructive stereotypes, which often led to popular violence. All these tendencies brought harm to the medieval scene and constituted – along with the positive developments – part of the legacy bequeathed to the modern West. The impact of the period between 1000 and 1500 has been in multiple respects both beneficial and harmful.

Christian Europe evolved by 1500 in ways that could not have possibly been anticipated five centuries earlier; the same is true for the Jews of western Christendom. By the year 1500, the expanded area of Christian control included a Jewish population that was no longer miniscule. To the contrary, it was close to parity with the older Jewish population of the Islamic world and was well on its way to superseding that population decisively. The center of gravity in Jewish life had shifted by 1500 in utterly unforeseen ways to Christian Europe – in numbers, in economic strength, in political and religious authority and creativity. Especially noteworthy is the emergence of an entirely new set of Jewish communities across northern Europe. Areas that in the year 1000 were devoid of Jewish life had by 1500 become centers of Jewish settlement and activity. This new northern European Jewry eventually became the largest element in world Jewish population by the eighteenth and nineteenth centuries.

Like the broader process that saw the evolution of Roman Catholic Europe move into its position of power, so too the evolution of western Christendom's Jewries was a slow and steady process, lacking drama and obvious turning points. This evolution was very much an offshoot of the larger changes in European life. The needs of this developing society convinced many European rulers that Jews could be useful in bringing the economic advantages and cultural riches of their more advanced competitors – the Islamic and Byzantine realms – into the orbit of western Christendom. The dynamism of this developing society and the rich opportunities it provided convinced many Jews that western Christendom offered options for a better life and stimulated such Jews to undertake the rigors of relocation.

Jewish population in Christian Europe expanded in two major ways. Many Jews were absorbed into western Christendom through the process of military conquest. In the year 1000, the largest concentrations of Jews in the western sectors of Europe were found in territories ruled by Muslims on the Iberian and Italian peninsulas. As these territories fell under Christian control, their Jewish populations faced a wrenching choice – to retreat with their former overlords or to remain under the rule of the new Christian authorities. These new Christian authorities were committed to persuading such Jews to remain in place and to contribute to the maintenance of societal stability after the conquest. These rulers attempted such persuasion in time-honored fashion, through the extension of appealing incentives that would convince these Jews to remain in place.[3] The new Christian rulers of the conquered territories seem to have been highly successful in their efforts, thus swelling markedly the number of Jews in Spain living under Christian rule.

---

[3] See Robert Chazan, ed. and trans., *Church, State, and Jew in the Middle Ages*, 69–75, for a number of the charters extended by conquering Christian rulers in order to entice Jews to remain in place.

Jewish population grew in a second way as well. Rulers desirous of attracting Jews to territories heretofore limited in Jewish population or even devoid of Jewish settlement used essentially the same techniques. They too offered incentives to Jewish settlement. In this case, the issue was not convincing Jews to remain during a period of transition; rather, the objective was to entice new Jewish settlers. To an extent, this drive for new Jewish immigrants can be seen in southern Europe, in the older areas of limited Jewish habitation. More striking is the desire of northern European rulers to attract Jews into their domains, areas in which Jewish settlements had not previously existed. Early sources tell us of the invitation extended by the Duke of Flanders to Jews to settle in his domain, of the establishment of a Jewish community in London by William the Conqueror, newly installed as king of England, and of the efforts of the bishop of Speyer to implant a Jewish enclave in his town.[4] In all these cases, the conviction of the Christian authorities that Jewish settlers would be useful was matched by the conclusion of Jews that such movement would serve their interests as well.

The opportunities offered by western Christendom that attracted Jews were balanced by liabilities. Especially problematic for Jews was the drive toward cohesion and uniformity. To the extent that this drive involved the strengthening of church-state integration, it gave the restrictive policies of the Church great influence over the everyday lives of Jews. To the extent that the yearning for uniformity fostered suspicion and animosity toward non-Christians, it moved many in Christian Europe to adopt a hostile attitude toward Jews and often to engage in anti-Jewish violence grounded in such hostility.

Medieval western Christendom exhibited growth and development in positive directions and – at the same time – evolved in problematic directions as well, and the same is true with respect to Jewish life in this dynamic ambiance. Out of the Jewish experience in medieval western Christendom emerged, first of all, the transition into the Christian world, which was destined to dominate the West for many centuries down to the present. Within that Christian world, the Jews made significant albeit not fully appreciated contributions to progress. Simultaneously, Christian Europe's intellectual and spiritual dynamism impacted the creativity

---

[4] See Chapter 5 for details.

of its Jewish minority in multiple ways, eventuating in a high level of creativity in multiple spheres of Jewish intellectual and spiritual life.

At the same time, the problematic aspects of medieval western Christendom took a heavy toll on its Jews. Entirely new dangers to Jewish existence appeared, including banishment of entire Jewish populations, wide-ranging popular violence that cost thousands of Jewish lives, and destructive stereotypes that portrayed Jews as an alien and dangerous element within Christian society. Both the positive and negative developments affected Jewish life profoundly between 1000 and 1500 and left a complex and multifaceted legacy for Jewish life in the modern West.

WHAT HAS BEEN SAID THUS FAR ABOUT THE STRIKING DEVELOPMENT of western Christendom between the years 1000 and 1500 represents an accepted consensus within the scholarly world. To be sure, these conclusions run counter to received popular wisdom. Citizens of the modern West find it difficult to comprehend that a thousand years ago the Islamic world was far advanced over Christian Europe in almost every way. The fact that in the year 1000 the major cities of the Muslim world – for example, Baghdad, Damascus, and Cairo – were large and prosperous at a level to which the inhabitants of London, Paris, and Frankfort could not aspire, indeed could not even dream of, has been rarely emphasized by Western historians and thinkers, making it difficult for modern inhabitants of the powerful West to grasp these realities. Present-day Muslims have a much better grasp of the earlier circumstances of Muslim power and European weakness. They are fully aware of the achievements of their ancestors and of the extent to which the Muslim sphere in the year 1000 outstripped western Christendom. For present-day Muslims, this prior reality poses the difficult question of what went wrong. Identifying what it was that enabled the formerly backward areas of Europe to overtake the medieval Muslim sphere and to maintain superiority down to the present constitutes a vexing issue in the contemporary Muslim world.

With respect to the changing position of the Jews of medieval western Christendom, the scholarly consensus is less fully developed, and the alternative popular consensus is stronger. For most Jews and for most non-Jews interested in the Jewish past, there is a broad sense of Jewish life in Europe as implanted in antiquity and an ongoing reality ever since. With respect to the Jewish presence in western Christendom, the dynamic change just depicted is extremely difficult to absorb. Let us look briefly at two colorful presentations of the purported rootedness of Jews in Christian Europe, one from the Christian side and one from the Jewish side.

Some years ago, while in Paris collecting data for a study of the Jews of northern France during the Middle Ages, I perused local histories of northern French towns in hopes of finding occasional but useful documentary evidence on Jews. My efforts were successful, and I discovered in these local histories many valuable testimonies to Jewish life during the twelfth and thirteenth centuries. As I read through these local histories, written generally by town archivists or local historians, I was struck by a recurring theme. Repeatedly, the local writers included the following sentences or slight variations thereof: "The Jews of Jerusalem rejected our Lord Jesus Christ and occasioned his crucifixion. In punishment, the Lord caused the destruction of Jerusalem and condemned the Jews to exile. The Jews left the Holy Land and settled in X [the particular town in question], where evidence of their sojourn has survived." The evidence of Jewish settlement in the towns of northern France presented in these local histories was in all cases from the twelfth or thirteenth centuries. However, widely accepted theological and folkloristic memories assumed Jewish presence in the many towns of northern France over the ages, stretching all the way back to the very first Christian century.

Jews have shared, to a significant extent, this perception of lengthy Jewish connections to Christian Europe. This conviction was recurrently articulated, nowhere better than in the post-1492 ruminations of Solomon ibn Verga in his *Shevet Yehudah*. There, ibn Verga laments the expulsion of the Jews of Spain by highlighting their long stay on the peninsula. He tells a delightful tale of the Babylonian king Nebuchadnezzar encountering difficulties in his siege of Jerusalem in 586 BCE and calling in reinforcements, led by the king of Spain. After achieving victory, the conquering and generous Babylonian monarch offered his Spanish ally choice of the spoils of war. According to ibn Verga, the wise Spanish king chose as his reward the Jews of the finest neighborhoods of the conquered Jerusalem, was accorded his recompense, and led his new subjects back to Spain, where their descendants remained for more than two millennia.[5] Thus, for ibn Verga as for many Jews, the expulsions of 1492–97 constituted an illegitimate rupture in the age-old presence of Jews in western Christendom. In fact, ibn Verga's view of Jewish presence in southern Europe serves as a counterargument to the claims of the local northern French archivists and historians. Taken seriously, ibn Verga is arguing that Jewish presence in southern Europe predated the crucifixion of Jesus by many centuries, meaning that Jewish settlement could by no means have been the result of that momentous event and the Jewish malfeasance associated in Christian thinking with it.

The claims of long-term Jewish settlement in northern and southern Europe by local northern French historians and by Solomon ibn Verga have considerable charm and appeal. In fact, however, the recollections of the former are simply incorrect. Jewish presence in northern France (the area upon which my study was then focused) and other areas of northern Europe did not emerge in any serious way until the beginning of the second Christian millennium; it postdated the crucifixion of Jesus by almost a thousand years.

The situation in southern Europe – depicted by Solomon ibn Verga – is a bit more complex. Jewish presence did develop there in late antiquity, although not nearly so early as ibn Verga claims. By the time of the crucifixion of Jesus, there surely were small Jewish enclaves on the Italian and Iberian peninsulas. However, as noted, the largest centers of Jewish life in southern Europe, including Italy and Spain, during the first half of the Middle Ages were located in areas controlled by the forces of Islam. Jewish presence in Christian areas of southern Europe during the period that predated the year 1000 was quite limited, confined – as we have seen – to fairly small numbers in areas of the Italian and Iberian peninsulas under Christian rule and in sectors of southern France. Thus, ibn Verga's claim of lengthy Jewish settlement on the Iberian peninsula is not actually wrong, as was the case for the local town historians of northern France. Jews did in fact populate Spain from late antiquity on. However, this did not mean unbroken Jewish settlement in Christian Spain. Even in Christian southern Europe, the notion of significant and stable Christian-Jewish interaction over the past two millennia is unsustainable.

---

[5] Solomon ibn Verga, *Shevet Yehudah*, 33.

The reality of ongoing Christian-Jewish interaction from the first century down through the twenty-first century has contributed substantially to the mistaken sense of unbroken Jewish presence in western Christendom. This ongoing interaction is indisputable, but its dimensions must be carefully understood. Given the role of Jews in the Gospels and the Pauline epistles, Judaism and Jews constituted a continuous and contentious issue for Christian thinkers and thinking, an issue that had to be regularly addressed, whether there was a significant Jewish presence or not. Thus, the thinkers of Latin Christendom consistently turned their attention to Jews and Judaism all through late antiquity and the early Middle Ages.[6] These considerations of Judaism and Jews cannot, however, be taken as indices of significant Jewish presence.

In effect, while Christianity was born within the Jewish community of Palestine in the first century, the paths of the two rival religious communities diverged markedly. The remarkable spread of Christianity took place by and large west of Palestine, throughout the Roman Empire. In contrast, the subsequent expansion of Judaism took place from the third century onward largely east of Palestine, in Mesopotamia. Interestingly, while Christian sources are rich in consideration of the issues raised by Judaism, Jewish sources down through the twelfth century are almost devoid of interest in Christianity. It was only with the emergence of sizeable Jewish communities within western Christendom that Jews began to concern themselves with Christianity and Christians.[7]

To be sure, the accumulated weight of Christian thinking vis-à-vis Judaism and Jews profoundly impacted the Jews who began to settle in western Christendom from the eleventh century on, as we shall see.[8] It is a mistake, however, to posit unwavering consistency in ecclesiastical doctrine, policies, and teachings from historical setting to historical setting. As the prior legacy of Christian thinking impacted the innovative circumstances of western Christendom, emphases and specifics changed, resulting in new doctrinal views, revised policies, and evolving imageries of Judaism and Jews. The interaction of Church and Jews in medieval western Christendom represents the amalgamation of older tendencies

---

[6] For valuable treatment of these early medieval thinkers, see Jeremy Cohen, *Living Letters of the Law*, chaps. 1 through 4.

[7] See Robert Chazan, *Fashioning Jewish Identity*.

[8] See throughout Part II.

introduced into a dynamically developing societal context. The result was a new and different stage in the history of Christianity's lengthy relationship to Judaism and Jews.

∾

MY OBJECTIVE IS TO REEXAMINE KEY ASPECTS OF JEWISH EXPERIENCE IN medieval western Christendom, to note the baneful facets of this experience, but to indicate as well productive elements in this experience. In approaching this task, it is important to note that medieval Europe and medieval European Jewry were hardly monoliths. Fissures and variations abounded on the medieval majority scene and were inevitably reflected in the experiences of the Jewish minority. Majority societies differed markedly across medieval western Christendom, creating alternative Jewish circumstances and experiences. This study is not intended to be a broad examination of the full range of medieval European treatment of Jews and of resultant Jewish experience.[9] Rather, I shall make an effort to highlight innovative tendencies in medieval majority treatment of Jews, in Jewish responses to this treatment, and in the resultant forms – both negative and positive – that Jewish life took.

A number of salient distinctions are notable in premodern Europe. The most significant division was between the areas of the south (Spain, southern France, and Italy) and areas of the north (England, northern France, Germany, Austria, Poland, and Hungary).[10] In the year 1000, the areas of the south – which had formed the heart of the Roman world – were far more advanced than those of the north, which had been the backward hinterland to Roman achievement. However, the great European leap forward during the period between 1000 and 1500 was very much centered in the north, which began its process of vitalization during the eleventh century and continued to lead the way during the ensuing centuries. It was northern warriors who initiated the effort to drive the Muslims out of their European enclaves in Italy and Spain and who subsequently led the crusading movements to the Holy Land that began at the end of the eleventh century. It was in the north that rapid

---

[9]   In chaps. 2–4 of my *The Jews of Medieval Western Christendom*, I treated sequentially the Jewries of the south, the northwest, and the northeast.

[10] For a helpful contrast of south and north, see Southern, *The Making of the Middle Ages*, 15–25.

economic and political development was most fully manifest, resulting in the fashioning of powerful and stable economies and monarchies in England and France. It was in these same areas of the north that new cultural institutions – for example the university – were created and new spiritual tendencies proliferated.

In the year 1000, as already noted, there was almost no northern European Jewry. Precisely the dynamic development of this heretofore backward area moved farsighted political leaders to become interested in fostering the settlement of urban business people, meaning *inter alia* Jews, and to convince adventuresome Jews to make their way northward. In northern Europe, the immigrant Jews encountered most directly the new civilization that was being spawned. In northern Europe, these Jews explored and exploited new business opportunities and achieved – at least briefly – considerable economic success; there, new relationships with the ruling authorities were forged; there, remarkable Jewish intellectual and spiritual creativity evolved. At the same time, it was in this same area that widespread popular hostility to Jews emerged – connected in part simply to their newness in the north but in part to the exclusionary tendencies of the new European civilization; it was in this same area that increasingly irrational fantasies of Jewish malevolence were spun out and disseminated; it was in this same area that the relationship with the ruling authorities turned destructive; it was from this area that the first major expulsions of Jews took place.

In the wake of the expulsions from Spain and Portugal in 1492 and 1497, northern Europe came to harbor the largest European Jewish settlements. At this point, a second major set of distinctions looms large, the distinction between the western areas of northern Europe on the one hand and the central and eastern areas on the other. Across the north in particular, the western areas of Christian Europe were quite different from the central and eastern areas, and these differences also had enormous implications for Jewish life.

In the north, where the development of a new Christian civilization was centered, the more westerly sectors – England and France – matured far more rapidly than the Germanic central areas and such easterly areas as Poland and Hungary. Jewish life was deeply affected, for good and ill, by the rapid political and economic maturation of England and France.

We have noted the multiple ways in which northern Europe innovated with respect to Jews – inviting them and establishing conditions under which Jewish life flourished on the one hand and limiting them and persecuting them on the other. This was also the area that pioneered in the eventual expulsion of Jews, which brought Jewish presence to an end in the northwestern areas of Europe from the late thirteenth through the late fourteenth centuries.

The situation in the central and eastern sectors of northern Europe was quite different. Much slower to mature, the central and eastern areas of northern Europe fostered a different kind of evolution for their Jewish communities. On the one hand, economic and political backwardness in north-central and northeastern Europe took a considerable toll on Jewish life. These Jewish communities did not enjoy the strong support and protection of powerful rulers and the economic opportunities of rapidly developing societies. At the same time, they did not suffer the liabilities associated with powerful rulers, who could ultimately squeeze their Jewish clients dry and/or expel them. By the end of the thirteenth century Jews were gone from England, and by the end of the fourteenth century the same was true for France as well. In central and eastern Europe, Jewish life was more precarious physically and economically; on the other hand, ongoing economic backwardness made the Jewish contribution enduringly useful, and the lack of strong central authorities precluded the kind of radical exploitation and wholesale expulsion suffered further westward. Thus, by the end of the fifteenth century, the slowly developing Jewish communities of north-central and northeast Europe had emerged as the demographic core of European – and eventually world – Jewry, destined to continue steady population growth down into the twentieth century.

Ultimately, the older civilization of southern Europe was eventually overwhelmed by the younger, more militant, less pluralistic, and less tolerant civilization of the north. In some instances, for instance southern France and large sectors of Italy, the armies and political authorities of the north invaded and subdued the south; in other areas, the new ideals of northern Europe slowly infiltrated the south and altered prior attitudes and practices. Thus, for example, the new Jewish economic specialization in the money trade that emerged in the north slowly made its way southward. To be sure, this new specialization never effaced completely the older diversity of Jewish economic activity; it did, however, alter the Jewish economic profile considerably.[11] Likewise, the new irrational perceptions of Jews only slowly made their way southward, but eventually they did so. Finally, it is striking to note that the new technique of expulsion was introduced into the south by such northern rulers as the Capetian king of France, to eventually be emulated by the kings of Castile and Aragon at the end of the fifteenth century.[12]

In our effort to discern the innovative elements in medieval Jewish circumstances, we shall often focus on the northern areas of Europe and indeed on the westerly sectors of northern Europe, in which the novel tendencies were most dramatically manifest. The focus on innovative Jewish circumstances in medieval Europe will necessarily eventuate in an emphasis on northern Europe, especially northwestern Europe. This is by no means intended to slight the Jewries of the south; rather, concern with the innovative necessitates a focus on those areas in which innovation was most pronounced.

ONE OF THE EXCITING YET PROBLEMATIC ASPECTS OF ALL RESEARCH IS its tendency to complicate simplistic imageries, to raise questions about views widely accepted and shared. Simplistic imageries have enormous appeal. They make the world readily understandable; they usually involve establishment of clearly demarcated good and evil; they eliminate much of the difficulty associated with complex judgments. Historians face a special challenge in encountering and challenging simplistic imageries. Because their task involves enormous quantities of data and complex judgments and because the issues with which they deal usually involve broad and widely held societal convictions, historians find that challenging broadly accepted notions is especially difficult and usually thankless. Replacement of simplistic views and easily comprehended goods and evils with complex realities is often thankless; it is, however, a task well

---

[11] For treatment of Jewish economic specialization in medieval Christian Europe, see Chapter 6.
[12] Study of the general impact of medieval northern European innovation on Jewish life in the south is a major desideratum.

worth undertaking. This is the potentially thankless task of the present book – to replace simplistic portraits of the Jewish experience in medieval western Christendom with a far more nuanced picture that makes ample room for both the baneful and the beneficial.[13]

---

[13] A few technical notes on citation of texts are in order. In general, when translations are available, I shall cite them. When no translation is indicated, then the translation is my own. Citations from the Hebrew Bible are taken from *TANAKH: A New Translation of the Holy Scriptures according to the Traditional Hebrew Text*; translations from the New Testament are taken from the *Revised English Bible*.

PART I

HISTORICAL SCHEMES

1

ᏉᏉ

The Jewish Middle Age: The Jewish View

*M*ANY HUMAN COMMUNITIES HAVE SEGMENTED THEIR SENSE of history into three parts: past – an early idyllic period; present – a period of serious decline; and future – an anticipated return to the idyllic past, replete with a sense of the everlasting nature of this third and final period. Christianity and Judaism each adumbrated a vision of its tripartite history, with of course differing perspectives on what constituted past, present, and future. In fact, Christians developed a sense of both tripartite Christian history and tripartite Jewish history. For our purposes, it is important to gain a sense of both the Jewish and Christian views of tripartite Jewish history, with a focus on the middle period of decline in Jewish fortunes.

In traditional Jewish thinking, this middle period of decline involved the loss of political independence, the destruction of Jerusalem and its sacred temple, and transformation of the Jews into a people in exile, all of which were attributed to Roman domination of Palestine in the first century and were clustered around the symbolic date of the year 70. In fact, two of these three developments actually took place over an extended period of time, predating and postdating the year 70. In the eighth pre-Christian century, the Judean kingdom had lost its political independence as a result of Assyrian conquest and remained a subjugated polity down through the second pre-Christian century – under the Babylonians, Persians, and Greeks. After a brief eight decades of renewed Jewish independence under the Hasmonean ruling family, in 63 BCE Rome bloodlessly asserted imperial domination of Judea. Thus, Jewish political independence ended long before the year 70.

On the other hand, the defeat of the year 70 did not transform the Jews into an exilic people. Rather, they became a predominantly exilic people only during the third century, when unsettled conditions in Roman Palestine caused significant numbers of Jews to emigrate and find refuge in nearby Mesopotamia, where conditions were far more peaceful and favorable. But Jews – and Christians as well – have collapsed loss of Jewish political independence, destruction of Jerusalem and its shrine, and exile, and assigned all of them to the year 70, in a way that distorts the historical realities but resonates symbolically and emotionally.

In the traditional Jewish worldview, the middle period of Jewish history consists of the lengthy epoch between independence in the Promised Land, the religious centrality of Jerusalem, and the integrity of Temple worship that symbolically ended in the year 70 on the one hand, and an eventual return to the Land of Israel, restoration of political independence, and enjoyment of religious fulfillment on the other.[1] This middle period is thus perceived as a lengthy hiatus between the greatness of the past in the Holy Land and the anticipated splendor of a future in the Land of Israel.

To be sure, even a cursory reading of the Hebrew Bible suggests that the pre-70 past was by no means unqualifiedly glorious. The narrative portions of the Hebrew Bible depict ongoing Israelite shortcomings, from the period of wandering under the leadership of Moses through the lengthy and convoluted history of the kingdoms of Israel and Judah and on to the period of return from Babylonian exile and resettlement of the Land of Israel. Prophetic fulminations highlight a wide range of Israelite and Judean failures. Nonetheless, the focus on the suffering of the middle period of the Jewish past and the hopes for eventual restoration have served to dampen the negative memories of earlier epochs and create a more sharply etched portrait of early happiness/exilic misfortune/redemptive splendor.

Traditional Jewish views characterize the middle period of exilic misfortune as radical dispersal of the Jewish people, incessant wandering,

---

[1] In fact, as we shall see shortly, there has been full recognition by Jews of a sequence of displacements and returns, but the one that began in 70 has had a special status in Jewish thinking. Note the Christian sense that the first two displacements can reasonably be called exile because of their limited duration, but that the third and lengthiest by far cannot be called exile – it must properly be labeled divine rejection.

intense persecution, and continuous suffering. Divine anger is the source of all this misfortune; God imposed punishment on his recalcitrant people. A multitude of ancient sins had purportedly occasioned this divine punishment, which was to be lengthy (but not everlasting) and excruciatingly painful.[2]

∿

JEWS PERCEIVED THE ROOTS OF THIS TRIPARTITE DIVISION AS SECURELY grounded in the Hebrew Bible, viewed as divinely revealed and thus indisputably true. This is the case for the Bible's narration of the past and equally the case for its predictions of the future. The historical books of the Bible, which cover a lengthy time frame, extending from the creation of the world through the return from Babylonian exile, include two sequences of land-exile-return.[3] The first of these sequences began with peaceable Israelite descent into Egypt and warm reception there, which then evolved into oppression and suffering and culminated in miraculous salvation through direct divine intervention. The second three-part sequence opens with the drama and tragedy of violence, destruction, and forced exile at the hands of the Babylonians. This second sequence ends on a far more prosaic note than the first, with the imperial order of Cyrus and the protracted and difficult return of a portion of the Judean people from Mesopotamia. In effect, subsequent Jewish embrace of a broad tripartite division of Jewish history borrows selectively from both these prior historical sequences, absorbing tragic and violent beginnings from the Babylonian exile and miraculous divine deliverance from the earlier sojourn in Egypt.

For this subsequent sense of violent exile and miraculous redemption, there is considerable predictive material in the Hebrew Bible. The book of Deuteronomy, composed largely of a series of lengthy addresses by Moses to his people on the eve of his death and their entry into the Holy Land, highlights the divine demand for compliance with the dictates of the covenant struck between God and the Israelite people. Moses details the demands of the covenant in his lengthy speeches. Fulfillment or non-fulfillment of the demands of the covenant will shape the contours

---

[2] Note the parallel and contrastive views in the Christian sense of the Jewish past, as described in Chapter 2.
[3] Genesis through 2 Kings, plus 1 and 2 Chronicles, Ezra, and Nehemiah.

of Israelite experience, with reward for fulfillment and punishment for non-fulfillment. Moses regularly projects the bounteous rewards that will flow from fulfillment of the covenant and the dire punishments that will eventuate from failure to fulfill the covenant, with emphasis on the latter.

The most well-known of such "rewards and punishments" passages is in chapter 28, toward the end of Deuteronomy. In the opening fourteen verses of the chapter, Moses spells out the rich rewards that adherence to the covenant will bring. Then for the succeeding fifty-four verses – an obvious imbalance – Moses depicts the horrific punishments that will be triggered by Israelite failure to fulfill the demands of the covenant. Descriptions of these punishments are graphic and grim, intended to inspire fear among Moses' immediate listeners and those who will subsequently hear or read these words through the ages.[4]

In the middle of these predictions of the dire consequences of failing to observe God's law, Moses makes initial and brief two-verse reference to exile.

The Lord will drive you and the king you set over you to a nation unknown to you or your fathers, where you will serve other gods, of wood and stone. You shall be a consternation, a proverb, and a byword among all the peoples to which the Lord will drive you.[5]

According to most modern scholars, the book of Deuteronomy was in fact composed subsequent to the exile forced on the Judean people by the Babylonians at the end of the sixth pre-Christian century and the return of a part of the Judean people under the rule of the Persians. Thus, modern scholars project this brief portrait of the punishment of exile – along with the lengthier prediction that follows later in the same chapter – as grounded in experienced realities, but predictive of a future exile. Traditional readers of the book of Deuteronomy, while dissenting from the late dating asserted by modern scholarship, have agreed nonetheless that these predictions of exile were surely intended to warn of the third and lengthiest exile.

The brevity of these two verses serves only as a prelude to the extended and more frightening picture sketched by Moses at the end of the same

---

[4] In synagogue ritual, the verses describing these future punishments are usually intoned in a hushed voice by the reader, in recognition of their frightening content.

[5] Deut. 28:36–37.

chapter. It is striking that the entire series of curses in Deuteronomy 28 closes with the ultimate punishment – that of wide-ranging and painful exile. The closing five verses of chapter 28 describe in terrifying detail this ultimate punishment.

The Lord will scatter you among all the peoples from one end of the earth to the other.

There you shall serve other gods, wood and stone, whom neither you nor your ancestors have experienced.

Yet even among those nations you shall find no peace, nor shall your foot find a place to rest.

The Lord will give you there an anguished heart and eyes that pine and a despondent spirit.

The life you face shall be precarious; you shall be in terror night and day, with no assurance of survival.

In the morning you shall say: "If only it were evening!" and in the evening you shall say: "If only it were morning!" – because of what your heart shall dread and what your eyes shall see.

The Lord will send you back to Egypt in galleys, by a route I told you that you should not see again. There you shall offer yourselves for sale to your enemies as male and female slaves, but none will buy.[6]

This graphic portrayal of the horrors of exile became deeply embedded in Jewish thinking, profoundly affecting the ways in which exilic experience was perceived and interpreted.

Horrific biblical projections of the suffering of exile are balanced by rapturous depictions of the joys of eventual redemption. No portrait of redemption is more glowing than that provided by the anonymous prophet whose utterances are collected at the end of the book of Isaiah. The entirety of chapter 60 of the book of Isaiah is devoted to a series of joyous images of the eventual redemption of God's people. We list here a mere sampling of these elated images:

> Raise up your eyes and look about.
> They have all gathered and come to you.
> Your sons shall be brought from afar,
> Your daughters like babes on shoulders.

---

[6] Deut. 28:64–68.

As you behold, you will glow;
Your heart will throb and thrill.
For the wealth of the sea shall pass on to you;
The riches of nations shall flow to you....
Aliens shall rebuild your walls;
Their kings shall wait upon you.
For in anger I struck you down,
But in favor I take you back.
Your gates shall always stay open,
Day and night they shall never be shut,
To let in the wealth of the nations,
With their kings in procession.
For the nation or the kingdom
That does not serve you shall perish;
Such nations shall be destroyed....
Bowing before you shall come
The children of those who tormented you;
Prostrate at the soles of your feet
Shall be all those who reviled you.
You shall be called
"City of the Lord,
Zion of the Holy One of Israel."[7]

This anonymous prophet was himself witness to the less than over-whelming return of a portion of the Judean people to their homeland under Persian hegemony. What he projects here is a far more magnif-icent and miraculous end to exile, through direct divine intervention. In this projected imagery, the entire world will recognize the majestic redemption of the Jewish people and, through that recognition, come to acknowledge the one true God. Here then, the frightful Deuteronomic depiction of exilic suffering gives way to its polar opposite – an exhila-rated vision of the remarkable blessings that will characterize the third and final period of Jewish history, blessings that will be eternal.

A similarly exhilarated vision of redemption/return is found in Psalm 126:

When the Lord restores the fortunes of Zion – we see it as in a dream – our mouths will be filled with laughter, our tongues with songs of joy.

---

[7] Isa. 60:4–5, 10–12, and 14.

Then shall they say among the nations: "The Lord has done great things for them!"

The Lord shall do great things for us, and we shall rejoice.

Restore our fortunes, O Lord, likes watercourses in the Negev.

They who sow in tears shall reap with songs of joy.

Though he goes along weeping, carrying the seed bag, he shall come back with songs of joy, carrying his sheaves.[8]

Once again, the redemption will be so extraordinary that other peoples will recognize the miraculous and acknowledge the power of the God of Israel.

The sense of a tripartite division of Jewish history was strongly reinforced by the influential apocalyptic imagery of the book of Daniel. In chapter 2 of the book, King Nebuchadnezzar was disquieted by a dream and imposed on his soothsayers the seemingly impossible task of recounting the dream and explaining it, which they were unable to accomplish. The Judean exile, Daniel, was brought to the king's attention and was able, with divine assistance, to accomplish this task. He reconstructed for the king the dream vision of a great statue. This statue, which was huge and its brightness surpassing, stood before you, and its appearance was awesome. The head of that statue was of fine gold; its breast and arms of silver; its belly and thighs of bronze; its legs were of iron; and its feet part iron and part clay. As you looked on, a stone was hewn out, not by hands, and struck the statue on its feet of iron and clay and crushed them. All at once, the iron, clay, bronze, silver, and gold were crushed, and became like chaff of the threshing floors of summer; a wind carried them off until no trace of them was left. But the stone that struck the statue became a great mountain and filled the whole earth.[9]

Having reconstructed the dream, Daniel proceeded to explain it. Reflected in this dream, he explained to Nebuchadnezzar, was a succession of kingdoms. To be sure, there is no reference in this succession of kingdoms to oppression of the Jews, but that was implied for Jewish readers by the reality of the Babylonian king and the exiled Judean lad and made manifest – as we shall see shortly – by the somewhat parallel

---

[8] Ps. 126:1–6.
[9] Dan. 2:31–35.

vision of chapter 7. The critical element in the chapter 2 royal vision is the stone that struck the statue and crushed it, growing into a mountain that filled the entire earth. Daniel explains that this element in the vision is a reference to eventual divine assertion of direct power over the entire world: "In the time of those kings [the kings symbolized by the gold, silver, bronze, iron, and clay], the God of Heaven will establish a kingdom that shall never be destroyed, a kingdom that shall not be transferred to another people. It will crush and wipe out all these kingdoms and make an end of them, but shall itself last forever."[10] Projected here is, once again, a redemption that would be everlasting.

Chapter 7 comes from the second part of the book of Daniel, which most recent scholars agree was composed at a very late date, probably during the second pre-Christian century, the period of Seleucid oppression of the Jews. In this later chapter, Daniel is no longer the interpreter of dreams of others. He himself is the dreamer, and he requires the assistance of heavenly figures to explain his dreams. In Daniel's dream, he sees four frightening beasts rise successively out of the sea. The imagery of the beasts makes it clear that they were fierce and harmful. In the explication of the fourth beast, the Jews are introduced overtly as the holy ones of the Most High. "He [the eleventh king of the fourth empire] will speak words against the Most High and will harass the holy ones of the Most High. He will think of changing times and laws; and they [the holy ones of the Most High] will be delivered into his power for a time, times, and half a time."[11] The sense of a middle period of suffering under a sequence of oppressive empires during a middle period of Jewish history is patent.[12]

Like chapter 2, the later chapter introduces a redemptive note. Daniel sees the divine court being convened, with a decision to destroy the last and most harmful of the kings of the fourth beast-empires. Daniel further sees:

> As I looked on, in the night vision,
> One like a human being
> Came with the clouds of heaven;

---

[10] Dan. 2:44–45.
[11] Dan. 7:25.
[12] Over the ages, Jews and Christians have disputed recurrently the identity of the four kingdoms symbolized by the four beasts and the implications of these identifications for messianic redemption.

He reached the Ancient of Days
And was presented to him.
Dominion, glory, and kingship were given to him;
All peoples and nations of every language must serve him.
His dominion is an everlasting dominion that shall not pass away,
And his kingship one that shall not be destroyed.[13]

Once again, there is a sense that the middle period of domination by others would end with divine intervention and establishment of Jewish authority that would be everlasting. This apocalyptic imagery powerfully reinforced the Deuteronomic and prophetic sense of a middle period of oppression and suffering, which would be succeeded by a redemptive epoch of unending success and joy. This tripartite division of Jewish history created important pre-judgments with which Jews over the ages have approached their experience as an exilic people.

IN HIS IMPORTANT BOOK *ZAKHOR*, YOSEF HAYIM YERUSHALMI HAS argued cogently and convincingly that, during the premodern period, Jewish historical memory was shaped largely by ritual and liturgy. While Yerushalmi's study was devoted ultimately to the emergence of modern Jewish historical writing as an alternative to Jewish memory, I believe he would further agree that, even during the modern period, much Jewish memory continues to be shaped through ritual and liturgy.[14] For premodern Jews overwhelmingly and for many modern Jews as well, an overall sense of Jewish history is encapsulated in ritual and liturgy and is disseminated across all sectors of the Jewish world and throughout all strata of Jewish society.

For Jewish memory as encapsulated in ritual and liturgy, the three-part dynamic of Jewish history is omnipresent. The sense of disruption is patent in fond recollections of pre-70 Jewish life and in the remembered pain of loss and dislocation. The feelings of loss and dislocation have been intensified by the perceived degradation of the middle period, often projected as punishment for and expiation of sinfulness. These feelings encountered the somewhat parallel Christian views of Jewish

[13] Dan. 7:13–14.
[14] Yerushalmi, *Zakhor*.

sinfulness and divine punishment, which reinforced the sense of loss and dislocation. Confronted at every turn by imagery of Jewish degradation, projected as punishment for rejecting the figure that Christians celebrated as their Messiah, Jews rebutted the specifics of the Christian case, but absorbed profoundly the broad notion of the degraded state of exilic Jewish circumstances.[15] Anticipation of eventual divine redemption suffuses Jewish ritual and liturgy as well. That hope was critical to preservation of Jewish identity, since a people without hope is doomed. Not surprisingly, there were major medieval Christian efforts to weaken or obliterate that hope.[16] The sense of loss, suffering, and hope for the anticipated redemption and renewal pervades Jewish law, liturgy, and lore over the long centuries that Jews denoted as exilic and characterized as the "middle age" of Jewish history.

Let us utilize prominent examples from the Jewish prayer service to highlight this vision of tripartite Jewish history. The standard Jewish prayer service, intoned multiple times on weekdays, Sabbaths, and holidays, revolves fundamentally around two poles – recitation of major biblical passages that proclaim and celebrate core Jewish beliefs and commitments (identified as the shem`a, after the first word of the first biblical passage) and a set of praises of and petitions to God (identified as the `amidah or the shemoneh-esreh). The biblical passages recited are: Deuteronomy 6:4–9; Deuteronomy 11:13–21; and Numbers 15:37–41. They focus on: belief in one God and the requirement of love of that one God; the covenantal relationship between the one God and his one people Israel, with the rewards and punishments that flow from fulfillment or non-fulfillment of the demands of the covenant; and core rituals that keep God and the covenant at the forefront of consciousness at all times.

In the very heart of the middle section, which highlights the rewards and punishments attendant upon fulfillment or non-fulfillment of the demands of the covenant, Jewish worshippers are regularly reminded that their fate is contingent upon meeting divine demands. The passage proclaims that, if Jews are faithful to the covenant, God will provide

---

[15] For the Christian views, see Chapter 2.
[16] Chazan, Fashioning Jewish Identity, chaps. 8 and 9.

splendid natural blessings. However, Jewish worshippers are warned of the alternative as well:

Take care not to be lured away to serve other gods, and bow to them. For the Lord's anger will flare up against you, and he will shut up the skies so that there will be no rain and the ground will not yield its produce; and you will soon perish from the good land that the Lord is assigning you.[17]

For many premodern and modern Jews, this passage served as an ongoing reminder of their own circumstances, their shortcomings, and the basis for these circumstances.

Moreover, the first two passages are embedded in sections of the book of Deuteronomy that are extremely rich in evocation of the reward-punishment scheme. The first passage – Deuteronomy 6:4–9 – is followed immediately by reference to God's beneficence in bringing the Israelites to the land he had promised and assigning to them "great and flourishing cities that you did not build, houses full of all good things that you did not fill, hewn cisterns that you did not hew, vineyards that you did not plant." The Israelites must be careful, however, to fulfill the demands of the covenant, "lest the anger of the Lord your God blaze forth against you and he wipe you off the face of the earth."[18] The second passage is even more strategically located. It is followed again by emphasis on God's beneficence in bringing the Israelites into the rich land they are to inherit, along with warnings of the fate that awaits them for failure: "See, this day I set before you blessing and curse: blessing, if you obey the commandments of the Lord your God that I enjoin upon you this day; and curse, if you do not obey the commandment of the Lord your God, but turn away from the path that I enjoin upon you this day and follow other gods, whom you have not experienced."[19]

The second core element in the Jewish prayer service – the benedictions of praise and petition – are post-biblical and express yet more strikingly the tripartite sense of Jewish history. This section begins with three benedictions that are standard for all services. These benedictions open – significantly for our purposes – with evocation of the glorious past of

[17] Deut. 11:16–17.
[18] Deut. 6:11 and 15.
[19] Deut. 11:26.

the patriarchs and the longed-for future redemption. "Blessed are you, O Lord our God and God of our fathers – God of Abraham, God of Isaac, and God of Jacob – the great, mighty, and awesome God, the sublime God, who confers wonderful kindnesses, controls all, recalls the kindnesses of the forefathers, and brings redemption to their children's children."[20] This initial benediction opens with evocation of the rich past and the glorious future. For Jews intoning this benediction repeatedly every day, there is deep satisfaction in the connection with both past and future, but inevitable awareness of the striking contrast with the present.

There are likewise three closing benedictions repeated in all services. Again, the first of the three focuses on the Jewish past and future. "Accept, O Lord our God, your people Israel and their prayer. Return [their] worship to the courtyard of your abode, and accept lovingly and graciously the sacrifices of Israel and their prayer. May the worship of Israel your people always be acceptable. May our eyes witness your return to Zion in mercy. Blessed are you, O Lord, who returns his presence to Zion."[21] The bounties of the past are recalled, and hopes for the future are articulated. Implicit again is the contrast with a present that is devoid of these bounties.

The weekday version of the middle portion of this set of blessings of praise and petition is given over to a sequence of requests, in which the themes of past, present, and future are again prominent. Following are some of the major themes of these petitions.

Sound the great ram's horn of our freedom, and raise the standard for ingathering of our exiles. Collect us together from the four corners of the earth. Blessed are you, O Lord, who gathers the far-flung of his people Israel.

Return our leaders as of yore and our councilors as of old. Remove from us agony and pain. Rule over us along with loving kindness and mercy, and provide appropriately justification for us. Blessed are you, O Lord, who loves righteousness and justice. . . .

[20] Seligman Baer, ed., *Seder Avodat Yisrael*, 87–88.
[21] Ibid., 98–99.

Return to Jerusalem, your city, with mercy. Dwell in it, as you have said. Build it speedily in our days in everlasting fashion. Reconstitute within it speedily the throne of David. Blessed are you, O Lord, who builds Jerusalem.

Revive the seed of your servant David speedily. Lift his horn through your salvation, for we hope for your salvation daily. Blessed are you, O Lord, who revives the horn of salvation.[22]

The focus on a glorious past and a splendid future inevitably serves to highlight the shortcomings of the present, which for Jews is the middle period of Jewish history, characterized by exile and degradation.

For one final example of evocation of the richness of the pre-exilic Jewish past and of aspirations for the post-exilic future, let us note the special prayer service added for festivals, a service constructed around recollections of holiday worship at the Jerusalem Temple. Central to this service is an expressive prayer that focuses on this glorious past, its destruction and loss, and hopes for a renewed future. Let us examine first the sense of the past and its glories.

You have chosen us out of all the nations; you have loved us and accepted us; you have elevated us above all other folk and have sanctified us with your commandments. Our King, you have brought us to your service and have designated us with your great and holy Name. You have lovingly given us, o Lord our God, appointed times for celebration, holidays and festivals for joyousness.[23]

The past is recollected as a period of divine-human closeness, with all the well-being such proximity implies.

The joyousness associated with the past gives way to the reality of painful loss and then – almost immediately – to hopes for a splendid future.

Because of our sins we have been exiled from our land and distanced from our home-terrain. We cannot ascend [to Jerusalem], to appear [there], to prostrate ourselves before you, and to fulfill our obligations in the house you

[22] Ibid., 92–97.
[23] Ibid., 351.

have chosen – the great and sacred house that bears your name – because of the violence done to your sacred place.

May it be your will, O Lord our God and God of our ancestors – merciful king – that you reconsider and have mercy upon us and upon your sanctuary out of your great mercy. May you rebuild it speedily and enhance its glory. Our father, our king, reveal speedily the glory of your kingship upon us; appear and be exalted through us in the eyes of all the living. Gather our scattered from among the nations, and collect our far-flung from the corners of the earth. Bring us happily to Zion your city and to Jerusalem, the site of your sanctuary, with everlasting joy. There we shall offer before you our obligatory sacrifices.[24]

The sense of loss of the Jerusalem Temple and the divine-human relationship it symbolized gives way immediately to hopes for renewal of the past, which will include restoration of the entire people to its promised homeland and reconstitution of the special divine-human relationship in a manner that will make a profound impression on all of humanity.

Given the role of liturgy in shaping the traditional Jewish sense of past, present, and future, the recurrent emphasis on the splendor of the Jewish past, the glories of the Jewish future, and the contrasting degradation and suffering of the middle period surely served to implant deeply among Jews a harshly negative sense of the Jewish "middle age."

THIS JEWISH SENSE OF BEING MIRED IN A MIDDLE PERIOD OF EXILE AND subjugation is prominent in many domains of Jewish creativity beyond liturgy – in poetry, philosophic rumination, and mystical speculation. Let us utilize premodern Jewish history writing, an admittedly secondary field of Jewish creativity, as a further portal through which to investigate the Jewish sense of a "middle age." As argued by Yerushalmi, up through the sixteenth century Jews were little preoccupied with history writing. Jewish historical memory was – as we have briefly seen – extremely well developed over the centuries, but historical writings played only a minor role in the formulation and dissemination of Jewish memory. To the extent that Jews wrote history, it was oriented to the pre-exilic

---

[24] Ibid., 352.

period, to developmental aspects of Jewish law, or to significant – often traumatic – contemporary events. It was only in the sixteenth century that overarching histories of the Jewish past began to be composed. These valuable compositions are highly revealing of the Jewish view of a "middle age" that had crystallized by that time.[25]

Of these new overarching histories, the most traditional and most influential was Joseph *ha-kohen*'s `*Emek ha-Bakha* (*Vale of Tears*). In a sense, the title says it all, as Joseph *ha-kohen* himself indicates:

Since the misfortunes that befell us from the day of Judah's exile from its land that was destroyed are scattered here and there, I committed myself to putting them together in a small volume, which will include all I have found in the booklets of writers who wrote before my time in Hebrew and in their books. I have entitled it `*Emek ha-Bakha*, because that title corresponds to its content. Everyone who reads it will be astounded and will gasp, with tears welling down from his eyes. Putting his hands to his loins, he will ask: "How long, O Lord?" I pray to God that the days of our mourning may come to an end. May he send us the Righteous Messiah, and may he redeem us speedily in our days, out of his mercy and loving kindness. Amen and amen.[26]

`*Emek ha-Bakha* begins precisely with the destruction of Jerusalem, which served as central symbol for the onset of the Jewish "middle age." Joseph depicts the killing of revered leaders by Titus and quickly proceeds to the Bar Kokhba revolt and its suppression. Joseph then moves rapidly across a number of centuries, describing isolated instances of persecution and suffering. The description becomes thick when Joseph reaches the eleventh century and Jewish life in western Christendom. The persecutions perpetrated against the Jews of western Christendom from the eleventh through the sixteenth centuries are numerous and form the core of `*Emek ha-Bakha*. To be sure, the gloom of the repeated persecutions – presented in staccato fashion, one after the other – occasionally gives way to reference to a major center of Jewish learning, a giant figure of Jewish creativity, or the composition of an important book.[27] Nonetheless, the sense of Jewish exile, subjugation, and incessant suffering is

---

[25] Yerushalmi, *Zakhor*, chapter 3.
[26] Joseph *ha-kohen*, *Sefer Emek ha-Bakha* (*The Vale of Tears*), Heb. pag., 1.
[27] This combination of Jewish suffering and learning had an important impact on the historical thinking of Heinrich Graetz, to be examined in Chapter 4.

palpable throughout and becomes increasingly sharp as the book progresses and as the suffering is increasingly centered in medieval western Christendom.

The double note of the introduction – suffering and redemption – is reprised by Joseph *ha-kohen* at the end of his work as well:

I praise the Lord who has inspired me to compose this little opus that contains most of the sufferings and persecutions that have befallen our people from the destruction of the Temple to this very day.... May the good Lord, in his mercy, always be at my side and dignify me to write about the advent of the Messiah, so that the words of the verse may be fulfilled with respect to us: "Rejoice with her [Jerusalem] in joy, all you who mourn over her."[28] Amen. Amen.[29]

While `*Emek ha-Bakha* focuses almost exclusively on persecution of Jews and Jewish suffering, in a curious way a positive message is embedded in this tale of woe. Both the introduction and conclusion close with reference to redemption. Since the pain and suffering detailed in `*Emek ha-Bakha* constitute expiation for sin, then precisely the ubiquity and extremity of the Jewish suffering suggest – according to the author – the possible completion of the process of expiation and the dawn of redemption. Joseph *ha-kohen* reflects well the broad Jewish perspective on the Jewish "middle age" as the unhappy period sandwiched between the splendors of past and future. His accessible and popular primer served to crystallize for many what were broadly perceived as the fundamental contours of the middle period of Jewish history and to disseminate that perception widely.

Not long before Joseph *ha-kohen* composed his `*Emek ha-Bakha*, a fellow émigré from the Iberian peninsula who had likewise found refuge in Italy – Samuel Usque – penned a somewhat similar historical work. Usque's *Consolacam as Tribulacoens de Israel* (*Consolation for the Tribulations of Israel*) is likewise focused on the long record of Jewish suffering; but it was written in Portuguese rather than Hebrew, was intended for a narrower audience (New Christians returning to the Jewish fold primarily), was broader in its scope, and was far more refined in its literary style. Usque created a rhetorically rich pastoral dialogue, with a Jacob

---

[28] Isa. 66:1.
[29] Joseph *ha-kohen*, *Sefer Emek ha-Bakha*, Heb. pag., 97.

figure rehearsing the tragedies that had befallen his people and with two prophetic figures offering the requisite consolations. Jacob's recitation of travails encompasses the entirety of the Jewish past, that is to say all three instances of exile and suffering, although the third and lengthiest of the exiles ultimately dominates. Most obviously shared with `Emek ha-Bakha is the focus on a redemption urgently hoped for and assumed to be in the offing. All the characteristics of the *Consolacam* noted – language, audience, and literary style – made it a far less influential work than `Emek ha-Bakha. Nonetheless, the confluence of themes makes it useful to our investigation of traditional Jewish perceptions of the middle period of the Jewish past.[30]

Usque begins his composition with a prologue that opens on a broadly humanistic note.

For troubled spirits, the recollection of past misfortunes will somewhat diminish the suffering from present ones, especially if those gone by have been more intense. And although one misfortune is hardly cured by another, this form of medicine was approved by the great worthies, whose broad knowledge has left us remedies for the soul's afflictions and who have counseled people how to endure the sufferings to which this wretched life of ours is so subject and subjected . . .

Indeed, if we wished to examine things closely and not allow ourselves to be overcome by emotion, there is no affliction – however great – whose might is now buffeting us that past generations have not seen and suffered more greatly.

And if there be any people that can exemplify and demonstrate this experience, surely it is our own toil-worn and harassed nation. Though our people has been suffering grave tribulations in our days, the tribulations that beset it in ancient times were yet much greater, and – compared to them – today's troubles can be considered small.[31]

Out of this desire to lessen the pain of recent tribulations, Usque extended the scope of his opus to include the suffering of all three exiles – the Egyptian, the Babylonian, and the Roman. In the process, he diminished the emphasis projected by Joseph *ha-kohen* on the third and lengthiest of

---

[30] Usque's work has been translated by Martin A. Cohen as *Consolation for the Tribulations of Israel*. For a valuable study of this composition, see Yosef Hayim Yerushalmi, "A Jewish Classic in the Portuguese Language," 1:15–123.

[31] Usque, *Consolation*, 38.

the exiles, thus offering the potential for reinterpretation of the tripartite sense of the Jewish past we have thus far encountered. In fact, however, this is a potential not realized.

Very quickly, Usque extends his prologue by offering a second line of consolation that in fact contradicts the first. Continuing the theme of amelioration of present suffering through consideration of past and more painful tribulations, Usque changes course in mid-sentence.

In my judgment, this can be easily believed [that present-day tribulations are less than those of the past], not only because our people is so reduced in numbers that the misfortunes – great as they are – cannot find a large enough target on which to spend their strength, but also, as I believe and trust, after this storm that has pursued us until this day, the dawn will break and the longed-for morning after winter's stormy night will graciously appear to us. Indeed, since all things are perfectly governed by the infinite Creator and composed without blemish, I cannot help but believe that, just as they [Jewish misfortunes] had a beginning, they will not lack an end, for he alone is without end and without beginning. Thus, since our sufferings are obviously so many and of such long duration and since their intensity has increased, it is certain that – unless our sins provide nourishment to sustain them – they will speedily come to an end, and the fair weather we look for will begin to appear.[32]

After arguing that present tribulations are mitigated by consideration of past and more intense suffering, Usque changes course and suggests that the accumulation of suffering over the lengthy stretch of the third exile and the intensity of the more recent persecution – in contradistinction to his prior argument – indicate that redemption is at hand. Here, Usque agrees totally with Joseph *ha-kohen*, both of them convinced that the length and depth of Jewish suffering during the third exile serves as sure indication of the impending onset of redemption.

This second view of Usque is well reflected in the organization of his composition. As noted, Usque – unlike Joseph *ha-kohen* – divides his work into three sections. In each, the Jacob figure laments the suffering of his progeny and is then comforted by the prophetic voices. In the first two sections, the incidents of suffering are few, but very well known, with lavish depiction of – for example – the destruction of the two

[32] Ibid., 38–39.

temples. As the author proceeds into the third and longest section of the composition, the style changes markedly. The incidents are no longer so well known, but they are far more numerous. Once again, as was the case in `Emek ha-Bakha, the author overwhelms his readers with the multitude of incidents, one following the other in swift succession, thus creating an overall impression of unceasing persecution and endless suffering.

Thus, differences notwithstanding, Joseph *ha-kohen* and Samuel Usque concur in reinforcing the sense of profound Jewish suffering during the middle period of the Jewish past, defined as the lengthy stretch of time between destruction of the Second Temple in 70 CE and the anticipated redemption of the Jewish people through direct divine intervention. In the realm of early modern Jewish history writing, the basic pattern rooted in the Hebrew Bible and strongly reinforced in the Jewish liturgy is once again clearly manifest.

THE JEWISH SENSE OF A THREE-PART JEWISH HISTORY PERVADED EVERY sector of medieval Jewish life and every corner of medieval Jewish culture. This view conditioned much of Jewish thinking about the experiences undergone by Jews in every area of Jewish settlement. Its impact was especially powerful in medieval western Christendom, where the Christian majority shared much the same outlook on Jewish history and Jewish suffering.

2

~

The Jewish Middle Age: The Christian View

CHRISTIANS HAVE VIEWED JEWISH HISTORY FROM THE PARALLEL perspective of a tripartite Jewish past, with agreement as to the broad time frames of the three periods of the Jewish past and radical divergences as to some of the specifics. There is a somewhat different Christian perspective on the first period of the Jewish past, with a tendency to highlight more prominently than Jews did the shortcomings of the early period of Israelite history. Especially noteworthy is the Christian focus on the purported Jewish role in the crucifixion of Jesus as the ultimate Jewish sin, which ignited final divine outrage and the onset of exilic suffering. Disagreement was more striking with respect to the third period. For Jews, the third period was to see bountiful divine blessings showered upon the long-suffering Jewish people. For Christians, there would indeed be great blessings for the Jews, but they would result from Jewish recognition of the truth of Christianity. Thus, divine bounty would be the fruit of Jewish rejection of Judaism and acceptance of Christianity. It is with respect to the middle period that there is fullest agreement, with both sides in accord on the drastic punishments visited by God upon the Jewish people for its sinfulness. To be sure, the two sides identified the Jewish sins in divergent ways. Nonetheless, whatever the sins specified, the empirical realities were viewed as the same – exile, powerlessness, subjugation, and suffering.

This view of the Jewish past was hardly a minor theme in Christian thinking. It was essential to Christian self-perception and self-worth. Jewish sinfulness, according to Paul and subsequent Christian thinking, resulted in God's rejection of the Jews, which in turn led to the divine turn to the Gentiles, meaning the beginning of Christianity as Paul conceptualized it. Thus, the sequencing of Jewish historical experience actually formed a critical element in Christian history and had to be regularly pondered, clarified, and disseminated to Christian believers. The tripartite division of Jewish history was a key building block in accurate understanding of Christian past, present, and future.

∾

THE ROOTS OF THIS CHRISTIAN VIEW OF THE MIDDLE PERIOD OF THE Jewish past lie ultimately in the same Hebrew Bible that underlay the Jewish view, interpreted in slightly but not overwhelmingly different fashion. Christian thinkers as well cited the predictions of Jewish suffering advanced in the narrative, prophetic, and apocalyptic sections of the Hebrew Bible. Although Christian observers saw the sins that occasioned divine punishment differently than their Jewish counterparts, the realities of Jewish circumstances projected by them for the middle of the three periods of Jewish history were very much the same.

The more proximate source for the Christian sense of Jewish suffering was Paul and his complex views of Judaism and the Jews. Paul's views of Judaism and the Jews have been the subject of intense scrutiny over the past few decades, largely as a result of the post-Holocaust effort to understand more fully the history and impact of Christian anti-Jewish imagery. Paul has been a center of attention in this effort, but the results have been murky.

For many scholars, Paul is the arch-villain of Christian-Jewish relations, the creator and purveyor of Christian notions of supersessionism. For these scholars, Paul is the clear source of the destructive sense of Jews as losing their place in covenantal history and being replaced by Christians. For many other scholars, however, matters are by no means so simple. In this alternative view, Paul did indeed suggest a shift in covenantal primacy from Jews to Gentiles, but that is hardly the end of the story. At the same time – urge these scholars – Paul was insistent upon God's everlasting relationship with the Jews, who were Paul's own people and God's "first love." God would not – in this view of Paul's perspectives – abandon the Jews forever. Rather, Jewish failures played a role in an ultimate divine plan to spread God's bounty more broadly across human society. With the passage of time, the Jews would eventually be reunited with their Creator and his new adherents.[1]

In the face of this sometimes intense scholarly disagreement regarding assessment of Paul, it seems to me the wisest course is to follow the lead proposed by Garry Wills and Jeremy Cohen. Wills, in his *What Paul Meant*, insists throughout on the difficulties of Paul's language and thus on the impossibility of certainty with respect to Paul's views. In his chapter on Paul and the Jews, he argues more specifically that the precise meaning of the Pauline attacks on Jewish law must be seen against the backdrop of three differing groups for which Jewish law had meaning – Jews who rejected Jesus; Jews who accepted Jesus; and Gentiles who accepted Jesus. To the extent that Paul is concerned with the third group, he is really not making overarching statements about the meaning of Jewish law and its efficacy; he is merely arguing against the imposition of the demands of Jewish law upon Gentile believers. Thus, great care must be exercised in assessing Paul's view of Judaism on the basis of these attacks.[2] In his *Living Letters of the Law*, Jeremy Cohen resolutely refuses to categorize Paul, but rather insists that there is fundamental ambivalence in the Pauline stance toward Judaism and Jews, an ambivalence that – according to Cohen – pervades much of Christian thought thereafter.[3]

The key passage on the Jews, their status, and their fate in the Pauline epistles is the complex and often puzzling Romans 9–11.[4] Paul opens by proclaiming: "I am speaking the truth as a Christian." At an important later point, he identifies himself a second time: "I am an Israelite myself, of the stock of Abraham, of the tribe of Benjamin."[5] This ambiguity in self-identification serves as fitting introduction to a passage that is complicated and convoluted.

---

[1] For a valuable summary of the two sides to this ongoing scholarly debate, see John Gager, *Reinventing Paul*.

[2] Garry Wills, *What Paul Meant*, especially chapter 7.

[3] Cohen, *Living Letters of the Law*, introduction.

[4] For important studies of Romans, see Krister Stendahl, *Final Account: Paul's Letter to the Romans*, and the essays in Cristina Grenholm and Daniel Patte, eds., *Reading Israel in Romans*.

[5] Rom. 9:1 and 11:1.

Paul proceeds immediately after proclaiming his Israelite identity to grieving for his Jewish brethren and singing their praises.

They are the descendants of Israel, chosen to be God's sons; theirs is the glory of the divine presence, theirs the covenant, the law, the temple worship, and the promises. The patriarchs are theirs, and from them by natural descent came the Messiah.[6]

He then quickly shifts gears and talks of the replacement of this group of God's children by others. Paul asks about the justice of this replacement of the initial covenant people and answers that God can show mercy to whomever he chooses to show mercy. As a reflection of God's ultimate power, Paul introduces the negative image of Pharaoh. God has – as it were – hardened the heart of the Jews as he had earlier hardened the heart of the ruler of Egypt, not really a flattering image for the people so lavishly praised a few verses earlier. Paul then proceeds to detail the key shortcoming of the Jews – their focus on law, rather than belief. Thus, the passage is replete with contradictions. The Jews are portrayed positively and negatively; God is portrayed as mysteriously hardening their hearts, as he did to Pharaoh, and then a reasonable explanation for God's decision is advanced. Given this tacking back and forth, it is hardly surprising that modern scholars have come to such profound disagreement as to the Pauline position vis-à-vis Judaism and Jews.

In chapter 11, Paul then asks about the future of the Jewish people. In answering this question, he adds yet further complication. After reprising the notion of God hardening the hearts of the Jews, he sets off in a new direction. The failure of the Jews – whether self-inflicted or mysteriously imposed by God – has had the beneficial result of opening the way for the Gentiles. What then does the future hold?

When they stumbled, was their fall final? Far from it!! Through a false step on their part, salvation has come to the Gentiles, and this in turn will stir them [the Jews] up to envy. If their false step means the enrichment of the world, if their falling short means the enrichment of the Gentiles, how much more will their coming to full strength mean![7]

---

[6] Rom. 11:4.
[7] Rom. 11:11–12.

This leads to powerful imagery drawn from the natural world and fated to have enduring impact on Christian perceptions of Jews.

If the root is holy, so are the branches. But if some of the branches have been lopped off and you, a wild olive, have been grafted in among them and have come to share the same root and sap as the olive, do not make yourself superior to the branches. If you do, remember that you do not sustain the root: the root sustains you.[8]

Finally, Paul draws an important conclusion as to the ultimate fate of the Jews:

This partial hardening has come on Israel only until the Gentiles have been admitted in full strength; once that has happened, the whole of Israel will be saved.[9]

The obscurity of all this is daunting. What is abundantly clear is that Paul advances a set of images of and teachings about Judaism and Jews that decisively influenced subsequent Christian thinking, required ongoing efforts at clarification, and gave rise to alternative views, as later readers focused on one or another of the conflicting Pauline themes.

Crucial for our purposes is the sense of Jewish failure (however explained), divine punishment, and eventual reconciliation. To be sure, Paul – preaching and writing before the decisive events of 66–70 – offers no details as to the nature of the punishment that God was imposing on the Jews, other than to project in abstract terms divine abandonment. In any case, Paul absorbs and transmits a tripartite sense of Jewish history, reinforces it, and to a significant extent, transforms it. He portrays the first period of Jewish history glowingly; the second period involves Jewish failures and dreadful punishment for these failures, variously understood; the third period will be resplendent once more as God, the new covenant people, and the original covenant people unite. For our purposes, the notion of the middle period as one of punishment for sinfulness is very much consistent with the Jewish sense of that middle period.

The Gospels, composed subsequent to the Pauline epistles, are in general less conflicted and more negative in their portrayal of the Jews. For the Gospels, the Jews – or at least the Jewish leaders – are the obvious foils

---

[8] Rom. 11:16–18.
[9] Rom. 11:25–26.

to the purity and goodness of Jesus and the identifiable enemy figures ranged against him. While Jesus was in a formal sense crucified by the Romans, the Gospels go to great lengths to exonerate Roman officialdom and to assign exclusive responsibility for this act to the leaders of the Jewish community, ostensibly overwhelming their Roman overlords. There is a potent sense of Jewish sinfulness and related punishment. Absent the Pauline speculation on the eventual fate of the Jewish people, there is little of the tripartite sense of Jewish history so dominant in Paul.

∽

THE NEW TESTAMENT — ESPECIALLY PAULINE — POSITION ON JEWISH history of course became determinative for subsequent Christian thinking, although it offered rich potential for alternative interpretations. The key interpreter of this issue — as of so many other issues as well — was the bishop of Hippo and monumental Christian thinker, Saint Augustine, who was deeply influenced by the Pauline perspective on Judaism and the Jews. Indeed, Augustine perceived himself to be merely explicating Pauline views.

Modern scholars have arrived at the consensus that the Augustinian doctrine vis-à-vis Judaism and the Jews was critical in establishing the framework for Jewish existence in Christian society all through late antiquity and the Middle Ages and down into modernity as well. Constantine, as a pivotal figure in the evolution of Christianity, laid the foundations for a Jewish place in Christian society in a most cursory way; Augustine erected upon these flimsy foundations an elaborate theory of the Jews, their role in cosmic history, and their utility to Christianity. His theory became critical for Jews over the ages. As we have seen, Jewish presence in medieval western Christendom was extremely limited down through the first millennium. When significant Jewish presence became a reality, the Augustinian doctrine became a critical – perhaps *the* critical – element in the Jewish status that eventuated.[10]

Augustine penned one specific treatise on Jews. It is primarily defensive in nature – a set of responses that Christians should be prepared to advance against Jewish claims. In the process, Augustine makes some

---

[10] The most comprehensive overview of the Augustinian position is that of Paula Fredriksen, *Augustine and the Jews*.

general observations – especially at the beginning and end of the treatise – on Judaism and Jews. He begins, not surprisingly, with Paul and Paul's exhortation to Christians to remain loyal to their faith, reminding them of God's kindness and God's severity: "Observe the kindness and the severity of God – severity to those who fell away, divine kindness to you, provided that you remain within its scope."[11] Augustine explains immediately that Paul was here talking of the Jews.

Assuredly, he said this about the Jews, who as branches of that olive tree that was fruitful in its root of the holy patriarchs have been broken off on account of their unbelief, so that because of the faith of the Gentiles the wild olive was grafted on and shared in the richness of the true olive tree after the natural branches had been cut off. . . .

By the just severity of God, therefore, the unbelieving pride of the native branches is broken away from the living patriarchal root, and by the grace of divine goodness the faithful humility of the wild olive is ingrafted.[12]

The impact of the Pauline imagery just now discussed is obvious here. Augustine was of course writing centuries after the year 70, which means that he was fully cognizant of the disaster occasioned by the Jewish rebellion against Rome. Indeed, by the time Augustine wrote, the center of Jewish population was no longer in the Land of Israel, giving rise to a deep sense of Jewish dispersion as well. Thus, Augustine interpreted Paul's message of divine punishment – the breaking off of the branches from the olive tree – in the light of these post-Pauline developments. Jewish failures and Christian successes – by Augustine's time, Christianity had become the ruling faith of the entire Roman Empire – thus had come to play an important pedagogic role for Christians, indeed for all humanity. The mechanism of divine reward and punishment, so central to the Hebrew Bible and thus to Christianity as well, was projected by Augustine as illustrated in remarkably clear fashion by the fortunes of the original branches of the olive tree and the wild branches grafted onto it. Anyone seeking reinforcement of belief in divine control of human history and in the role of sin and divine punishment need only attend to the contrasting fates of the Jewish and Christian communities. In the multifaceted Augustinian doctrine that established essential justification

---

[11] Rom. 11:22.
[12] Augustine, "In Answer to the Jews," 391.

for Jewish presence in Christian societies, this pedagogic notion of the illustrative value of Jewish and contrastive Christian fate plays a central role.

Thus, for Augustine the tripartite division of Jewish history was clearer than it had been for Paul. The first period – up until the year 70 – began with the patriarchs and their greatness; this greatness was subsequently compromised by their errant descendants, who sullied the legacy of Abraham, Isaac, and Jacob. The sinfulness of the Jews – the original branches of the olive tree – culminated in rejection of Jesus, responsibility for his crucifixion, and resultant rejection by God. This latter rejection set in motion election of the Gentiles to fill the void in the divine-human covenant. The realities of post-70 Jewish and Christian history show – in Augustine's view – punishment of the Jews on the one hand and rewards for the Gentiles on the other. Ultimately, along the lines suggested by Paul, there would be a reconciliation of the old branches of the olive tree, the new branches, and God. The closeness of these views to the Jewish sense of three-part Jewish history is patent, as is the divergence.

This same sense of tripartite Jewish history pervades Augustine's historiosophic masterpiece, *The City of God*. As was usually the case, Augustine sought to achieve multiple objectives in this work. One level with which he was concerned involved worldly history, more specifically the historical achievements of pagan Rome. Stung by the suggestion that the sack of Rome in 410 by the Visigoths had been occasioned by its embrace of Christianity, Augustine devoted the first five books of the *City of God* to the history of Rome, with the argument that worship of the gods – instead of the one true God – lay at the core of the failed experience of that earthly city. Embedded within this lengthy counter-history of Rome is a brief but intriguing contrast with the saga of the Jews, which comes at the close of Book IV. This capsule history of the Jews highlights all the negatives associated with Rome. According to Augustine, "those earthly blessings – the sole object of breathless desire for those who can imagine nothing better – are dependent on the power of the one God, not on that of the many false gods, whom the Romans believed they ought to worship."[13]

In order to prove his point, Augustine offers the contrastive portrait of Israel, whose people worshipped the one true God and whom the

[13] Augustine, *Concerning the City of God against the Pagans*, 177.

one true God blessed abundantly. Augustine highlights God's consistent intervention on behalf of the Israelites. He focuses heavily on the Egypt experience and the exodus, citing God's rapid increase of the Israelite population, the succoring of the young in the face of Egyptian persecution, the miraculous signs and wonders produced against the Egyptians, the parting of the Red Sea, the manna in the wilderness, and the provision of water for the thirsty wanderers. Subsequently, the Jews succeeded in their wars and in their peacetime pursuits as well. These successes flowed from the support of the one true God who rules the universe. "In fact, the Israelites received from the one true God all the blessings for which the Romans thought it necessary to pray to all the host of false gods, and they received them [these blessings] in a far happier manner."[14]

To be sure, Augustine limited the extent of this positive portrait of the early history of the Jews. Jewish well-being involved the material realm only. Augustine insists that the ultimate Jewish shortcoming was the inability to rise above the material level to genuine spirituality. This was the ultimate cause of the failure of the Jews and their eventual downfall. Once again, in this different setting, Augustine reinforces the imagery of a three-part Jewish history, now projected as material achievement, followed by spiritual sin and material/spiritual punishment, and culminating in ultimate reunion with God and his true, that is, Christian adherents.

CHRISTIAN DEPICTION OF THE MIDDLE PHASE OF JEWISH HISTORY, with strong emphasis on the intense suffering endured by the Jews in the wake of their sinfulness, is prominent from the Church Fathers onward. Especially noteworthy in this regard is the highly influential history of the Church penned by Eusebius of Caesarea.[15] Flush with the exhilaration of the shift in Roman policy introduced by Constantine, Eusebius set out to describe the heroes and villains of the first three centuries of Church history. In his plan for the work, he identifies five issues he intends to address. Two involve heroes, viz. the leaders of the Church and its martyrs, and two involve ongoing villains, viz. the persecuting Roman

---

[14] Ibid., 178.
[15] Eusebius, *The History of the Church.*

authorities and the internal dissidents determined to lead the faithful astray. The fifth issue involves the Jews, who were the initial enemies of the church and who – according to Eusebius – paid a terrible price for their rejection of Jesus.[16]

Much of Book 2 of *The History of the Church*, which proceeds from the Crucifixion down through the uprising against Rome, is taken up with evidence of extreme Jewish suffering throughout this forty-year period. The beginning of Book 3 is devoted to the culminating horrors of the failed war against Rome.

The calamities which at that time overwhelmed the whole nation in every part of the world; the process by which the inhabitants of Judea were driven to the limits of disaster; the thousands and thousands of men of every age who together with women and children perished by the sword, by starvation, and by countless other forms of death; the number of Jewish cities besieged and the horrors they endured, especially the terrible and worse than terrible sights that met the eyes of those who sought refuge in Jerusalem itself as an impregnable fortress; the last scene of all when the Abomination of Desolation announced by the prophets was set up in the very Temple of God, once world-renowned, when it underwent utter destruction and final dissolution by fire – all this anyone who wishes can gather in precise detail from the pages of Josephus's history.[17]

For Eusebius and other major Church thinkers, these horrific disasters were worthy of full depiction and deep Christian consideration, since they were the direct and obvious result of divine anger with the Jews for their rejection of Jesus.

As Jewish presence in medieval western Christendom grew, this tri-partite sense of Jewish history evolved from a broad claim designed for internal Christian purposes to a tangible sense of the situation of a grow-ing Jewish minority. Given the reality of the Jews as a small numerical element in Christian society and as a powerless element at that, the more remote portrait of the middle period of Jewish history took on enhanced and immediate meaning. In addition, this sense of Jewish history played a major role in the accelerating commitment to missionizing among the Jews. One of the most persuasive arguments advanced by Christians on both the informal and formal levels was the evidence from the historical

---

[16] Ibid., 1.
[17] Ibid., 68–69.

sphere, that is to say the obvious historical reality of Jewish subjugation and Christian ascendancy. The evidence of Jewish polemical literature shows the ubiquity and impact of this powerful missionizing thrust.[18]

To cite but one salient example of this medieval Christian sense, let us note the important twelfth-century work composed by a major convert from Judaism to Christianity, Petrus Alfonsi. Petrus wrote his polemical tract in the form of a dialogue between a Jew named Moses and a Christian named Petrus, in effect suggesting an inner conversation between a former Jewish self and a new Christian identity. In the second chapter, the author attempts to show his Jewish interlocutor the importance of the Jewish rejection of Jesus and the resultant impact on the subsequent history of the Jews. Central to the argument for the special quality of the sin that set in motion the present exile is a striking contrast between the previous and present Jewish exiles.

According to the Christian spokesman in the dialogue, the Babylonian exile was a relatively comfortable affair. During that exile,

They [the Jews] sustained no punishment other than servitude. They tilled the fields, they planted vines, they built houses, and they lived in safety with their wives and children.[19]

The contrast between this prior exile and present exile is – according to Petrus (the interlocutor and author) – stunning and proves that the sin for which the present exile eventuated was of a unique nature.

Petrus's description of the horrors of the present exile is one of the richest available in medieval literature and deserves lengthy citation:

In the second [exile, that is to say the current exile], however, they bore so many, so great, and such unheard-of scandals that ones like them or equal to them have never been seen or heard among them.

Indeed, they were slain and burned and sold as captives, and the sale increased so much, until thirty captives were given for one piece of silver.[20] Nevertheless, no one was found who would buy, just as Moses promised when he

---

[18] Chazan, *Fashioning Jewish Identity*, chapter 8. See Chapter 9 of this text.
[19] Petrus Alfonsi, *Dialogue against the Jews*, 103.
[20] An ironic reference to the thirty pieces of silver Judas Iscariot is supposed to have received for betrayal of Jesus.

said: "There you shall offer yourselves for sale to your enemies as male and female slaves, but none will buy."[21]

There were ships filled with them that were released upon the open sea to drift without oar or helmsman, to their disgrace and shame.

Moreover, after you were cast into this captivity, you were given intolerable commands – not to read the law or to teach it to your children. If anyone was found either reading the law or teaching it to his children, either he was burned by fire, or he was flayed by very sharp iron combs.[22] Besides this, you were not permitted to observe either the Passover or the Sabbath. Truly, if anyone was found doing so, he was punished very harshly. . . .

Thus, throughout the passage of all ages, diverse commandments of evil were proclaimed against you, as is proved by the testimonies of your own books.[23]

Thus, the Christian sense of Jewish history shows obvious signs of absorption of the three-part historical scheme of the Hebrew Bible, with the modifications necessary to advance the conclusion of the superiority of Christianity over its Jewish roots. The concurrence of Jewish and Christian thinking was important in reinforcing many of the shared conclusions for the Jewish minority. The relative agreement of Jewish tradition and Christian tradition, in tandem with the everyday evidence of the limited numbers and secondary status of post-70 Jews, served to reinforce powerfully for Jews their sense of living in a middle period of abysmal decline.

THE SENSE OF A "MIDDLE AGE," SANDWICHED UNHAPPILY BETWEEN A glorious past and an even more splendid future, was deeply embedded in premodern Jewish consciousness. The larger environment within which the rapidly growing Jewish communities of the Christian West found themselves reinforced this sense markedly. The Christian majority of medieval Latin Christendom regularly projected the present as a hiatus between the First and Second Comings of Jesus as Messiah and Redeemer. The initial appearance of Christ was glorious; his subsequent appearance

---

[21] Deut. 28:68.
[22] A reference to rabbinic sources that depict the Roman punishment inflicted upon Rabbi Akiba.
[23] Petrus Alfonsi, *Dialogue*, 103–4.

was to be yet more splendid. Medieval Christendom harbored a powerful vision of tripartite Christian history.

In addition, medieval Christians projected a potent vision of tripartite Jewish history as well, a vision rooted in the Hebrew Bible and sharing many Jewish assumptions while simultaneously negating central Jewish convictions. Christians agreed on a happy period of the Jewish past, on its painful disruption, and on a splendid Jewish future as well. The major Christian divergence from the Jewish view involved the precise nature of the splendid Jewish future. For Christians, redemption for the Jews – intimately related to the Second Coming of Christ – would involve the effacing of Judaism and disappearance of the Jews; it would involve absorption of Judaism and the Jews into the Christian faith and community.

The Jews of medieval Europe were profoundly aware of this Christian version of their history, in many ways so consonant with their own, and of the profound threat that it posed. They were regularly confronted with graphic representations of the majority sense of Christian success and Jewish suffering throughout the towns of medieval Europe, in stained glass windows accessible to all, in artistic frescoes, and in striking statuary. The common contrast of the female figures of Ecclesia and Synagoga – the former regal and victorious, the latter defeated and humbled – captured effectively the Christian sense of debased Jewish circumstances during the "middle age" of Jewish history. Christians in medieval Europe challenged their Jewish neighbors by contrasting sharply Christian success with Jewish failure.

Jews were fully sensitive to this Christian view of a Jewish "middle age." It is the key to one of the most probing of the Christian missionizing thrusts and is widely reported in Jewish writings from medieval western Christendom. Jewish sources regularly portray Christian antagonists – some perceived as genuinely friendly – urging Jewish neighbors and friends to acknowledge the reality of degraded Jewish circumstances, to recognize that these circumstances reflect divine rejection, to absorb this painful truth, and to take the obvious step of conversion. Thus, for example, the oldest of the Hebrew First-Crusade narratives depicts seemingly well-disposed Christian associates urging a prominent Jewess who had survived the 1096 assaults in Worms by hiding with supportive Christians outside of town to take in the reality and reach the inevitable conclusion. "Know and see that God does not wish to save you, for they [the Jews of Worms] lie naked at the corner of every street, unburied. Sully yourself [a pejorative reference to baptism]."[24]

The important mid-twelfth-century Jewish polemical work *Milhamot ha-Shem* of the unknown Jacob ben Reuben reflects in far more peaceful terms Jewish awareness of the same set of Christian views. The author depicts a comfortable relationship between himself and "a priest expert in logic and sophisticated in esoteric wisdom." The two met regularly, and the Jewish author describes himself as learning a great deal from their conversations. At some point, however, the Jewish author portrays the priest as addressing him in the following terms: "How long will you waver on the threshold, not allowing your heart to understand, your eyes to see, and your ears to hear – you and all your brethren who are known by the name of Jacob. You become poorer and lower and weaker in obvious ways; your numbers decline daily, both yesterday and tomorrow. Our enemies are trampled under our feet, while our friends as resplendent as the sun as it goes forth."[25] Jews were well aware of the extent to which their Christian contemporaries shared their sense of tripartite Jewish history, while turning that tripartite history into a convincing argument for Christian truth.

For medieval Christians, the tripartite division of Jewish history – obvious at every turn – served as a constant reinforcement of Christian truth; for medieval Jews, the challenge was to maintain a firm grasp on the Jewish sense of tripartite history with its conviction of eventual redemption of Jews *qua* Jews; for us, the confluence of the two views of Jewish past, present, and future indicates how firmly rooted the imagery of endless Jewish suffering in general and on the medieval scene in particular has been.

---

[24] Robert Chazan, *European Jewry and the First Crusade*, 231–32.
[25] Chazan, *Fashioning Jewish Identity*, 185.

3

‿

The European Middle Ages

THE TRADITIONAL TRIPARTITE VIEW OF CHRISTIAN HISTORY ruled supreme well into what has come to be called the European Middle Ages. Despite the vigor and vitality of the rapidly developing and highly innovative society of post-1000 western Christendom, members of this society continued to believe themselves in a middle period between Jesus' First and Second Coming, with a far happier future in the offing. During the fourteenth century, the successes of medieval western Christendom began to unravel somewhat, with both natural and human catastrophes interrupting the continuous growth of the preceding three centuries, and new views began to emerge on major issues. Many of these innovative views challenged prior practical and theoretical assumptions regarding Christian life and society. Not the least of these new views focused on the traditional Christian sense of historical development.

An innovative sense of tripartite European history emerged, with nontraditional perceptions of antiquity as the age of Greco-Roman freedom and creativity, a middle period of decline associated with Churchdominated Europe, and an anticipated modern period of return to the freedoms and values of Greece and Rome. This radically new tripartite history evolved from dissatisfaction with and criticism of the existing order. The notion of history divided into this new sequence of ancient, medieval, and modern periods quickly took hold in European and subsequently worldwide thinking, despite the obvious difficulties in applying this scheme to non-European societies. While the division was quickly accepted, assessments of the nature and quality of the three periods have elicited profound disagreement. For our purposes it is important to note the ongoing debate over the middle element in the sequence. For some, the "Middle Ages" constitute a period of abysmal decline, which modernity has attempted to reverse; for others, the "Middle Ages" bequeathed to modernity the noblest achievements of the human spirit.

∾

THE VERY NOTION OF THE "MIDDLE AGES" *AB INITIO* IMPLIES NEGATIVity. To identify an epoch as "middle" defines that period in terms of what preceded and succeeded it, rather than its own intrinsic characteristics and merits. To be defined as a time frame between a prior and a subsequent suggests at least drabness and colorlessness; more often, it implies pejorative assessment. Fourteenth-century European coinage and utilization of the term "Middle Ages" in fact reflect a distinctly negative view of medieval European civilization.

Indeed, a related terminology emerged that is clearer and more obviously damning. The terms "Middle Ages" and "Dark Ages" have sometimes been utilized interchangeably. With the term "Dark Ages," we are no longer in the domain of implied negativity; the negativity is overt. The term "Dark Ages" is no longer fashionable, in recognition of some of the positive developments to be detailed shortly. Scholars have increasingly restricted the term "Dark Ages" to the sixth through ninth centuries, the nadir in European fortunes. For the purposes of this discussion, we shall focus on the term "Middle Ages," the conceptualizations of this period, and the conflicting and ambivalent evaluations of it.

The new European term "Middle Ages" reflects a profoundly negative assessment of medieval western Christendom. It began to appear in fourteenth-century Italy among the circle of humanists led by Petrarch and offered a revolutionary division of Western history. The Italian humanists of the fourteenth and fifteenth centuries perceived early signs of the fraying of the medieval synthesis. The papacy had begun to lose its historic powers; many of the most potent medieval sovereignties seemed be in decline; vexing and divisive spiritual issues had begun to proliferate. Surrounded by the impressive physical remains of Roman antiquity and conscious of their own connections to the glories of that Roman past, the Italian humanists saw the Middle Ages as a period of steep decline between the achievements of ancient Greece and Rome and what they hoped would be the renewal and eventual extension of those achievements into an exciting future. They projected the medieval interlude as a declivity in human history, an unfortunate hiatus between a glorious past and – hopefully – an even more splendid future.

The leaders of the slightly later Reformation saw medieval society and the medieval Roman Catholic Church from quite a different, but equally negative perspective. They remained deeply committed to the Christian vision, but were convinced that the medieval Church under the leadership of the papacy represented a distortion of and defection from the genuine vision of Jesus himself. The objective of the Reformation leadership was to reach back into the past, not in the direction of Greco-Roman antiquity, but rather in the direction of the original message of Jesus and his immediate followers. Luther and Calvin were unsparing in their criticism of the Roman Catholic Church, thus negating major aspects of medieval civilization. The Reformation stances on the Middle Ages have remained operative and influential down to the present, substantially affecting the imagery of medieval life and civilization well beyond Protestant circles.

Enlightenment thinkers developed yet further the humanist sense of break between the creativity of the Greco-Roman past and resumption of that creativity in a fruitful new era of human history. In the period between the fourteenth-century Petrarch and such eighteenth-century thinkers as Voltaire, the medieval synthesis disintegrated radically. The religious unity of medieval western Christendom under the leadership of the Roman Catholic Church gave way to the fragmentation produced by the Reformation. This fragmentation in turn made the prior alliance of church and state no longer tenable. Wars grounded in the earlier vision of an intimate church-state linkage threatened to tear apart European societies. Equally important, the old structures of knowledge dissipated as well, with science displacing for many the prior certainties provided by divine revelation.

Out of all this turmoil emerged new visions of societal structuring and new perspectives on human understanding. The earlier political arrangements and the prior patterns of knowing associated with the European Middle Ages were projected as superannuated, intellectually and morally bankrupt, and cruelly destructive. For the leadership of the Enlightenment, the European Middle Ages stood as the antithesis of what was innovative and desirable; the medieval legacy constituted the decisive barrier to the successful emergence of a new and improved order. Major medieval institutions, such as the Roman Catholic Church, and related medieval developments, such as papal power and the inquisition, took on symbolic significance as highlighting all that was lamentable in the European past, which would surely give way to a better European future. Only obstinate loyalty to superannuated medieval institutions and values threatened the onset of a brighter new world.

The major Enlightenment thinkers were unanimous in condemning the medieval Roman Catholic Church and the society they believed it spawned and controlled. The tone generally involved derision and mockery. Voltaire's *Philosophic Dictionary* is rich in ridicule of what he saw as medieval credulity and cruelty. In the article he provided for the *Encyclopedia* on history, Voltaire dismisses the Middle Ages in the following terms:

The ages after the fall of the Roman Empire, as one has elsewhere remarked, are only barbarous adventures under barbarous names, excepting the time of Charlemagne. England remained practically isolated until the time of Edward III. The northern countries were savage until the sixteenth century, and Germany was in anarchy for a long time. The quarrels of emperors and popes ravaged Italy for six hundred years. It is difficult to detect the truth in the passions of the unlearned writers who have written ill-constructed chronicles of this miserable time. The Spanish monarchy witnessed only one noteworthy event under the Visigoth kings, and that was its destruction. Everything was confusion until the reign of Isabella and Ferdinand. Until Louis XI, France fell victim to the dark misfortunes of an unregulated government.[1]

For many in the twentieth and twenty-first centuries, the term "medieval" retains its negative humanist, Protestant, and Enlightenment connotations. As the contemporary media depict horrors across the globe, they regularly describe these horrors as "medieval." The locution is regularly synonymous with barbarity and cruelty and usually designates actions inspired by traditional religious visions seen as opposed to modern secular sensibilities. That these recent "medieval" horrors are often associated with Islam and with a renewed commitment to the kind of church-state integration that characterized the European Middle Ages and was subsequently rejected by Western modernity serves to reinforce use of the pejorative term "medieval" to designate them.

[1] Denis Diderot and Jean d'Alembert, *Encyclopédie ou dictionnaire raisonné des sciences, des arts et des métiers*, 8:223.

Nonetheless, a more benign view of the European Middle Ages emerged fairly quickly as well. Numerous fifteen-century thinkers accepted the new notion of a Middle Ages, without absorbing the negativity just now indicated. In part, this resulted from geographic considerations. By the fifteenth century, major centers of Western civilization had coalesced in northern Europe, in countries like England, France, and Germany.[2] Lacking historic connections to the Greco-Roman world – indeed defined as barbaric and dangerous by the Romans – Englishmen, Frenchmen, and Germans could not share so readily in the admiration of Greece and Rome expressed by their Italian counterparts; they had to seek historical roots in their own sectors of Europe. While some invoked the pre-medieval cultures of northern Europe as their sources of historical validation, the more common reaction was to turn to the Middle Ages – the period during which these new centers of Western civilization had first coalesced and achieved greatness – and to seek the genius embedded therein.

There was more than sheer geography at work, however. With the passage of time, segments of learned society came to investigate the complex medieval experience more fully and to make increasingly available the riches of that period. This led to enhanced appreciation for some of the towering achievements of the European Middle Ages, ranging from the political and economic through the intellectual and on into the aesthetic. The creation of powerful and effective states, the development of increasingly sophisticated economies, the fashioning of stunning works of architecture and art, and profound exploration of the intellectual and spiritual spheres all served to buttress the sense of a dynamic and creative period.

Just as the early humanist negativism toward the Middle Ages evolved into the more intense opposition of the Enlightenment, so too did the early positive assessments deepen with the onset of nineteenth-century Romanticism. Part of the Romantic reaction (against both the Enlightenment in general and its assessment of the Middle Ages in particular) involved heightened appreciation for the achievements of medieval England, France, and Germany; part of the reaction involved intensified identification with the ideals of the medieval Church and its core

[2] See the Introduction.

religious values. Medieval political accomplishments, ostensible societal stability, ecclesiastical ceremony, aesthetic sensibility, and chivalric ideals contrasted tellingly for many with the seemingly more pedestrian values of an industrialized and democratized nineteenth-century Europe. A romanticized Middle Ages offered enormous appeal, and such romanticization made its appearance in scholarship, literature, and the arts.

Thus, assessment of the Middle Ages became yet one more touchstone in the battle between those desirous of change and those committed to prior institutions and values. For the former, the European Middle Ages constituted the unfortunate interruption of a trajectory that began with promise and was being resumed with high hopes; for the latter, the European Middle Ages constituted the repository of virtues and values that were in the process of being jeopardized by irresponsible and dangerous agents of destructive change.

BY THE LATE NINETEENTH CENTURY, GLOBAL AND MONOLITHIC ASSESS-ments of the Middle Ages both negative and positive had begun to recede, making way for more aggressive collection of data and more nuanced evaluation of the European Middle Ages. Ultimately, appreciation of the complexities of the medieval period – both its achievements and its shortcomings – won out.

The composite picture of a lengthy period of approximately a thousand years involving an entire continent has quite properly given way to internal differentiations, to awareness that medieval western Christendom underwent important changes over the period of one thousand years and that Roman Catholic Europe included a wide range of lands, climates, societies, and cultures. There has been, for example, accelerating awareness of major differences between the first and second half of the thousand-year period often designated as medieval. To the extent that the term "Dark Ages" is used at all these days, it refers to the period that precedes the year 1000, to that period during which western Christendom lay in the shadows – and often at the mercy – of its more powerful rivals, the Byzantine Empire and the vast and potent world of Islam. The momentous changes that took place around the year 1000 and began the process that transformed western Christendom from the backwaters to the vanguard of the Western world have drawn increasing attention.

There has likewise been an enhanced focus on the differences among the diverse geographic and cultural areas of medieval western Christendom – between the southern, Mediterranean lands and the northern territories, between the westerly areas of Europe and those of central and eastern Europe.

Scholars no longer portray the civilization of medieval Latin Christendom in monolithic terms, either wholly negative or wholly positive. There is growing awareness of a complex civilization, with much that was laudable and much that was lamentable. Older monochromatic stereotypes have by and large disappeared, at least in the academic world, replaced by the sense of a dynamically changing civilization moving in directions that were extremely fruitful and, at the same time, fraught with dangers.

To illustrate this new awareness of complexity, let us focus on treatments of a particularly important period in the history of medieval western Christendom – the creative and problematic twelfth century. In 1927, Charles Homer Haskins published a path-breaking work provocatively entitled *The Renaissance of the Twelfth Century*. Haskins himself was fully aware of the reactions that his carefully chosen title would evoke.

The title of this book will appear to many to contain a flagrant contradiction. A renaissance in the twelfth century! Do not the Middle Ages, that epoch of ignorance, stagnation, and gloom, stand in the sharpest contrast to the light and progress and freedom of the Italian Renaissance which followed? How could there be a renaissance in the Middle Ages, when men had no eye for the joy and beauty and knowledge of this passing world, their gaze ever fixed on the terrors of the world to come?

Haskins's response to the ostensible contradiction in his title and to the probing questions he posed to himself contains important insights.

The answer is that the continuity of history rejects such sharp and violent contrasts between successive periods, and that modern research shows us the Middle Ages less dark and less static, the Renaissance less bright and less sudden, than was once supposed. The Middle Ages exhibit life and color and change, much eager search after knowledge and beauty, much creative accomplishment in art, in literature, in institutions. The Italian Renaissance was preceded by similar, if less wide-reaching movements; indeed it came out of the Middle Ages so gradually that historians are not agreed when it began, and some would go so far as to abolish the name, and perhaps even the fact, of a renaissance in the Quattrocento.[3]

Haskins negates here the Renaissance's (if we allow use of the term) own self-image and the contrastive portrait it projected of the period that preceded it. On a theoretical plane, he argues that historical change does not take place as sharply and decisively as the Renaissance notions suggest. Change is slower and more cumulative, and Haskins argues that the roots of the new lay very much in what preceded it. More specifically and perhaps more importantly, Haskins disputes the negative portrait of the European Middle Ages. He urges that this lengthy period includes major episodes of "life and color and change," the "eager search after knowledge and beauty," and "creative accomplishment in art, in literature, in institutions." His book focuses on what he perceived to be one particularly energetic and robust segment of the European Middle Ages, the twelfth century.

The Haskins sense of the twelfth century as a period of remarkable creativity has become standard for subsequent twentieth- and twenty-first-century medieval studies. Recent medievalists share Haskin's projection of the twelfth century as an epoch of unusual creativity. On the fiftieth anniversary of the appearance of *The Renaissance of the Twelfth Century*, Harvard University convened a major conference in which the basic insights of Charles Homer Haskins were celebrated and expanded, both conceptually and topically. Robert L. Benson and Giles Constable edited the proceedings of the conference as *Renaissance and Renewal in the Twelfth Century*, with the title pointing to conceptual expansion. The conference and volume advanced notions of both a rebirth and a renewal. In addition, the conference and volume of papers also enlarged the scope of the original study of twelfth-century developments, moving into numerous areas that Haskins had not addressed.[4] The basic continuity with the original Haskins volume lay in projection of the twelfth century as an epoch of monumental creativity and achievement, a perspective far removed from that of the thinkers who originally coined the term "Middle Ages."

---

[3] Charles Homer Haskins, *The Renaissance of the Twelfth Century*, v–vi.
[4] Robert L. Benson and Giles Constable, eds., *Renaissance and Renewal in the Twelfth Century*.

To the terms "renaissance" and "renaissance and renewal," one of the editors of the anniversary volume, Giles Constable, added yet a third alternative in *The Reformation of the Twelfth Century*. Again, Constable adopted a term coined for a later period and argued for use of this term for the twelfth century. For Constable, use of the term "reformation" highlights the centrality of religion and religious institutions in western Christendom's remarkable twelfth-century changes.

The terms most frequently used for religious change in the eleventh and twelfth centuries were *reformare* and *reformatio*. These, like reform today, were multi-purpose words and could refer either to restoration and revival in a backwards-looking sense, or to rebirth and re-formation, as a forward-looking change. In its traditional Christian sense, as Paul used it in Romans 12.2, *reformatio* described the ideal of personal renewal, but in the eleventh and twelfth centuries it was also applied to institutions, including the church, the empire, and society as a whole. It is a less exclusively cultural and secular term than renaissance, as it is used today, and is thus a reminder that the movement of renewal included religious life and institutions as well as intellectual and artistic developments.[5]

Here Constable takes the expansion of the early Haskins insights yet further. The twelfth century emerges as a period of the widest possible societal vitalization.

Almost all contemporary medievalists share the Haskins-Benson-Constable sense of a creative twelfth century. Yet, at the same time, voices have pointed to the underside of this same period, to the negative developments observable alongside the positive, to destructive aspects of a period of creativity and progress. Perhaps the most influential voice in this view of the twelfth century as both positive and negative has been the English medievalist R. I. Moore, especially in *The Formation of a Persecuting Society*, first published in 1987 and widely cited and debated ever since.

Moore makes it clear that he by no means disagrees with the view that the twelfth century saw remarkable achievement in a variety of domains. "This book neither pretends nor attempts to offer in any sense a complete or even a fair account of the nature and achievements of European society and institutions in one of the most vigorous and creative periods of their

---

[5] Giles Constable, *The Reformation of the Twelfth Century*, 3.

history."[6] Rather, Moore sets out to show that this "vigorous and creative" period had an underside as well. "Whether we choose to see the epoch since 1100 as one of progress or decline, to step back a little further is to see that around that time Europe *became* a persecuting society."[7]

Moore advanced two major theses in his book. The first is that persecution of a number of disparate groupings simultaneously indicates that explanation for the persecution must lie with the persecuting majority, rather than the persecuted minority.

That three entirely distinct groups of people, characterized respectively by religious conviction, physical condition, and race and culture, should all have begun at the same time and by the same stages to pose the same threats, which must be dealt with in the same ways, is a proposition too absurd to be taken seriously. The alternative must be that the explanation lies not with the victims but with the persecutors. What heretics, lepers, and Jews had in common was that they were all victims of a zeal for persecution which seized European society at this time.[8]

Moore's second thesis is that the explanation of this zeal for persecution does not lie with the masses, that it is not a "bottom-up" inclination for persecution. Rather, in Moore's view, the zeal for persecution was fostered from the top down, through the emergence of a new social class – functionaries of both church and state with a vested interest in expanding the power of their institutional masters and in the process safeguarding and solidifying their own positions. Thus, according to the Moore view, one of the most important advances of the twelfth century – the maturation of organizational structures in both church and state – resulted in the development of a class of functionaries who were responsible for an extremely destructive development, a persecutory zeal that engulfed a number of out-groups on the European scene (Jews very much included).

Another major formulation of the new exclusionist tendencies in twelfth-century Europe is that of the French historian Dominique Iogna-Prat, in his *Order and Exclusion*. Iogna-Prat's focus is quite different from that of Moore; he is largely concerned with changes in the socio-religious

[6] R. I. Moore, *Formation of a Persecuting Society*, vii.
[7] Ibid., 5.
[8] Ibid., 67. Note the identification of medieval Jews as distinguished by race and culture.

ambience, rather than the socio-political sphere. For Iogna-Prat, the religious sphere and the social sphere – and indeed the political sphere as well – had by the twelfth century been fused. Iogna-Prat suggests that, during the second half of the Middle Ages, "Christianity had remodeled itself into Christendom,"[9] which is to say that the religious, social, and political spheres had become one.

The expansionist logic of this entity – Christendom – moved western Christendom in the direction of ever-clearer definition of "others" and the determination to emerge victorious over these "others." Iogna-Prat focuses on

the emergence, during the eleventh century, of the all-embracing notion of Christendom, which no longer simply described a spiritual community but connoted a social and temporal structure. Institutionally, the Christendom (*Christianitas*) defined by eleventh- and twelfth-century clerics was a unitary whole, with a center, Rome, and boundaries that were to be both defended against external enemies – the pagans and infidels – and extended until they encompassed the whole world (*Universitalitas*). In this sense, Christendom was an institutional entity that steadily affirmed its differences from the outside – the Orthodox, Judaism, and Islam – and a universalist utopia that accompanied, justified, and spurred on the expansion of the Latin west in the eleventh and twelfth centuries.[10]

While Iogna-Prat analyzes many of the same exclusionary and persecutory tendencies examined by Moore, he locates the causative core of these tendencies in the religious vision of vigorous and creative twelfth century Christianity/Christendom itself.

Thomas Bisson's study of twelfth-century European power and governance points the way toward connecting the recent positive and negative assessments of the twelfth century and in fact the European Middle Ages altogether. Significantly, Bisson entitles his study *The Crisis of the Twelfth Century: Power, Lordship and the Origins of European Government*.[11] Especially important for our purposes is Bisson's sense that the alterations in power and governance during the twelfth century constituted a crisis. To be sure, the changes that Bisson highlights are generally considered positive, yet he designates the period of change a crisis juncture, pointing

---

[9] Dominique Iogna-Prat, *Order and Exclusion*, 1.
[10] Ibid., 2.
[11] Thomas N. Bisson, *The Crisis of the Twelfth Century*.

to the reality that change – especially rapid change – is in and of itself disorienting and disconcerting, even when the shifts are in a broadly positive direction. In the case of twelfth-century Europe, the process of change moved the leadership of the Church, which was a highly conservative body, to insist on clarification of traditional doctrine and policy and to press for adherence to all elements of this traditional doctrine and policy. On the popular level, awareness of change was distressing to many, creating a sense of loss of moorings and a concern with the forces or agents of change. Both these reactions to change bore problematic implications for Europe's growing Jewish population, as we shall see. The growing scholarly sense of medieval Europe as moving in simultaneously positive and negative directions indicates, above all else, the dynamism of medieval European society, the rapid change taking place within it, and the complex and often contradictory reactions to this rapid change.

Thus, the study of medieval western Christendom in recent research is no longer grounded in simplistic bifurcation into what is viewed by some as a "negative" Middle Ages and by others as a "positive" Middle Ages. Rather, scholars have come to treat the European Middle Ages as a complex human phenomenon, comprised of diverse periods and geographic/societal areas, each of which shows the normal human combination of constructive and destructive elements. This is a valuable perspective from which to engage the study of the Jewish experience in medieval western Christendom.

4

ॐ

The European Jewish Middle Ages

_T_HE NEW DIVISION OF HISTORY THAT SURFACED TOWARD THE
close of the European Middle Ages reconfigured the traditional
Christ-centered triad of glorious past, decadent present, and splendid
future. The new glorious past centered on Greece and Rome, rather than
Jesus; the decadent middle period involved the triumph of Christianity;
the splendid future would revive the values of Greece and Rome and
repudiate the values of Christianity. Enlightenment thinkers reinforced
and sharpened this new tripartite division of history.

The changes in European society associated with modernity included
altered status for European Jewry. Slowly and subtly, some Jews began
to integrate themselves into majority society.[1] The process of integration
accelerated explosively with the formal restructuring of Western polities as a result of the American and French revolutions. Increasingly large
numbers of Jews found themselves absorbed into drastically reconfigured
Western societies. Integration proceeded at many different levels, including the demographic, the economic, the political, and – not least – the
cultural. An inevitable result of this integration was assimilation of the
new ideas, ideals, and values of Enlightenment and post-Enlightenment
thinking. The challenge – keenly felt within nineteenth- and twentieth-
century Western Jewry – was somehow to engage the new patterns of
thought while remaining grounded in the core legacy of the Jewish
past.

---

[1] For a sense of this process, see Jacob Katz, _Out of the Ghetto_, and David Sorkin, _The
Transformation of German Jewry, 1780–1840_.

Since a central feature of Enlightenment thinking involved new stances toward history, attitudes toward the Jewish past inevitably underwent considerable change for many Jews. Jewish historians quickly accepted the drive toward accumulation of fuller data on the Jewish past. Scholars ransacked libraries in search of manuscripts and early printed books neglected by publishers and cultural authorities. These scholars began to investigate areas of cultural achievement previously given short shrift, for example philosophic speculation and secular poetry. In a more far-reaching way, a new conceptual framework for understanding and presenting Jewish history slowly emerged. The traditional tripartite division of Jewish history – pre-exilic, exilic, and redemptive – had to be accommodated to the newer European sense of ancient, medieval, and modern. More important yet, the older notions of divine causation as the driving mechanism of history had to give way to the new humanistic sense of human efficacy in historical process.

As was true for the Christian majority, Enlightenment thinking – with its removal of God from historical process, its celebration of Greco-Roman values, and its denigration of medieval Christianity – dictated the initial thrusts of the changing perspectives on the Jewish past. Some aspects of this new posture were relatively easy for Jews to assimilate; other aspects were considerably more difficult. Like their Christian contemporaries, Jews too proceeded from infatuation with Enlightenment ideals toward Romantic and/or nationalistic celebration of alternative values. Eventually, historians of the Jews, like their general medievalist counterparts, moved toward less programmatic historical research, more detailed and more textured study of the Jewish past, and a more nuanced understanding of the balance sheet of negatives and positives in medieval Jewish experience.

JEWS LIVING THROUGH THE GREAT REVOLUTIONS OF THE LATE EIGHTeenth century felt an exhilarated sense of the onset of a new era, which almost inevitably evoked associations with traditional Jewish aspirations for redemption. The well-known letter of Berr Isaac Berr, celebrating the granting of rights to the Jews of France, reflects this conviction of the dawning of long-anticipated and divinely ordained salvation. At the same time, the author perceived unprecedented human achievement as well.

So late as the 27th of September last [1791], we were the only inhabitants of this vast empire who seemed doomed to remain forever in bondage and abasement. On the following day, on the 28th, a day forever sacred among us, you inspired the immortal legislators of France. They pronounce, and more than sixty thousand unfortunate beings, mourning over their sad fate, are awakened to a sense of happiness by the liveliest emotions of pure joy. Let it be acknowledged, dearest brethren, that we have not deserved this wonderful change by our repentance or by the reformation of our manners. We can attribute it to nothing but the everlasting goodness of God. He never forsook us entirely; but, finding that we were not yet worthy of seeing the accomplishment of his promises of a perfect and lasting redemption, he has not, however, thought it proper to aggravate our sufferings. For surely our chains had become the more galling from the contemplation of the rights of man, so sublimely held forth to public view.

Therefore our God . . . has chosen the generous French nation to reinstate us in our rights and to operate our regeneration, as in other times he has chosen Antiochus, Pompey, and others to humiliate and enslave us. How glorious it is for that nation, which has in so short a time made so many people happy.[2]

Palpable here is the profound conviction of the dawning of a new historical era. Abasement of the Jews, which Berr Isaac Berr interestingly pushes back to the days of Antiochus and Pompey, rather than Vespasian and Titus (and Jesus), has come to an end.[3] To be sure, the careful author distinguishes between this exciting new epoch and the ultimate redemption, which he mentions but upon which he does not dwell; nonetheless, the exhilaration of this new epoch suffices for an outpouring of joy and thanksgiving. The sense of historical causation is in the process of alteration. God is still very much in the picture, but the French nation comes in for a considerable share of approbation as well.

Fairly quickly, the Jews of nineteenth-century Europe adapted themselves to their new circumstances and assumed many Enlightenment

---

[2] *Transactions of the Parisian Sanhedrin*, trans. M. Diogene Tama, 11–12.
[3] Recall the traditional Christian emphasis of the year 70, Vespasian, Titus, and the Crucifixion, discussed in Chapter 2.

commitments and attitudes. Among these was the commitment to the historiographic emphases in majority society, which included new, more open, and ostensibly more objective study of the past. In 1819, a group of young German Jews articulated a program of innovative historical study.[4] This program was to begin with the amassing of fuller data on the Jewish past, data no longer controlled and filtered by the rabbinic leadership of the traditional Jewish world. Scholars would unearth new sources reflecting the historic diversity of Jewish populations and attitudes. From these long ignored data, they would compose new Jewish communal histories, which would eventuate in sufficient historical data and perspective to allow for a grasp of the essence of the Jewish people, their culture, and their faith. The achievements of this enterprise – labeled *Wissenschaft des Judentums* (The Scientific Study of Judaism) – were most impressive.

The first great modern historian of the Jews – Heinrich Graetz – utilized the newly unearthed data on the Jewish past to write a multi-volume history of the Jews that proved highly appealing, especially to Jewish readers struggling to absorb innovative patterns of thinking while remaining loyal in some fashion to Jewish tradition. Graetz's history was a strained but effective amalgam of the valuable new evidence unearthed by his scholarly confreres. It was a monumental attempt to synthesize traditional Jewish views with nineteenth-century cultural values – a combination that resonated most appealingly among Graetz's liberal Jewish contemporaries.

Graetz was fully aware of the European notions of antiquity, the Middle Ages, and modernity that had been developing for centuries. In the introduction to the fourth volume of his *History of the Jews* (the first volume he actually published), Graetz made some striking generalizations about the history of the Jewish people (to which we shall return shortly) and about the larger settings within which Jewish history unfolded from late antiquity until the nineteenth century. For Graetz, the world within which Jewish life developed went through three major stages, reflecting the newer ancient, medieval, and modern distinction – Greco-Roman

---

[4] For valuable documentary evidence of this program, see Paul Mendes-Flohr and Jehuda Reinharz, eds., *The Jew in the Modern World*, 211–40.

antiquity; the Christian Middle Ages; and Enlightenment modernity. Here is the beginning of Graetz's formulation:

The senile Roman Empire languished and sank into its tomb; in its mouldering body the chrysalis of European and Asiatic nations was developed; they attained the brilliant butterfly-form of Christian and Moslem chivalry; and from the ashes of its castles the phoenix of civilization soared triumphantly aloft.[5]

Graetz's traditional Jewish thinking did not permit him to share the general Enlightenment enthusiasm for Greco-Roman civilization. He did share fully, however, the broad European exhilaration over modernity, when "the phoenix of civilization soared triumphantly aloft."

With respect to the middle period of European history, Graetz imbibed fully the general Enlightenment castigation of the Middle Ages. While "the brilliant butterfly-form of Christian and Moslem chivalry" suggests a positive view of the medieval period, Graetz quickly reverses course with the following:

Universal history also thrice changed its spiritual standard. From the refined but hollow culture [a reference to the Roman Empire, of which Graetz was hardly enamored], mankind degenerated into barbarism and dark ignorance [the Middle Ages]; from ignorance it again rose to the luminous sphere of a higher civilization [modernity].[6]

Graetz's sense of Greco-Roman antiquity is ambiguous; his perception of modernity is unabashedly positive; his view of the middle period is thoroughly and unqualifiedly negative.

Throughout his presentation of the Jewish experience in medieval western Christendom, Graetz criticizes unsparingly the larger medieval ambience in which Jewish life took place. Following is one of many

---

[5] Heinrich Graetz's eleven-volume opus, *Geschichte der Juden*, was published between 1853 and 1876, with new editions of the various volumes following subsequently. A somewhat problematic English translation was published in five volumes as *History of the Jews* by the Jewish Publication Society of America from 1891 through 1895. Ismar Schorsch translated important sections of the Graetz history and important Graetz essays as *The Structure of Jewish History and Other Essays*. Because of the felicity of the Schorsch translation, I shall cite material from Graetz's introduction to his fourth volume from it. Note also Schorsch's valuable introductory observations, 1–62. This passage can be found on p. 126.

[6] Ibid.

passages in Graetz's *History of the Jews* that illustrate his radically negative assessment of medieval western Christendom, even apart from its treatment of the Jews.

There sprang up against it [Judaism], in the early part of the thirteenth century, a power exercising ruthless, inexorable oppression, such as had not been practiced against it since the time of Hadrian – Pope Innocent III. He was the father of all the evils experienced by the European nations up to the time of the Lutheran Reformation: the tyrannical domination of the Roman Church over princes and peoples; the enslaving and abasing of the human mind; the persecution of free thought; the institution of the Inquisition; the auto-da-fe against heretics, i.e. against those who dared doubt the infallibility of the Roman bishop.[7]

Heinrich Graetz, poised between traditional and innovative views of the Jewish past, struggled to synthesize these two currents and did so. In effect, he melded the traditional Jewish triad – pre-exilic, exilic, and redemptive – with the modern European sense of antiquity, the Middle Ages, and modernity. This meant, above all else, conflating the Jewish sense of an exilic period replete with suffering and woe and the Enlightenment sense of a degenerate Middle Ages, with the villainous Roman Catholic Church setting the tone of barbarism and cruelty. The exilic suffering predicted in Scripture in fact took place, as a result of the widely condemned cruelty of the medieval Church.

The conflation of the traditional Jewish triad and the modern European sense of antiquity, the Middle Ages, and modernity is immediately obvious in the way that Graetz defines the middle period of Jewish history that he begins to depict in the fourth volume of his history. For Graetz, this middle period began in the year 70 and extended down to 1780, breaking down into three subperiods: (1) the talmudic period (70–1040); (2) the rabbinical-philosophical period (1040–1230); (3) the rabbinical period per se (1230–1780).[8] This middle period opens traditionally with the year 70, but concludes in consonance with European thinking with the changes in Jewish life attendant upon the French Revolution. While European historians dated the end of the Middle Ages earlier than did Graetz, he clearly espoused the same criteria utilized by his European

---

[7] Graetz, *History of the Jews*, 3:496.
[8] Graetz, *The Structure of Jewish History*, 129–30.

peers, that is, the growing reliance on human reason, which took longer to reach and impact the lives of Europe's Jews.

In the process of this conflation, Graetz distorted the broad Jewish experience of late antiquity and the early Middle Ages, which predated the onset of rich Jewish life in medieval Europe and during which the overwhelming majority of Jews was to be found outside the borders of Christian Europe. Himself a descendant of medieval European Jewry and deeply immersed in its lore, Graetz transformed the experience of the Jews in medieval and early modern Europe into the paradigm of exilic Jewish history; he projected Jewish exilic history as the medieval European Jewish experience writ large. This tendency, already discernible in Joseph *ha-kohen*'s `*Emek ha-Bakha*, takes on far greater significance in the modern synthesis crafted by Heinrich Graetz.[9]

One of the most evocative statements in Graetz's *History of the Jews* is found at the very beginning of the fourth volume, which – as previously noted – was the very first that Graetz published. This lengthy lament over Jewish suffering and panegyric to Jewish spiritual greatness – while ostensibly highlighting the major characteristics of Jewish life in exile altogether – obviously draws most of its force from Graetz's perception of the Jewish experience in medieval and early modern western Christendom. For Heinrich Graetz, the experience of medieval European Jewry was projected as the quintessential experience of premodern Jews everywhere.

The long era of the dispersion, lasting nearly seventeen centuries, is characterized by unprecedented sufferings, an uninterrupted martyrdom, and a constantly aggravated degradation and humiliation unparalleled in history – but also by mental activity, unremitting intellectual efforts, and indefatigable research. A graphic, adequate image of this era could only be portrayed by representing it in two pictures: the one represents subjugated Judah with the pilgrim staff in hand, the pilgrim pack upon the back, with a mournful eye addressed toward heaven, surrounded by prison walls, implements of torture and red-hot branding irons; the other exhibits the same figure with the earnestness of the thinker upon his placid brow, with the air of a scholar in his bright features, seated in a hall of learning, which is filled with a colossal

---

[9] For Joseph *ha-kohen*, see Chapter 1. Recall Salo Baron's criticism of this projection of the medieval European Jewish experience onto the totality of Jewish exilic history in his 1928 essay, discussed in the Prologue.

library in all the languages spoken by man and on all the branches of divine and human lore – the figure of the servant with the proud independence of the thinker.[10]

This depiction of exilic (read medieval European) Jewish circumstances is highly reminiscent of Joseph *ha-kohen*'s `*Emek ha-Bakha*, with its focus on physical woes mitigated by Jewish learning. In fact, Graetz went well beyond his sixteenth-century predecessor in highlighting the combination of suffering and learning. With respect to both these aspects of Jewish circumstances, Graetz drew heavily on premodern Jewish thinking, much of it polemical, and at the same time portrayed his Jewish heroes in terms meaningful and attractive to nineteenth-century audiences, both Jewish and non-Jewish.

Graetz constructed his striking imagery out of two sharp contrasts: the materially powerful Christian majority and the materially weak Jewish minority; the spiritually barren Christian majority and the spiritually fecund Jewish minority. These contrasts were bequeathed to Heinrich Graetz by his medieval Jewish forebears. Both Graetz and his medieval Jewish predecessors intended these contrasts to undercut key majority Christian convictions. Early Christianity had constructed a Christian-Jewish binary grounded in the material-spiritual dichotomy that pervaded Greco-Roman civilization. For the Church Fathers, Jews represented the physical and the material – they were the biological descendants of biblical Israel; Christians represented the opposite – they were the spiritual heirs of the patriarchs and the prophets and hence *Verus Israel*, the true Israel. Medieval Jews seized upon this binary and reversed it. They projected themselves as truly spiritual, with their Christian neighbors taking on the role of the brutish, loutish, and physical.[11] For medieval Jews and by extension for Heinrich Graetz, the weak, suffering, and cerebral Jews, through their combination of material degradation and spiritual elevation, clearly deserved to be designated the true Israel.

In the process of drawing these sharp contrasts between Christian majority and Jewish minority, Graetz defined for himself and his readers the essence of the Jewish experience in medieval western Christendom.

---

[10] Schorsch, *The Structure of Jewish History*, 125. Note the reference to seventeen centuries and recall Graetz's definition of the middle period of Jewish history as extending from 70 to 1780.

[11] Chazan, *Fashioning Jewish Identity*, chapter 14.

It was a two-part experience – unmitigated horrors on the physical level, projected as a protracted martyrdom, and the capacity to overcome these physical sufferings through extraordinary spiritual creativity. In portraying these sharp contrasts, Graetz fused traditional Jewish polemical motifs with major nineteenth-century European values.

The first of Graetz's two pictures depicts "subjugated Judah with the pilgrim staff in hand, the pilgrim pack upon the back, with a mournful eye addressed toward heaven, surrounded by prison walls, implements of torture and red-hot branding irons," resulting in what Graetz claims to be "unprecedented sufferings, an uninterrupted martyrdom, and a constantly aggravated degradation and humiliation unparalleled in history." This portrait brilliantly conflates traditional Jewish thinking with nineteenth-century European sensibilities.

Suffering and martyrdom were of course central themes of Christian thinking throughout the ages. Christianity was grounded in imagery of suffering and martyrdom, with its central figure sacrificed for the benefit of humanity. During the early centuries of its history, the Christian communities produced a sequence of martyrs who emulated their Messiah in offering their lives as testimony to the truth of their faith. During the Middle Ages, the crusading enterprise called upon Christian warriors to take up the cross of their Savior and to undergo suffering on his behalf.

In reaction, medieval Jews in western Christendom internalized the commitment to martyrdom and claimed for themselves a martyrdom unprecedented in the annals of human history, a martyrdom that far surpassed that of their Christian neighbors.[12] For Christians, Jesus was the "Suffering Servant" predicted by Isaiah 52:13–53:12; for Jews, in contrast, the humble and despised figure depicted by the prophet was none other than the Jewish people. Thus, Heinrich Graetz, following in the footsteps of his medieval forebears, made the imagery of Jewish martyrdom central to his portrait of the middle period of Jewish history.

At the very same time, Graetz updated this powerful premodern Jewish imagery and made it appropriate to the nineteenth-century environment in which he lived and for the nineteenth-century readers he addressed. In

---

[12] Chazan, *European Jewry and the First Crusade*, 105–36; Chazan, *Fashioning Jewish Identity*, chapter 16; Shmuel Shepkaru, *Jewish Martyrs in the Pagan and Christian Worlds*; Simha Goldin, *The Ways of Jewish Martyrdom*, especially chapter 1.

the Graetz view, the villainous figure responsible for the horrors endured by the [Jewish] "Suffering Servant of the Lord" was the Roman Catholic Church, much vilified in the Enlightenment and Protestant environment in which Graetz wrote. To portray the Jews as major victims of the cruelty of the Roman Catholic Church was to arouse enhanced sympathy on the part of Jewish and even non-Jewish readers – the sympathy normally evoked by human suffering and the augmented sympathy due those who suffer gratuitously at the hands of a despised enemy figure.

The same combination of traditional and innovative motifs suffuses Graetz's second image – that of "the same figure with the earnestness of the thinker upon his placid brow, with the air of a scholar in his bright features, seated in a hall of learning, which is filled with a colossal library in all the languages spoken by man and on all the branches of divine and human lore." Here Graetz once more drew on the polemical convictions of his medieval Jewish predecessors. Challenged covertly and overtly by the Christian environment in which they found themselves, medieval Jewish thinkers regularly adumbrated a contrast between the loutish – albeit powerful – Christian majority and the cultivated – if weak – Jewish minority. In this contrast, Jewish intellectuality and spirituality were regularly projected as vastly superior to the brutishness of the Christian milieu.[13] Given the Enlightenment valorization of learning and intellect, this traditional Jewish polemical motif acquired new and augmented resonance for Graetz's nineteenth-century European audience – both Jewish and non-Jewish – deeply committed to learning and reason.[14]

Graetz's portrait of the Jewish past, steeped in traditional Jewish thinking while at the same time absorbing modern sensibilities, was highly attractive to at least many of Graetz's Jewish and non-Jewish contemporaries on a number of levels. In the first place, it was dramatic and exciting, rich in (Jewish) heroes and (non-Jewish, essentially Christian) villains; at the same time, it reprised in modern idiom traditional Jewish (and Christian) perceptions of the medieval Jewish experience as an exercise in suffering; additionally, it reformulated prior Jewish

---

[13] Chazan, *Fashioning Jewish Identity*, chaps. 14 and 16.

[14] Not surprisingly, introduction of these medieval Jewish polemical motifs aroused considerable ire among many of Graetz's Christian readers.

polemical claims, thereby assisting Jews in asserting the dignity of their history and faith and combating the appeal of the history and faith of the Christian majority. On the other hand, the Graetz portrait raised for some contemporary and many subsequent readers a host of questions. Some of these questions involved the accuracy of the Graetz portrait; some involved the values embedded in the Graetz narrative. Graetz, as the most eloquent formulator of the synthesis of Enlightenment historical thinking and Jewish values, became the object of far-reaching criticisms leveled from many directions.

We have noted earlier the 1928 challenge by Salo Baron to the regnant consensus as to the dividing line in Jewish history created by the French Revolution, with all that came before it, painful and humiliating to Jews and all that came subsequently, an uplifting blessing.[15] The central target of this assault was obviously the Graetz formulations we have just examined. Graetz's sense of the horrific medieval period and the bountiful modern period seemed to Baron and many others after him decidedly one-sided. In his 1928 essay, Baron dealt with a limited aspect of the contrast, the sixteenth through eighteenth centuries on the one hand and post-revolutionary Jewish life on the other. Throughout his subsequent monumental *oeuvre*, Baron remained true to the principles he laid down in 1928. History – he firmly believed – was complex and must not be treated in the monochromatic terms of Heinrich Graetz, as ideologically and emotionally appealing as these monochromatic terms might be. In everything he wrote, Baron insisted on nuanced understanding of complex phenomena.

Let us note just one aspect to the subsequent Baron analysis of Jewish life in medieval western Christendom as illustration. As we have just seen, Heinrich Graetz identified the Roman Catholic Church as the arch-villain of the European Middle Ages, both as regards majority Christian experience and minority Jewish experience.[16] Baron addressed the medieval Roman Catholic Church at numerous points in his *Social and Religious History of the Jews*, but always as a complex phenomenon in general and as regards its impact on Jewish life in particular.[17]

[15] See Prologue.
[16] See note 7.
[17] See especially Baron, *A Social and Religious History of the Jews* (rev ed.), 4:5–20 and 9:3–134.

The closing overview statement on the place of the Church in medieval European Jewish life in the ninth volume of Baron's history contrasts strikingly with the earlier-cited Graetz strictures.

Sharp repudiation of Judaism and its teachings, aspersions against its ethics as well as theology, and yet basic toleration of it in the Christian world uniquely among all non-Christian faiths and unorthodox Christian sects – were the principles governing the medieval Church's attitude toward the mother religion. Similarly, the Jewish people, permanently accused of "blindness," stubbornness, and even baser motives, discriminated against economically and rigidly separated socially, was nevertheless to be allowed to continue its historic career to the very end of days, which would be ushered in by its final conversion.[18]

The gulf separating Graetz and Baron on this issue and many others as well was monumental. The explanation for this gap lies with a change in setting and the broad progress of historical research over the century that separates these two giants. Baron spent the bulk of his scholarly career as a member of one of the most respected history departments in America, in which he was regularly exposed to the latest in medieval research. Thus, the kind of distancing from the one-sided and reductionist already noted in general medieval historical studies constituted the ambience in which Baron carried on his own efforts.[19] Little wonder, then, that the earlier Graetz tendencies toward monolithic judgments dissipated so totally in Baron's voluminous writings.

A ROMANTIC REACTION TO THE ENLIGHTENMENT COALESCED DURING the nineteenth century and challenged the latter's view of the cosmos and human history, and this Romantic reaction had important implications for Western perceptions of antiquity, the medieval period, and modernity. Romantic and especially Romantically inclined nationalist thinkers reevaluated the virtues and shortcomings of the three periods. They developed once again a tripartite scheme of an idealized past, an undignified middle period, and a glorious future, however they radically reformulated the specifics of the three periods.

[18] Ibid., 9:132.
[19] See Chapter 3.

Jewish nationalist-Zionist thinkers constructed an innovative tripartite scheme of Jewish history, built very much along general Romantic-nationalist lines. The Romantic-nationalist-Zionist perspective dismissed Graetz's definition of the boundaries of the middle period in Jewish history, which synthesized the traditional Jewish triad and the new Western sense of antiquity, the medieval period, and modernity. However, it shared with Graetz an evaluation of the middle period of Jewish history as suffused with persecution and suffering and likewise shared Graetz's conviction that the third period of Jewish history would be initiated by changes on the human scene that would end Jewish suffering and enhance Jewish well-being and creativity. To be sure, in identifying the human factors that would trigger the onset of the third phase of Jewish history, the Zionists dissented radically from the Graetz perspective.

Like traditional premodern Jewish thinkers and nineteenth-century Enlightenment-oriented Jewish historians, the nationalists-Zionists too projected this middle period as a vale of tears, an unremitting saga of persecution and suffering. To be sure, the Zionist movement split into a number of subgroups with slightly differing perspectives on the middle period of the Jewish past. For the political and secularly oriented wing of the Zionist movement, the middle period of the Jewish past involved endless suffering and little else. The religious and cultural Zionists took a position much closer to that of Heinrich Graetz; for them, the persecution endured by the Jews during this middle period was a reality, but had to be balanced against the remarkable creativity generated by these Jews. For this latter group, Jewish creativity did not cancel out the reality of suffering and did not ameliorate the need for a Zionist solution to the endless cycle of persecution; Jewish creativity in the face of persecution did, however, strengthen the sense that, freed from the suffering they had long endured, Jews in their own land and in charge of their own destiny could and would reach greater heights of achievement.

Two major innovations distinguished nationalist-Zionist perceptions of the underlying dynamic of Jewish history. Zionists accepted neither traditional Jewish belief in divine redemption nor the Enlightenment faith in liberal Western societies as the solutions to age-old and seemingly interminable Jewish suffering. Both alternatives involved misplaced confidence. Neither God nor the liberal West could or would solve the problems of the Jewish people. Like other nationalists, the Zionists believed that only Jews themselves, asserting their own identity and their power as a collective, could effect the changes that would end the disastrous middle period of group history and usher in the redemptive era.

The second major innovation involved dismissal of the traditional and Enlightenment valorization of the spirit over the body. As we have seen, this shared emphasis on the spiritual enabled Graetz to fuse traditional Jewish views and Enlightenment perspectives in his depiction of the Jewish Middle Ages. The Zionists broke with this shared emphasis, seeing in it a distinctly apologetic purpose. Zionists accused their Enlightenment predecessors (not unfairly) of highlighting Jewish spirituality in order to evoke the esteem of the larger European environment. Beyond the craven apologetics, the Zionists saw in valorization of the spiritual a dangerous misreading of the dynamics of Jewish and in fact all human history, a misreading that encouraged Jews to bend their energies in fruitless and counterproductive directions. In the Zionist view, change in Jewish circumstances required a commitment to the material aspects of Jewish peoplehood and to mobilizing Jewish physical resources toward achieving political independence, safety, and security.

These new perspectives on the fundamental dynamics of Jewish fate led to some alternative dating for the ancient, medieval, and modern periods of Jewish history. Arguably, the most authoritative statement of Zionist historiography has been the three-volume history of the Jewish people composed by distinguished members of the Hebrew University's Department of Jewish History and subsequently translated into a large one-volume opus in English.[20] The middle volume/section was written by Haim Hillel Ben Sasson, who defines the period that he will describe in the following terms:

From the viewpoint of Jewish history, the Middle Ages may be defined as the period stretching from the early Moslem-Arab conquests, which commenced in 632 CE to the spiritual crisis experienced by Jewry during the second half of the seventeenth century, after the collapse of the messianic Sabbatean movement.[21]

---

[20] Haim Hillel Ben Sasson et al., *Toldot `Am Yisrael*; Haim Hillel Ben Sasson, *A History of the Jewish People*.

[21] Ibid., 385.

Interestingly, Ben Sasson and many others in the Zionist camp abandoned the traditional dating of the year 70 as the onset of the Jewish Middle Ages.[22] Ben Sasson explains his choice of the seventh century by arguing that the seventh century ushered in a period during which almost all Jews lived under the domination of monotheistic rivals and thus suffered from the conflict and persecution inherent in monotheistic control of other monotheists. More interesting yet is the new dating of the third period of Jewish history. The Zionists rejected the traditional Jewish sense of divine intervention at some unspecified point in the future as setting in motion the third and redemptive period. The same is true for the Enlightenment sense of a new Western civilization as marking the end of the Jewish Middle Age and the onset of a new and happier era. Given their convictions as to the fundamental dynamic of Jewish history, Zionists saw this Enlightenment view as well as erroneous. A date that would reflect internal Jewish activity – with a focus on the physical – would supply the missing key, but that key proved difficult to find.

The Ben Sasson dating of the seventeenth century reflects Gershom Scholem's influential suggestion that the Sabbatian movement of the mid-seventeenth century serves as the dividing line between the Jewish Middle Ages and Jewish modernity. According to Scholem, this is precisely the point at which the Jewish masses first broke out of their passivity and asserted their active and physical commitment to wide-ranging change. Scholem's assessment of the Sabbatian movement involved a radical inversion of the standing of that movement. Scholem rehabilitated in a number of ways the Sabbatian movement, vilified by both traditional and Enlightenment-oriented Jews as a misguided messianic fantasy. In the first place, Scholem insisted that the movement was a major phenomenon in Jewish history. Scholem projected the movement as an uprising that stretched all across the far-flung Jewish diaspora, involved every sector of Jewish society, and included leaders at the very center of Jewish communal life. Equally important, he described it as nothing like the religious chimera of fevered Jewish imaginations; rather, it was the spontaneous uprising of the Jewish masses, aware at last that the time had come to take Jewish fate in their own hands.

---

[22] Note especially the extensive collections of sources organized by Ben Zion Dinur. The first collection was called *Yisrael be-Arzo* (*Israel in Its Land*); the second was *Yisrael ba-Golah* (*Israel in Diaspora*). Both collections begin with the Muslim conquests of the seventh century.

Speaking of the social composition of the Sabbatian movement, Scholem says the following:

The "small man" was more easily drawn into the emotional vortex generated by the messianic proclamation; he had neither reason nor strength to resist. All the more surprising is the real proportion of believers and unbelievers within the ruling class. All later statements notwithstanding, the majority of the ruling class was in the camp of the believers, and the prominent and active part played by many of them is attested by all the reliable documents. No doubt there was pressure from below, yet most of the communal leaders did not wait for this pressure; as a matter of fact, they did not require it in order to be spurred into action.[23]

Scholem laid out a powerful case for the Sabbatian movement as a massive Jewish awakening and the beginning of a new epoch in the history of the Jewish people, the beginning of the modern period as viewed through the Zionist lens.

There were powerful and effective ideological forces at work in the Zionist movement. Within the movement, there was also an intense drive toward reconstruction of the Jewish past in ways consistent with the basic premises of the enterprise. Out of this drive toward yoking historical study to the Zionist undertaking emerged the very early commitment to building a modern university at the center of the nationalist endeavor. The historians of this university would provide the historical data to reinforce the ideological thrusts of the movement. And indeed, the so-called Jerusalem School of historians did provide powerful academic leadership for the burgeoning university and movement. There was, however, one major limitation on the utility of these historians. The reality was that the leading figures of the young Jerusalem School arrived in Palestine as fully formed historians, trained in the best European centers of historical research. This enhanced the intellectual authenticity of their research and their teaching; at the same time, it extinguished the possibility of overly simplistic evaluation in their analyses. There was no Graetz-like figure in the Jerusalem School – its adherents were too sophisticated for Graetz-like monochromatic formulations.[24]

The first of the Jewish historians hired at the Hebrew University – Yitzhak (Fritz) Baer – is a case in point. Baer arrived in Palestine in 1930

[23] Gershom G. Scholem, *Sabbatai Sevi, the Mystical Messiah, 1626–1676*, 5.
[24] For a fine discussion of the "Jerusalem School," see David N. Myers, *Re-Inventing the Jewish Past.*

a very well trained historian, who had already ransacked the archives of Spain in search of new data on the history of medieval Spanish Jewry, thereby laying the foundation for sophisticated reconstruction of the history of the Jews in medieval Spain.[25] In 1945, Baer published his pathbreaking *History of the Jews in Christian Spain,* a major milestone in the writing of medieval Jewish history.[26] While important facets of the history of Jews in medieval Christian Spain have been explored more fully in the intervening decades, in many cases by Baer's students or students of his students, the Baer synthesis remains one of the most effective and illuminating reconstructions ever achieved of a set of medieval Jewish communities, distinguished by Baer's mastery of both sets of sources for Jewish life in medieval Iberia – the archival materials that he had gathered prior to leaving Germany and the Jewish sources of which he was a master.

To be sure, there are obvious ideological overtones to the book. Baer – like Scholem – highlighted the power of myth and mysticism in medieval Jewish life, indeed in Jewish history overall. Thus, he created a somewhat essentialist portrait of the Judaism of the Iberian Jews. Those inclined toward the mythic and mystical were truly Jewish, and their efforts were salutary for the preservation of Jewish faith and values. On the other hand, those Jews attracted to philosophy were seduced into non-Jewish ways. They deviated from the true Judaism and inflicted incalculable damage – according to Baer – on Jewish life. When the Jewish communities of Spain suffered the traumatic attacks of 1391, the corrosive effects of philosophy became manifest. In Baer's view, the massive wave of conversions was the direct result of immersion in philosophy and indicated the extent to which authentic Judaism had been betrayed by looking to the outside world. This is simultaneously a perception of the truly genuine in medieval Jewish life and history and an argument for the validity of the Zionist dream and movement, grounded likewise in a mythic sense of authentic Jewish peoplehood.

This essentialist view has been widely criticized, as well it should be. However, it should not be allowed to diminish the overall sophistication of the Baer opus. Baer understood well the dynamics of the medieval

[25]   Fritz Baer, ed., *Die Juden im christlichen Spanien.*
[26]   Yitzhak Baer, *A History of the Jews in Christian Spain.*

Roman Catholic Church, medieval Iberian governments, the internal tensions in Spanish society, and popular sentiment – at least as they had been delineated by scholars up to his times. His mastery of the Jewish materials entailed a full grasp of the internal dynamics of Jewish communal life, clear understanding of the diverse factions within the Spanish Jewish community, and comprehensive treatment of the various facets of Jewish intellectual and spiritual creativity. Baer was clearly offended by a figure like Abner of Burgos, who was a major defector from the Jewish community and proselytizer among his former co-religionists. Despite Baer's scorn for such defectors and proselytizers, he was obviously fascinated by Abner as well and understood him to be an important figure in late-thirteenth- and early-fourteenth-century Iberian Jewry. He painstakingly alerted his readers to the importance of Abner and himself made major contributions to the study of this significant albeit problematic figure.

Baer and his colleagues at the Hebrew University created an academic environment that did not allow for the development of reductionist portraits of medieval Jewish life, such as that composed by Heinrich Graetz. Although Baer and most of his colleagues were profoundly committed to the Zionist dream, they were at the same time highly professional scholars, whose scholarship was by and large free of simplistic overstatement. What was true in the early decades of the Hebrew University became even more the case as the writing of Jewish history branched out into a number of Israeli university settings and as Israeli scholars circulated ever more freely in the world of international scholarship. The medieval Jewish history written by these scholars bears no special Zionist-Israeli stamp; it is essentially professional scholarship and is widely acknowledged as such.

THUS, RECONSTRUCTION OF THE MEDIEVAL JEWISH EXPERIENCE HAS proceeded through much the same evolution as general study of the Middle Ages. Initially reductionist perspectives have largely given way to an expanding body of sophisticated scholarship. Centered in the universities of North America, Israel, and Europe, this scholarship has increasingly distanced itself from the simplistic formulae of traditional Jewish and Christian thinking and the early monolithic phases of modern research into the Jewish past. The syntheses offered by twentieth- and twenty-first-century scholars in all these worldwide centers of research are for the most part fully cognizant of the complexities of medieval European Jewish life, its problems, and its achievements.

One major, but understandable, shortcoming of the new scholarship is its failure to penetrate popular thinking. For most popular thinking, among both Jews and non-Jews, the Middle Ages remain the locus of unremitting Jewish suffering, in effect the same kind of vale of tears projected in traditional Jewish and Christian thinking. Although lamentable, this shortcoming is hardly unique to Jewish scholarship on the Middle Ages, since the larger body of scholarship on medieval Europe in general has done little to efface the popular sense of medieval as synonymous with the barbaric and benighted. Countering deeply ingrained popular stereotypes is extremely difficult, perhaps even impossible. Yet such an effort lies at the heart of the present book.

PART II

HISTORICAL THEMES

5

~

Demographic Movement and Change

*M*EDIEVAL DEMOGRAPHIC DEVELOPMENTS ARE EXTREMELY
difficult to reconstruct, but exceedingly important. Genuine
statistics are impossible to come by, and researchers are left with only
shards of impressionistic data. Despite the difficulties, scholars have
reached important general conclusions about medieval Jewish demographic movement and change from the available sources and have
achieved considerable consensus on these issues. Distinguishing between
such scholarly consensus and a variety of theological and ideological
prejudgments is no easy task, but it is crucial. For the realities of Jewish demographic movement and change form the essential backdrop to
understanding Jewish experience in medieval Christian Europe.

The starting point for any discussion of Jewish demographic developments in medieval Latin Christendom must be recognition of the fact
that, in the year 1000, the Jews of this area constituted only a tiny fraction
of worldwide Jewry. In the year 1000, the overwhelming majority of Jews
lived under Muslim rule, which stretched vast distances from western
India all the way to the Atlantic Ocean. Even on the European continent,
the numbers of Jews living under Muslim rule in southern Italy and southern Spain greatly exceeded the Jewish population of Europe's Christian
territories. The old centers of Jewish life in the Byzantine Empire still
housed Jewish communities that far outstripped those of Latin Christendom. Thus, the fundamental demographic developments of the period
between 1000 and 1500 involve the overall growth of the Jewish population of western Christendom in general and the emergence of an entirely
new set of Jewish communities in northern areas of Europe in particular.

This radical shift in world Jewish population is key to a full grasp of Jewish fate in medieval Latin Christendom.

THE WANDERING JEW

Powerful imagery shared by the Christian majority of the West and the Jewish minority has impeded accurate comprehension of the demographic changes that affected the Jews of medieval Latin Christendom. Jews and Christians both medieval and modern have projected the medieval Jewish experience – especially but not exclusively in western Christendom – in somber terms. They have portrayed Jewish suffering as ubiquitous, with one of the most salient indices of this suffering radical demographic instability. We recall readily Heinrich Graetz's imagery of "a subjugated Judah with the pilgrim staff in hand, the pilgrim pack upon the back." As we have noted, the roots of this perception lie in biblical predictions of exile and exilic suffering, with an emphasis on the scattering of the exiled "among all the peoples from one end of the earth to the other."[1]

While Jews have absorbed this sense of biblically predicted dispersion fully, it has been yet more prominent in Christian circles. For Christians, emphasis on Jewish sinfulness and divine punishment has played a critical role in explaining the passing of the divine-human covenant from Jewish to Christian auspices. Jewish exilic suffering has served Christians as clear and irrefutable proof that God had indeed punished the Jews for their monumental sin of rejecting and killing the promised Messiah. This Jewish sin in turn has served as the basis for understanding what Christians claim as the second element in the divine response to Jewish malfeasance – selection of the Gentiles as replacements for the original and subsequently rejected Jewish bearers of the covenant. Emphasis on Jewish suffering at the hands of God served as one of the fundamental elements in the Augustinian doctrine that posited the useful role played by Jews in Christian society and hence the need to maintain such valuable Jewish presence.[2]

---

[1] See Chapter 1 for the biblical predictions and Chapter 4 for Graetz.
[2] See Chapter 2.

Christian thinkers reinforced the broad biblical predictions of exilic wandering by invoking a powerful biblical image, that of the fratricide Cain. Given the Gospel view of the responsibility of Jews for the crucifixion of Jesus, it is not difficult to understand how Cain, the killer of his brother, became identified in Christian thinking with Jews. In the Genesis story, God admonishes Cain in the following terms:

What have you done? Your brother's blood is crying out to me from the ground. Now you are accursed and will be banished from the very ground which has opened its mouth to receive the blood you have shed. When you till the ground, it will no longer yield you its produce. You shall be a wanderer, a fugitive on the earth.[3]

The triple themes of fratricide, banishment from the land, and a lifetime of wandering much enriched Christian imagery of Jewish post-Crucifixion fate.

The next element in the biblical account enhanced identification of Cain and Jews. Cain pleads to God that the punishment decreed for him is unbearable. He notes: "I shall be a wanderer, a fugitive on the earth, and I can be killed by anyone." God responds by putting a mark on Cain, "so that anyone happening to meet him should not kill him."[4] Here the elements of fratricide, banishment from the land, and wandering are supplemented with notions of protection from unwarranted murder, which was a fundamental element in Christian doctrine concerning Jews, and of the imposition of a sign, variously interpreted as Jewish adherence to the law, the mark of circumcision, and – eventually in medieval western Christendom – distinguishing garb. Thus, the Cain-Jew identification seemed incontrovertible to medieval Christians.

Note the potent expression of this identification in the following opening passage in a letter of Pope Innocent III from the year 1208:

The Lord made Cain a wanderer and a fugitive over the earth, but set a mark upon him, making his head to shake, lest any finding him should slay him. Thus, although the Jews – against whom the blood of Jesus Christ calls out – ought not be killed, lest the Christian people forget the divine law, yet as

---

[3] Gen. 4:10–12.
[4] Gen. 4:14–15.

wanderers ought to they remain upon the earth, until their countenance be filled with shame and they seek the name of Jesus Christ, the Lord.[5]

Here, almost all the elements in the Cain story appear – fratricide, blood calling out from the earth, banishment, wandering, a sign, and protection from random killing. The concatenation of themes assured the impact of this imagery on medieval Christian thinking.

The realities of Jewish life in medieval western Christendom have seemed to dovetail perfectly with the biblical predictions of suffering through wandering and the Cain imagery. Jews were in many sectors of medieval Europe – especially in the north – accurately perceived as new-comers, hence reinforcing the theme of wandering. As these newcomers settled into the northern sectors of medieval Europe, they continued to move about regularly, pursuing economic opportunity and forming new Jewish settlements. Moreover, beginning in the late twelfth century and continuing throughout the ensuing centuries, large numbers of Euro-pean Jews suffered banishment from their home territories – dramatic reflection of the broad biblical predictions and the specific punishment imposed on the fratricide Cain.

To be sure, the confluence of imagery and reality has been highly exaggerated. Closer inspection of Jewish demography indicates that the suggestive imagery and the realities of Jewish demography in late antiq-uity and the first half of the Middle Ages diverged markedly. While traditional Jewish and Christian thinking posited defeat at the hands of the Romans, exile from the Land of Israel, and the onset of Jewish wandering as occurring simultaneously in the year 70, in fact this was not at all the case. Historians of Jewish life in late antiquity note that the defeat of the year 70 – for all its impact on Jewish religious life – did not alter significantly the basic demographic distribution of Jews. Palestine remained the largest center of Jewish population, with the diaspora com-munities of the east (Mesopotamia) and the west (the Mediterranean basin) remaining secondary. Even the second major defeat at the hands of the Romans, during the failed Bar Kokhba uprising of 132–135, does not seem to have altered Jewish demographic patterns. In the wake of this second defeat, the centers of Jewish population in Palestine seem to have

---

[5] Solomon Grayzel, ed. and trans., *The Church and the Jews in the XIIIth Century*, 1:126–127, #24.

drifted northward out of Judea and into Galilee, but Palestinian Jewry continued to dominate on the worldwide scene. With the compilation of the Mishnah around the year 200, the centrality of Palestinian Jewry deepened further.

The decline of Palestinian Jewish life does not seem to have occurred in the year 70 or to have resulted from overt clashes with the Roman authorities. Instead, the broad third-century upheaval in the Roman world and its destructive impact at the eastern fringes of the empire, including Roman Palestine, seem to have inspired growing numbers of Jews to seek better circumstances in the relatively peaceful Sassanian Empire, with its flourishing Jewish centers. The voluntary migration of large numbers of Palestinian Jews ended the demographic and spiritual centrality of the Jewish community in the Land of Israel in late antiquity. These historical realities challenge two stereotypes – first, the traditional Jewish and even more so the traditional Christian sense of the simultaneity of the defeat of the year 70 and the onset of Jewish exile from the Land of Israel and, second, the assumption of Jewish removal from the land as forced, the result of divinely ordained Roman persecution.

Likewise, the conviction that the defeat of the year 70 inaugurated incessant Jewish wandering over the globe does not square with demographic realities either.[6] In fact, once the new pattern of Jewish settlement was established by the year 300, with Mesopotamian Jewry dominating and with smaller Jewish centers in Palestine and further westward throughout the Mediterranean basin, Jewish demographic distribution remained remarkably stable for more than seven centuries. From 300 through the onset of the second Christian millennium, the same demographic pattern is discernible. While Jews certainly did move around – as almost all human communities do – there are no major demographic upheavals and no indications of a divinely ordained punishment that made the Jews "wanderers" or "fugitives on the earth."

The stability of Jewish demography is all the more striking, given that the sectors of the world the Jews of the early Middle Ages inhabited underwent monumental change. The Muslim conquest was one of the most remarkable military achievements in Western history. Quite unexpectedly, a new force inspired by a new faith erupted from the peripheral

---

[6] Recall the northern French histories cited in the Prologue.

area of the Arabian peninsula, spread with stunning rapidity northeastward, toppled the venerable Sassanian Empire, and simultaneously swept westward and significantly reduced both the Greek and Latin sectors of the Roman Empire. When the dust had settled, the new Islamic authorities controlled a vast empire, which stretched from the western areas of India across the Near East and the eastern and southern littorals of the Mediterranean Sea and over onto the mainland of Europe.

Such remarkable overthrow of the old order might well have disrupted Jewish life – perhaps even markedly. Yet, the Muslim conquests did no such thing. In fact, Jewish demographic distribution remained remarkably constant, maintaining the constellation of Jewish population centers that had been created during the third century and – if anything – strengthening many of them. The older centers in Mesopotamia, which had assumed spiritual leadership in the Jewish world and had begun the compilation of the Babylonian Talmud, remained dominant, and the creative centers of Jewish life in Palestine, Syria, Egypt, all across North Africa, and over onto the Italian and Iberian peninsulas exhibited ongoing or even enhanced vitality. Jewish population distribution looked much the same in the year 1000 as it had in the year 300, long before the Muslim conquests.

FORCED DISLOCATION

While no real case can be made for the onset of incessant wandering across the face of the globe subsequent to defeat at the hand of Rome and for demographic instability through the early centuries of the Middle Ages, at least the realities of Jewish life in medieval western Christendom subsequent to the year 1000 might seem to support fully the traditional Jewish view of ongoing wandering as part of the divine decree of exile and the Christian identification of Jews with Cain, consigned to endless displacement as part of the divine edict of punishment for the Crucifixion. Jewish life in medieval western Christendom seems to show a very high level of demographic instability, with an entirely new phenomenon – forced banishment of entire sets of Jewish communities – becoming especially prominent. Medieval Jews and even more so medieval Christians might easily interpret this demographic instability as the divine punishment posited in both religious traditions.

Prior to the twelfth century, wholesale banishments of sets of Jewish communities were hardly known. To be sure, the Assyrians in the eighth pre-Christian century had expelled most of the inhabitants of the northern kingdom of Israel, and in the sixth pre-Christian century the Babylonians had done the same to most of the inhabitants of the southern Judean kingdom. However, these two expulsions hardly fit the traditional Jewish and Christian paradigms. Modern scholarship now projects such expulsions as standard procedure for breaking the cohesion of defeated peoples in the Ancient Near East. More important, they long preceded the onset of the sinfulness and divine punishment that both Jewish and Christian traditions associate with the year 70.

There are reports of forced expulsions from areas of the Iberian peninsula and southern France during the seventh century. These reports are, however, extremely fragmentary, and some modern scholars question the reality of such expulsions altogether.[7] More important for our purposes, these early events seem to have been little known in the post-1000 period. The rulers of northern Europe did not invoke these early banishments as precedents for the sequence of expulsions that began in twelfth-century northern France, nor do Christian thinkers cite them as evidence for the traditional claims of Jewish wandering across the face of the globe. The expulsions that began in the latter part of the twelfth century much enhanced the sense of medieval Jewish life as fulfillment of the divine edict that transformed the Jews into a community of wanderers knowing no rest or respite.

Given the Augustinian doctrine of toleration of Jews in Christian society, we may well ask how forced banishment could take place at all. The simple answer to this question is that the Augustinian position by no means implied *carte blanche* for all forms of Jewish behavior. A safe and secure place in Christian society for Jews required lawful behavior on the part of these Jews. Individual Jewish malfeasance occasioned normal judicial procedures. Jews accused of crimes could be and were subject to prosecution and – if proven guilty – could be and were duly punished. On occasion, individual Jews were executed for serious crimes. At the same time, there was a strong sense on the medieval scene of the corporate identity of Jews – and indeed of others as well. Not infrequently,

---

[7] See Bernard S. Bachrach, *Early Medieval Jewish Policy in Western Europe*, chapter 1.

Christian authorities held entire Jewish communities responsible for criminal behavior and prosecuted and punished these communities *en masse*. The sense of corporate Jewish culpability and harmfulness lay at the root of the mass expulsions of Jewish communities from sectors of medieval western Christendom. Banishment found justification, even under the Augustinian doctrine, as a legitimate way of dealing with widespread Jewish transgressions and harmfulness that seemed intractable.

The first significant expulsion of Jews in medieval western Christendom took place at the very center of the vitalization of Christian Europe. In 1182, King Philip Augustus banished Jews from the royal domain of France. The monarch's father, King Louis VII, who reigned from 1137 to 1180, had assiduously protected the growing Jewish community of the royal domain. Strikingly, King Louis VII had rallied to the defense of his Jewish subjects in the wake of the execution of numerous Jews in the neighboring county of Blois in 1171, for which his Jewish clients were profoundly grateful.[8] In 1179, King Louis VII associated his son Philip with him on the throne, dying only a few months later. This son, known to posterity as Philip Augustus, was the first of the great Capetian kings who transformed a small and weak royal domain into one of the major political forces in thirteenth-century and subsequent Europe. King Philip Augustus, viewed by present-day historians as a clever and wily monarch, managed to outwit and out-maneuver a wide range of opponents, in the process exploiting maximally the limited but important resources at his disposal.[9]

We do not possess documents that provide directly the royal perspective on the sequence of steps taken by the newly installed monarch against his Jewish subjects. We are dependent on the detailed portrait of these steps sketched by his clerical biographer, Rigord of Saint Denis.[10] Rigord depicts three distinct royal actions: confiscation of Jewish property in March of 1180; subsequent forgiving of Jewish loans, with a fifth part of these loans reverting to the king; and then in April of 1182 an edict of

---

[8] See Robert Chazan, "The Blois Incident of 1171," 13–31.
[9] On the statecraft of Philip Augustus, see John W. Baldwin, *The Government of Philip Augustus.*
[10] There is a valuable new edition of this important work – Rigord, *Histoire de Philippe Auguste.*

expulsion that eventuated in the removal of Jews from the royal domain three months later.[11] The royal domain at this point in time was quite small, meaning that the banished Jews could find refuge in neighboring principalities without traveling long distances or adjusting to radically new circumstances. Nonetheless, royal banishment of an entire set of Jewish communities was a highly significant precedent; the actions of King Philip Augustus set an important example for a sequence of greater and lesser rulers of northern and eventually southern Europe.

Rigord of Saint Denis goes to considerable lengths to identify Jewish misdeeds that served as goads to and justifications for the three royal steps. He mentions: royal belief in the charge that Jews kill innocent Christian youngsters (a charge that Philip Augustus's father had explicitly disavowed); royal recognition that Jewish wealth had facilitated the hiring of Christian menservants and maidservants to work in Jewish homes, with resultant deviation from Christian practice and belief; royal indignation that Jews had contravened biblical law by lending money at interest to Christians, as a result of which the Christian populace allegedly suffered deeply. While it is tempting to treat the Rigord reconstruction as a distorted clerical reworking of the political realities, in fact there is considerable evidence to support his correlation of alleged Jewish misdeeds with royal actions. When we begin to have at our disposal actual decrees of expulsion, they regularly anchor banishment of Jews in one or another set of alleged Jewish misdeeds. For the late twelfth and on through the thirteenth and fourteenth centuries, the central Jewish misdeed adduced was an addiction to usury that the authorities could not reform.[12]

While rationalization and legitimization of expulsion was a constant from Philip Augustus onward, so too is the evidence that there were more tangible considerations on the minds of rulers who elected to remove their Jews. In Philip's case, there was clearly substantial royal profit from both the pre-expulsion actions and the expulsion itself. According to Rigord, in advance of the actual expulsion Jews were allowed to sell their moveable goods, but their immovable property escheated to the royal treasury. In all likelihood, this was a substantial windfall for a revenue-starved government. We may also readily surmise that obligations owed

---

[11] Ibid., 144–59.
[12] For a number of edicts of expulsion, see Chazan, *Church, State, and Jew*, 309–19. See below for late-fifteenth-century Spain.

to Jews were likewise taken over by the royal authorities, as this was a constant feature of the later and better documented expulsions. The sums realized from expulsion of the Jews were regularly considerable, although of course the immediate revenues always had to be reckoned against subsequent profit from the Jews lost over time.

While the most tangible advantage enjoyed by authorities that expelled their Jews was financial gain on a substantial – often massive – scale, there were significant ancillary benefits as well. As reflected in Rigord's enthusiastic account of the royal anti-Jewish steps, various elements in the subject population approved of the moves, especially of the expulsion of Jews. Rigord's catalogue of Jewish misdeeds suggests that many in the Christian population would have seen Philip Augustus's edict of expulsion as removing a Jewish threat to physical safety (the killing of Christian youngsters), a Jewish threat to the economic well-being of the Christian populace (the suffering engendered by Jewish moneylending), and a Jewish threat to the religious purity of Christian society (the religious backsliding encouraged by Jews). For a young and embattled monarch, such popular approbation was no small matter.

In addition, if Rigord is taken to be characteristic, ecclesiastical enthusiasm for the royal moves was considerable. It is clear that Philip Augustus's anti-Jewish actions resonated positively for Rigord, who regularly designates Philip "the most Christian king" throughout his account of these anti-Jewish moves. Not coincidentally, he reports only briefly and grudgingly the same monarch's decision to reintroduce Jews into his domain in 1198.[13] Additionally, Rigord reports prominently royal consultation with Bernard of Vincennes, a respected hermit, who suggested the second of the three royal moves. Rigord further reports that, upon enactment of the edict of expulsion, some Jews chose to be baptized. These Jews King Philip Augustus treated properly and liberally, returning to them all their property and ensuring them perpetual liberty. Finally, Rigord indicates an important post-expulsion step, designed to win even further ecclesiastical approbation.

All the synagogues of the Jews, which are called schools by them and where the Jews – in the name of a false faith – convene daily for the sake of feigned prayer, he ordered cleansed. Against the will of all the princes, he caused

---

[13]   Rigord, *Histoire de Philippe Auguste*, 352–53.

those synagogues to be dedicated to God as churches, and he ordered altars to be consecrated in these synagogues in honor of our Lord Jesus Christ and of the blessed mother of God, Virgin Mary.[14]

Just as Philip gained for himself wide-ranging popular approbation, so too did he win important ecclesiastical support as well.

The expulsion of 1182 – as useful as it was to the young king – was profoundly painful to the Jewish victims, again on many levels. On the simplest level of all, individuals and families were torn from their moorings. We have noted recurrently that the Jewish communities of northern Europe were young, emerging as a result of the vitalization that began in the late tenth century and accelerated rapidly thereafter. However, we must not confuse the relatively recent origins of the Jewish communities of northern Europe with the feelings of rootedness of individuals and families. The Jewish communities of northern Europe, viewed from the broad sweep of the Jewish past, were young; Jews settled in a given locale for a few decades were sufficiently embedded in their environments to feel enormous pain and upheaval upon being constrained to leave precipitously. Beyond this significant psychological reality, there were important financial losses as well. As Rigord indicates, the Jews expelled by Philip Augustus – while permitted to sell their moveable goods or take them into exile – lost their immoveable possessions and (although Rigord does not mention this) lost obligations owed to them. Just as the royal profit was considerable, so too were the Jewish losses extensive and painful.

In 1182 the French royal domain was extremely small. One of the major challenges the young monarch faced was the fact that powerful barons surrounded his small domain on all sides. This meant, for the exiled Jews, that finding refuge did not entail movement over long distances and did not require profound social and economic adjustments. On the other hand – as we shall see extensively in the next chapter – Jewish economic outlets in northern Europe were quite constricted. As a result, Jews often had to move about in order to find new markets for their limited economic repertoire. Thus, forced banishment meant hardship for the exiled Jews, as they strove to find new places of residence and business, and for the Jews into whose towns and domains the displaced

---

[14] Ibid., 154–55.

Jews made their way. Expulsions affected both the refugees and those Jews whose towns and domains subsequently absorbed them.

We have focused on the earliest of the royal expulsions and have noted that it served as an important precedent. Beginning at the end of the thirteenth century, expulsion of Jews proceeded from an occasional feature of Jewish life in Europe to a regular phenomenon. In 1290, King Edward I of England expelled his Jews, who found refuge in areas of northwestern France from which their ancestors had two centuries earlier made their way into England.[15] In 1306, the Jews of the greatly expanded royal France faced a similar fate. The expulsion of 1306 involved the largest number of Jews to be formally banished up to that point in time; it also encompassed for the first time southern European Jewish communities, since by 1306 the tentacles of Capetian authority had extended southward all the way to the Mediterranean Sea. The exiled Jews of southern France largely moved westward onto the Iberian peninsula; the exiled Jews of northern France largely moved eastward into Germanic areas.[16]

All these late-thirteenth- and early-fourteenth-century expulsions involved the same combination of religiously based rationalization, financial advantage to the authorities expelling their Jews, and suffering for the Jewish victims. The grounds advanced for these late-twelfth and thirteenth-century expulsions centered regularly on Jewish usury – the suffering it created within the Christian populace, its ultimate illegitimacy, and the unwillingness of the Jews to give up their moneylending business, despite repeated governmental efforts to suppress it. Again, the expelling authorities enjoyed considerable financial gain. By this time, the principalities of northwestern Europe had created sprawling and effective bureaucracies. Large, well-staffed offices emerged for realizing maximal profit from the Jewish lands and loans that had escheated to the authorities. Likewise, the expulsions won for their instigators wide-ranging approbation in numerous sectors of the societies over which they ruled. Church leadership and broad swaths of the populace were profoundly pleased with the expulsion of the Jews and grateful to the expelling authorities. The Jews, on the other hand, suffered painful uprooting and profound economic loss. Again, as already noted for 1182, the hardships

---

[15] For full treatment, see Robin Mundill, *England's Jewish Solution*.
[16] William Chester Jordan, *The French Monarchy and the Jews*, chapter 13.

extended to those Jewish communities in which the exiled Jews sought refuge. Given the limited options for Jewish economic activity, Jews living in these host Jewish communities saw their economic activities come under enhanced pressure.

There was yet one further broad liability to be noted. As a result of the sequence of late-thirteenth- and early-fourteenth-century expulsions, Jewish life in northern Europe was detached from the advanced and exciting centers of the new European civilization and removed to the lagging areas of central and eastern Europe. There, the desire to enjoy some of the progress palpable in the western areas of northern Europe made the authorities receptive to fostering the immigration of Jews, who were viewed as potentially useful in transplanting the economic culture of the advanced western sectors into backward regions of central and eastern Europe.

The period between the late thirteenth and late fourteenth century saw a spate of expulsions that removed Jews from the most advanced and exciting areas of northwestern Europe. A second wave of expulsions began in the late fifteenth century and continued down through the first half of the sixteenth century, affecting Jewish life all across southern Europe and northward into the Germanic territories as well. While attention has focused heavily on the most famous and painful of these expulsions – those affecting the Jews of the Iberian peninsula in the 1490s – the broad scope and potent impact of these expulsions deserve notice as well. Jewish life was affected across much of late-medieval western Christendom.[17]

Let us begin with the most well-known of this new spate of expulsions – those from the Iberian peninsula in the 1490s. Like the earlier expulsions from the north, those from the Iberian peninsula display the same combination of religiously grounded rationalization and ulterior motivations. The expulsions from Spain and Portugal were – like the earlier banishments – formally grounded in rationalizations of religious and social necessity. However, these formal grounds shifted in the late fifteenth century, as a result of the special circumstances of Iberia and Iberian Jewish life. The rationalizations of the earlier northern European banishments lay exclusively with Jewish usury. In fifteenth-century

---

[17] For treatment of the overall wave of expulsions, see Jonathan I. Israel, *European Jewry in the Age of Mercantilism*, chapter 1.

Iberia, the grounds for expelling Jews lay in the phenomenon of massive conversion of Jews during the late fourteenth and on into the fifteenth centuries, the resultant creation of a large class of New Christians, and the difficulties in assimilating these New Christians effectively into their new religious identity and community. In the face of growing evidence of backsliding among these New Christians, the remedy proposed regularly involved a twin assault on the problem: inquisitorial proceedings launched against the backsliders themselves and elimination of the Jews, who allegedly served as a constant stimulus – both overtly and symbolically – toward return to Jewish mores and Jewish beliefs. Rather than an emphasis on Jewish usury in the expulsion documents of the late fifteenth century, the focus is very much on the religious impact of the overt Jews on the New Christians.[18]

Once more, it is clear that there was considerable governmental profit from the expulsion of the Jews. Again to be sure, there was short-term gain at the expense of long-term profit. Many observers have concluded that the expulsion of Jews (and subsequently of Muslims as well) signaled the onset of long-term economic decline for Spain, a conclusion still widely debated in Spanish society and academic circles. In any case, the expulsion of Jews won the Spanish crown widespread approbation in many sectors of late medieval Spanish society. The populace at large, hostile baronial elements, and the ecclesiastical leadership all seemed by and large to agree on the benefits of removal of the Jews from Iberia. In fifteenth-century Spain, there seems to have been one further motive as well – the desire to create a homogeneous Christian population in the area of Europe historically most diverse. The benefits and liabilities of this effort likewise continue to be debated in contemporary Spanish society. It is striking that the area of medieval Europe that showed the greatest heterogeneity during the Middle Ages evolved into the most uniformly Catholic area of modern Europe.

Like the northern banishments, the expulsions from the Iberian peninsula also took a heavy toll on the Jews who were displaced from their ancestral homes – both psychologically and materially. The psychological dimension is especially noteworthy. Much more deeply than their

---

[18]   The fullest treatment of the major expulsion, that of 1492, is Haim Beinart, *The Expulsion of the Jews from Spain.*

northern confreres, the Jews of Spain felt an age-old identification with Iberia, a sense that their residence on the peninsula had preceded the birth of Islam in the seventh century and in fact even the birth of Christianity. We recall the charming tale told by Solomon ibn Verga, in his *Shevet Yehudah*, of the participation of the Spanish king in the Babylonian conquest of Jerusalem in 586 BCE and of the gift of the Jews of the best Jerusalem neighborhoods bestowed upon the Spanish monarch. This tale suggests that the expulsion of 1492 uprooted a community that had enjoyed more than two millennia of settlement on Iberian soil and that was devastated by the loss of its millennia-old home.[19]

While the Jews of northern Europe were able – and in fact desired – to find refuge in areas of Christian Europe still open to them, the Iberian Jewish refugees found few options for remaining within the borders of western Christendom. Upon expulsion from Castile and Aragon in 1492, the largest number of refugees made their way by land into Portugal. Southern France had long been closed off as a result of the expulsion of 1306 and the final expulsion from France in 1394. Some Jews found refuge in areas of Italy still open to Jewish settlement. When the king of Portugal was pressured into expelling his Jews in 1497, only sectors of Italy remained as possible areas of resettlement within southern Christian Europe.[20] Thus, the bulk of Iberian Jewry was forced to leave western Christendom and to find refuge eastward in the Turkish Empire, struggling (like the areas of central and eastern Europe in the north) to match the gains of the westerly kingdoms of Christian Europe. Just as northern Jews were perceived by the rulers of central and eastern Europe as useful tools in their efforts to emulate the achievements of the northwestern areas of Europe, so were the Iberian Jews perceived as potentially helpful by the Turkish authorities.

The expulsions noted thus far were largely the result of edicts enacted by major European monarchs – the kings of England, France, Aragon, Castile, and Portugal. Further expulsions were decreed at the end of the fifteenth century by the king of France for the Jews of Provence and by the king of Aragon for the Jews of Sicily and Sardinia. Simultaneously, all across southern Italy and up into the Germanic territories, more

---

[19] See the Prologue.
[20] Areas of eastern Europe in the north simply did not come into view as options.

limited expulsions were decreed by local authorities. Popular discontent and resentments fed these expulsions, which were reinforced by both Reformation and Counter-Reformation tensions and issues. The thorough removal of Jews from the western sectors of Europe that culminated in the expulsions from Iberia in the 1490s was augmented by further forced demographic movement through the central areas of Europe – from Italy in the south northward into Germany. The net result was reinforcement of the eastward movement of medieval European Jewry, with most of the Jews of the south relocating outside western Christendom altogether in the Ottoman Empire and the Jews of the north moving further eastward into the developing areas of eastern Europe.[21]

VOLUNTARY MIGRATIONS

In most instances, human decisions to change locale are complex, involving assessments of the areas being abandoned and the areas into which relocation is contemplated. When the latter areas are perceived to be clearly advantageous over the former, the decision to move is made. The expulsions upon which we have thus far focused involved no such weighing of pros and cons; they were forced upon Jews, who exercised no choice whatsoever in the matter. However, these banishments, as painful as they might have been, constituted the minority of instances of Jewish demographic movement during the period between 1000 and 1500. In the majority of Jewish relocations, Jews were in a position to evaluate the advantages and disadvantages of the locales they considered leaving and the locales into which they contemplated moving. Comparative evaluation and voluntary decision-making were the norm in most of Jewish demographic movement throughout medieval western Christendom, traditional Jewish and Christian imagery of such movement as imposed as divine punishment notwithstanding.

Indeed, the very immigration of Jews into northern Europe, which established this important new set of Jewish communities, was entirely voluntary. We know of no banishments that set Jews in involuntary motion around the turn of the millennium. Rather, the movement of Jews beyond the usual perimeter of their prior settlement into Jewishly

---

[21] Again, see Israel, *European Jewry in the Age of Mercantilism*, chapter 1.

underpopulated areas of southern Europe and into the Jewishly unpopu-
lated reaches of northern Europe seems to have involved decisions on the
part of a small number of adventuresome Jews that economic opportunities in these developing areas warranted the gamble of attempting to settle
in them. To be sure, this decision may well reflect limitations encountered
in prior places of settlement, but it is difficult to see these decisions as
reflective of the traditional Jewish and Christian sense of Jewish movement as a divinely imposed punishment. Rather, Jewish migration into
northern Europe looks much more like the entirely human drive toward
betterment for self and family.

Jewish readiness to immigrate into northern Europe dovetailed nicely
with the desire of northern European political authorities to attract these
adventuresome Jews by affording them a variety of forms of support.
While we possess little detailed data that clarify the early Jewish population movement into and within northern Europe, we do have brief
narrative accounts of Jewish population movement into the county of
Flanders in the early eleventh century, the kingdom of England in the
middle of the eleventh century, and the town of Speyer toward the end of
the eleventh century.[22] In the case of Speyer, we also have the document
of invitation extended by the bishop of the town, acting in his capacity
as temporal ruler.[23] In all three cases, we learn of the decision of a ruler –
the count of Flanders, the king of England, and the bishop of Speyer – to
support the immigration of Jewish clients.

Especially noteworthy is the clarification offered by the bishop of
Speyer: "When I wished to make a city out of the village of Speyer, I
Rudiger, surnamed Huozmann, bishop of Speyer, thought that the glory
of our town would be augmented a thousandfold if I were to bring Jews."[24]
Quite clearly, the contribution that the Jewish immigrants were projected
to make to the town of Speyer revolved around its economy and the
extent to which Jewish presence might stimulate economic development.
The specifics of the charter of invitation suggest that the anticipated
immigrants were merchants and that their anticipated contribution was

[22] For Flanders, we have a brief Hebrew narrative that can be found in Abraham Habermann, ed. *Sefer Gezerot Ashkenaz ve-Ẓarfat*; for England, we have the brief twelfth-
century statement of William of Malmesbury; for Speyer, we have a short Hebrew
narrative that can be found in Chazan, *Church, State, and Jew*, 59.

[23] Chazan, *Church, State, and Jew*, 58–59.

[24] Ibid., 58.

in the realm of business affairs. In the cases of Flanders and England, we know far less. However, the sense is once again of anticipated Jewish contribution to the economy. The invitation to settle in Flanders involved an especially prominent Jew, who was empowered to bring along with him a number of fellow Jews. The invitation to England was issued by the duke of Normandy turned king of England, already familiar with Jewish economic contribution in Normandy and seemingly desirous of extending that contribution to his newly conquered kingdom.

In the case of Speyer, the extant Hebrew narrative source suggests a factor that had distressed some of the Jewish migrants and stimulated thoughts of relocation. According to this narrative, a fire had broken out in the Jewish neighborhood of the town of Mainz, which moved the burghers of the town to anger against their Jewish neighbors.[25] This eruption of hostility may well have stimulated the bishop of Speyer to extend his invitation. It may at the same time have convinced some Mainz Jews to respond positively to the Speyer overtures. It would seem exaggerated, however, to see in the move to Speyer evidence of Jews being forced to relocate. Clearly, the Mainz community remained viable and continued to house a major Jewish community for many centuries. Rather, what this episode suggests is the normal human situation of assessing the advantages of remaining in place against the advantages of relocating. Most of the Mainz Jews opted to stay in place; some of them decided to make the move. This move thus involved the normal human weighing of alternatives and the normal human exercise of volition.

This paradigm of the pressures of violence – real or potential – affecting the decision to move became common in northern Europe from the fourteenth century onward. By the fourteenth century, the process of elimination of Jews from the more westerly sectors of northern Europe was well under way. Jews had been banished from England in 1290 and by and large from France in 1306. While Jews were permitted to return to France in 1315, the returnees were unable to reconstitute the flourishing Jewish life of the twelfth and thirteenth centuries.[26] The Jewish population of northern Europe was thus concentrated in the Germanic lands

---

[25] Ibid., 59.

[26] Ibid., 80–83. On Jewish life in fourteenth-century France, see Roger Kohn, *Les Juifs de la France du Nord*.

of the central areas of northern Europe. There, Jews encountered twin difficulties, both long-term and more immediate.

By virtue of economic and political backwardness, this area had long been less secure for Jews than the more effectively governed westerly sectors of northern Europe. This was the area in which the unusual crusade-related violence of 1096 broke out, in part as a result of the lack of effective governmental control.[27] Periodic persecution during the twelfth and thirteenth centuries was far more common in this area than in France and England. In addition, the backwardness of governments meant that the general European crisis of the fourteenth century struck more deeply in the Germanic areas than elsewhere in Europe. From the late thirteenth century onward, Jews living in the Germanic lands suffered periodic episodes of popular violence.[28] As was the case with the Jews of Mainz in 1084, however, all this did not mean an automatic decision to relocate. It did, however, mean a high level of receptivity to consideration of alternatives.

At precisely this point in time, the governing authorities in eastern Europe began the arduous process of attempting to achieve what the bishop of Speyer had set out to do in 1084 – to improve the economic circumstances of their realms. This process was especially noteworthy in Poland and Hungary. In both cases, the key to economic improvement lay in attracting urban settlers, and the Jews were part of the urban populace of the Germanic lands that might reasonably be attracted. A number of charters suggest that once again rulers concerned with attracting Jews offered promises of security and economic opportunity to potential Jewish settlers.[29] These charters reflect a significant change from the late eleventh century in the economic profile of the potential immigrants. The Jews addressed in these documents were no longer merchants, as had been the case in 1084; they were moneylenders of the more limited type, that is, moneylenders who insured their disbursal of funds through accepting pawns in exchange for the money loaned. The authorities in Poland and Hungary viewed this kind of business as useful

---

[27] See Chazan, *European Jewry and the First Crusade.*

[28] For a valuable overview, see Jorg R. Muller, "*Erez gezerah* – 'Land of Persecution,'" 245–60.

[29] See, e.g., the charters for Austria and Poland in Chazan, *Church, State, and Jew*, 84–93.

and promised valuable support for Jews and the Jewish lending business as an inducement to immigration.

Once again, Jews were in the position of making decisions about relocation. The disadvantages of their circumstances in the Germanic lands were weighed against the advantages offered in the developing areas of eastern Europe, with their supportive rulers and enticing business opportunities. Many Jews opted to make the move into eastern Europe, laying the foundations for the great population centers of early modern and modern Jewish life. While there were certainly pressures that impacted the decision to move, that decision involved nonetheless a weighing of benefits and liabilities and genuine Jewish decision-making.

Yet another kind of pressure for migration emanated from the limitations of Jewish economic activity. The Jewish immigrants into northern Europe found themselves constricted economically from the very beginnings of their settlement. Immigrating northward largely as merchants, these Jews were never successful in creating for themselves a diversified economy. Rather, they continued to fill limited and useful niches in the general economy. To be sure, the specific niches evolved with the passage of time, but real diversification eluded the Jews of medieval northern Europe.[30] Jewish economic specialization had enormous impact on Jewish settlement patterns and Jewish mobility. In effect, any given town or areas could absorb only a limited number of Jewish merchants or Jewish moneylenders. These limitations necessitated a constant search for new markets for Jewish trade or Jewish moneylending, forcing Jews to consider at all times options available for relocation.

Jews regularly began by settling in large urban centers and then slowly fanning out into the surrounding towns and villages. Due to the availability of unusually rich archival materials from England, scholars have traced the movement of Jews into a growing number of English towns in some detail. From the beginning of the reign of King Henry II in 1154, treasury records indicate organized Jewish communities in London and nine other relatively important English towns. During the peaceful three and a half decades of the reign of Henry II, the number of organized Jewish communities seems to have trebled. The founding of new Jewish settlements came about as a result of the limitations of Jewish

---

[30] See Chapter 6 for fuller detail on evolving Jewish economic activity and its limitations.

economic activity and the resultant need to strike out in search of new markets.[31]

The evidence from northern France is less voluminous, and it is impossible to trace the same detailed process. Nonetheless, there is a strong sense of much the same developments at work. By the late thirteenth century, Jews had spread themselves across much of the length and breadth of the ever-expanding royal domain and many of the major baronies of northern France.[32] The evidence from the Germanic lands suggests a parallel process. In an extremely important study, Michael Toch has provided copious data on the ongoing diffusion of the Jewish population all across the German lands. Toch has provided a series of eight maps, which shows graphically the expanding number of Jewish settlements. He has then reinforced this map evidence with a table that delineates the growing number of Jewish settlements by fifty-year time blocs. The end result is incontrovertible evidence of a growing and rapidly spreading Jewish population.[33]

As Jews made their way into developing areas of eastern Europe, starting during the thirteenth and accelerating during the fourteenth century, the pattern of settlement shows the same dynamic. The early centers of Jewish life in Poland and Hungary were located in towns close to the German lands from which the Jewish immigrants originated. With the passage of time, economic limitations once more forced Jews to contemplate relocation in search of new business opportunities. Again, many went beyond contemplation to the decision to seek opportunity in new settlements.[34]

The voluntary forms of migration encountered in this section indicate considerable demographic movement that was by no means totally forced. There were pressures that made the Jews receptive to the notion of moving, but there was voluntary decision making in the process. In all the cases just now examined, Jews had options, with some Jews choosing to stay put and others to move. This is a far cry from the traditional

[31] Cecil Roth, *A History of the Jews in England*, 11–12.
[32] See Robert Chazan, *Medieval Jewry in Northern France*, 207–20.
[33] Michael Toch, "The Formation of a Diaspora," 55–78.
[34] See the table of Jewish settlement in Bernard D. Weinryb, *The Jews of Poland*, 31, and the map of non-Christian settlement in Nora Behrend, *At the Gates of Christendom*, 59.

Jewish and Christian imagery of Jews hounded from place to place as a result of divine fiat.

∾

THE JEWS OF MEDIEVAL EUROPE WERE UNUSUALLY MOBILE FOR THEIR era. Many of them chose to settle in the foreboding, challenging, and exciting environment of medieval western Christendom. Once settled in this new environment, they began a pattern of ongoing relocation. To be sure, some of the relocation of the new Jewish communities of the north and the older Jewish communities of the south was forced upon the Jews and reflects negative attitudes on the part of the host majority. The formal expulsions were traumatic and harmful in many ways. They are not, however, the whole of the story of Jewish demographic movement. The Jews of medieval Europe regularly assessed their circumstances and often decided to move in search of improving their lives and the lot of their families.

Ultimately, the most significant achievement of the Jews of medieval Christian Europe lay in the area of demographic change. The myriad Jewish decisions to relocate from the Islamic realm into western Christendom and likewise to leave the Mediterranean ambience for the wilds of northern Europe resulted in a monumental shift in world Jewish population distribution. As a result of these many individual decisions, the center of gravity in the Jewish world shifted from the Islamic lands into the exciting and problematic territories of western Christendom. The price paid for relocation into those areas destined to dominate the West from the late Middle Ages well into the twentieth century was steep. On the other hand, it is difficult to imagine Jewish fate without these decisions. Remaining mired in the realm of Islam as it began to lose ground to its Christian competitor bloc surely would have exacted a high price as well, a price that is difficult to imagine.

6

ॐ

Economic Activity

$\mathcal{E}$ CONOMIC SUCCESS WAS THE KEY TO THE WELL-BEING OF THE Jews in medieval western Christendom, as it is for all human communities. As in the preceding chapter, so too in this chapter we must begin by noting major differences between the older Jewries of southern Europe and the newer Jewish communities of the north. The largest Jewish communities of the south lived from the seventh century on under Muslim rule, until the vitalization that affected all of western Christendom beginning at the end of the tenth century. As a result of this vitalization, the largest of the Jewish communities of the south – on the Iberian and Italian peninsulas – joined the ever-expanding orbit of western Christendom. Even more striking was the impact of this vitalization in the north, where entirely new sets of Jewish communities emerged.

Economic factors impacted the emergence of medieval northern European Jewry in a number of ways. The first involved simply the normal importance of economic success to any society and was common to all the Jews of medieval western Christendom. Economic factors also played a special role for the new Jewish settlers of northern Europe. In effect, economic considerations fostered the creation of this new Jewry. Perceptions of potential economic opportunity moved some Jews to consider venturing forth beyond the prior perimeters of Jewish settlement and trying their luck in this backward but rapidly developing area. Jewish perceptions of economic opportunity paralleled the conviction of major northern European rulers that immigrant Jews, bringing their economic expertise from the more developed Mediterranean basin, might contribute to the process of growth and maturation already under way. The combination of Jewish economic interest and governmental support for anticipated Jewish economic contribution set the stage for the emergence and development of medieval northern European Jewry.

At the same time, economic attitudes and issues set important constraints on the evolution of medieval northern European Jewry. The Jews venturing northward seem to have migrated with the intention of filling certain niches in the young economy, and supportive rulers reinforced these intentions. The optimal evolution of the new Jewish settlements would have been toward diversification, in the direction of an increasingly variegated Jewish economy and the strength that would have flowed from diversified economic activities and contributions. But such diversification did not take place. Societal resistances of many kinds to the new Jewish settlers precluded "normal" economic diversification. Instead, the basic pattern of a Jewish niche economy remained. We shall examine this aspect of Jewish life in medieval northern Europe, the extension of an increasingly specialized Jewish economy down into the older areas of Jewish settlement in southern Europe, and the liabilities and benefits that eventuated from this abnormal Jewish economic profile.

SHYLOCK

While wandering was a fundamental feature of the traditional Jewish and Christian views of Jewish exilic fate, a specialized Jewish economic profile was not part of the traditional imagery that preceded the development of an augmented Jewish presence in medieval western Christendom. It might conceivably have been, since the dire biblical predictions of divine punishment speak recurrently of God making the land barren, suggesting movement out of agriculture.[1] However, even this limitation of Jewish economic activity does not appear in traditional imagery, since Jews remained fully involved in agriculture in all their areas of settlement throughout late antiquity. During the first half of the Middle Ages, the only significant shift in Jewish economic life involved movement off the land, as a result of the tax structure imposed by the Islamic authorities, which adversely affected non-Muslim agricultural activity.[2] Nonetheless, the overall profile of Jewish economic activity remained highly

---

[1] See Chapter 1.
[2] Baron, *A Social and Religious History of the Jews*, 4:151–58.

varied – with the exception of agriculture – throughout the early centuries of the Middle Ages.[3]

In medieval western Christendom, imagery of Jews as limited in economic interests and abilities – especially focused on banking and moneylending – and as profoundly harmful to their neighbors through their financial activities emerged for the first time. This imagery has no validity as a portrait of Jewish economic life over the ages; later observers – non-Jewish and Jewish – have inappropriately projected a feature of Jewish life in medieval western Christendom onto the broad canvas of premodern Jewish life. Jewish economic activity in medieval northern Europe was from the beginning of Jewish settlement constrained and narrow. Initially, the economic activities of the Jews of the north involved predominantly trade; with the passage of time and for reasons to be clarified shortly, these Jews turned their focus – and indeed were encouraged to turn their focus – to moneylending. Eventually, moneylending as a Jewish specialty made its way into the Jewish communities of the south as well. Thus, ultimately Jewish behaviors in both the north and south of Europe created the image of the Jewish moneylender as a figure of Western folklore – as a pernicious and odious figure at that.

To an extent, the negative views of Jewish moneylending-banking-financial activity flowed from standard and ubiquitous hostility to such activities, whether carried out by Jews or anyone else. There is a traditional perception of banking/moneylending as a sterile activity, which parasitically feeds off the creative productivity of the farmer, laborer, and artisan. While understandable, this perception is obviously misguided in fundamental ways. Bankers and lenders are clearly indispensable to almost all societies; this is especially true for societies in the throes of rapid development, as was the case in medieval western Christendom from the eleventh century on. Nonetheless, the image of the banker/moneylender has never been truly positive, and this is surely a factor in the potency of the anti-Jewish economic imagery spawned in medieval Europe.

There was, however, a second and more specifically Jewish element in the negative imagery of the Jewish moneylender that emerged in medieval western Christendom. From their earliest days, Christians projected Jews as quintessential enemy figures. In the Gospel depictions of

[3] S. D. Goitein, *A Mediterranean Society*, vol. 1.

the life and crucifixion of Jesus, Jews are the only oppositional figures depicted. Romans – to the extent they appear – are benign onlookers. Indeed, the special circumstances of the emergence and development of Christianity required these Jewish foes. Since Christians perceive their faith community as developing out of the missteps of the Jews, Jewish shortcomings in general and failures vis-à-vis Jesus as promised Messiah in particular were critical to the theoretical underpinnings of Christian legitimacy.[4] The imagery of Jews as quintessential enemy figures was destined for a long and influential history on the Christian scene.

As the Jewish move into moneylending and finance took place, initially in northern Europe and then more widely across medieval western Christendom, the broad antipathy toward moneylenders and the intense sense of Jews as enemy figures coalesced into potent imagery of the Jewish moneylender as a rapacious and implacable enemy of Christendom and Christians. We recall, for example, Rigord's suggestion of Jewish moneylending as one of the stimuli to the royal anti-Jewish actions of the first years of the reign of Philip Augustus. According to Rigord, Jewish moneylending involved the following damages to Christian society and Christianity: (1) Many Christian borrowers were forced to abandon their ancestral holdings. (2) Some Jewish creditors actually incarcerated insolvent Christian debtors. (3) Surely the most heinous form of harm associated with Jewish lending – and the one depicted most fully by Rigord – involved alleged Jewish desecration of sacred objects taken by Jews as pledges for loans. Rigord describes the blasphemous Jewish maltreatment of these sacred objects and underscores how reprehensible these actions were by calling up a number of biblical passages that announce the punishments associated with desecration of *sancta*.[5]

Rigord quickly and unhappily passes over the decision by Philip Augustus to readmit Jews to his domain. King Philip Augustus made this move in the wake of demographic instability aroused by a popular reformist preacher, Fulk of Neuilly. Specifically, Fulk urged the barons of northern France to rid their domains of Jews because of the sinfulness of Jewish usury and the harm caused by Jewish moneylending. That a number of barons complied with this urging suggests the intensity of

---

[4] See Prologue and Chapter 2.
[5] Rigord, *Histoire de Philippe Auguste*, 146–49.

the hostility toward Jewish lending that had crystallized across northern France by the end of the twelfth century.[6]

The sense conveyed by Rigord in his account of Philip Augustus and by the reformist preaching of Fulk of Neuilly – the details of which are lost to us – finds expression in a papal letter of 1205, written by Pope Innocent III and addressed to King Philip Augustus himself.

Know then that the news has reached us to the effect that in the French kingdom the Jews have become so insolent that by means of their vicious usury, through which they extort not only usury but even usury on usury,[7] they appropriate ecclesiastical goods and Christian possessions. Thus seems to be fulfilled among Christians that which the prophet bewailed in the case of the Jews, saying: "Our heritage has passed to aliens, our homes to strangers."[8]

The powerful Pope Innocent III laments forcefully the perceived damage to Christian debtors and to the *sancta* of Christianity that we have seen in Rigord.

In 1289, Count Charles of Anjou and Maine – who was simultaneously lord of a number of important polities on the Italian peninsula – expelled the Jews from his northern French counties. He projected the grounds for this expulsion as threefold: Jewish seduction of Christians out of their faith, Jewish cohabitation with Christian maidens, and Jewish usury. The count portrays the impact of the last of these three factors in the following terms: "They despoil these Christians of their movable and immovable goods by their devious deceits and by the endless abyss of usury, and thus they force these Christians to beg for alms."[9] King Edward I of England and King Philip IV of France cite the failure to curb Jewish usury – despite ongoing efforts – in the royal expulsion edicts of 1290 and 1306 respectively as the factor that ultimately moved them to banish Jews from their realms.

---

[6] On Fulk, see Chazan, *Medieval Jewry in Northern France*, 74–75.
[7] This is a reference to compounded interest. Elimination of compound interest was one of the first reforming steps taken by the French monarchy in its constriction of Jewish lending.
[8] The biblical verse is Lamentations 5:2. The entire passage is in Grayzel, *The Church and the Jews in the XIIIth Century*, 1:106–107, #14.
[9] Chazan, *Church, State, and Jew in the Middle Ages*, 314–15.

This imagery of the devious and harmful Jewish moneylender assumed classical form in Shakespeare's Shylock. To be sure, many have suggested that Shakespeare in fact set out to subvert the traditional imagery by portraying a Jewish moneylender whose animosity to his Christian clients is readily understandable as a reaction to humiliating mistreatment. Shakespeare's Shylock has genuine grievances and is seemingly moved by these grievances, rather than by amorphous hatred of Christianity and Christians. While this may well have been the great author's intention, the remarkable portrait he drew of a Jewish lender, his hostile calculations, his implacable hatred, and his undoing served to cement rather than subvert the imagery that Jewish economic experience in medieval western Christendom had created. For the post-medieval world, the Jewish merchant of Venice has very much defined Jewish economic proclivities.[10]

The medieval and post-medieval imagery of Jewish economic activity – initially created in medieval western Christendom – projected Jews as economically limited, moneylending as the special economic province of Jews, the fundamental impropriety of this economic specialization, Jewish moneylending as profoundly harmful to Christian society, and moneylending as a potent weapon in the ongoing Jewish battle against Christianity, Christendom, and Christians. While nowhere near so old as the imagery of Jewish wandering, this more recent image took hold in medieval European folklore and formed an important element in majority and minority perceptions of exilic Jewish history altogether and of the fundamental nature of Jews.

LIMITED ECONOMIC OUTLETS

It must again be emphasized that pre-1000 Jewish history shows no signs of limited Jewish economic activities. The sources for Jewish life in late antiquity offer no hint of specialized Jewish economic activity in either Palestine or the various diasporas in which Jews were settled. To the extent that Jewish economic life can be reconstructed from the limited sources at our disposal, we see Jews occupied in every facet of economic

---

[10] On the Shakespeare imagery, see the observations in Robert Chazan, *Medieval Stereotypes and Modern Antisemitism*.

activity, with no propensity for any sort of specialization, and this is true for the Jews living in Palestine, in the eastern diaspora in Mesopotamia, and in the western diaspora throughout the Roman Empire.

When we reach the first half of the Middle Ages, sources begin to proliferate. Especially noteworthy is the rich documentation of everyday Jewish life at the eastern end of the Mediterranean basin that has been gleaned from the treasure trove of the Cairo Genizah. The documentation is truly remarkable; more remarkable yet is the creativity of the late S. D. Goitein in reconstructing from this documentation the life of what he called "a Mediterranean society," that is to say the Jewish communities of the eastern Mediterranean basin from the ninth through the eleventh centuries. The very first of Goitein's five-volume study of these communities focuses on Jewish economic activity and shows impressive Jewish economic diversity, with the sole exception of agriculture.[11] Jews occupied every stratum of the economy in the eastern Mediterranean, from bottom to top. Goitein was able to identify the widest possible range of Jewish economic endeavor.[12] At no point were Jews associated with any particular economic specialization.

During the first half of the Middle Ages, the largest Jewish enclaves on the European continent were in precisely those areas that had fallen to the conquering Muslims, especially Sicily and the southern sectors of the Iberian peninsula. In these areas, as well as in the smaller Jewish communities in the Christian areas of Italy, Spain, and southern France, there is still no evidence of Jewish economic specialization. Again, with the exception of agriculture Jews appear in every sector of the economy, ranging from the most menial labor to such high-end endeavors as medicine and banking. This last field of economic activity deserves special mention. It is clear that Jews throughout the Muslim world were involved *inter alia* in finance – they owned and operated large, successful banking establishments.[13] Yet this reality gave rise to no imagery whatsoever of

[11] Goitein, *A Mediterranean Society*, vol. 1.

[12] I vividly recall a lecture given by Goitein in the mid-1970s at Tel-Aviv University. At the time, I was teaching a course on medieval Jewry in western Christendom, and I urged my students to attend the Goitein lecture, even though it would ostensibly be removed from our focus. To my surprise and enormous pleasure, Goitein specifically contrasted the multifaceted economy of the Jews in the medieval Muslim world with the limited economic outlets of the Jews in medieval western Christendom.

[13] Goitein, *A Mediterranean Society*, 1:chapter 3.

special Jewish affinity for finance. Rather, finance was yet one more facet of a variegated Jewish economy.

Thus, evidence for imagery of Jewish economic specialization does not predate the arrival of Jews in northern Europe; rather, it is a result of the special circumstances of this new milieu. Attracted to the rapidly developing areas of northern Europe, Jews were welcomed by some elements in society for the economic contribution they might make, while they were simultaneously viewed with suspicion and hostility by other segments of society. This combination of acceptance and rejection shaped an unusual economic profile for the immigrant Jews – what we might well identify as a Jewish niche economy.[14]

The earliest stage of the Jewish niche economy in northern Europe involved trade. The charter of Bishop Rudiger that invited Jews to settle in Speyer, for the economic contribution they might make to urban development, includes the following major stipulation vis-à-vis Jewish economic activity:

I have accorded them the free right of exchanging gold and silver and of buying and selling everything they use within their residential area and outside it, beyond the gate and down to the wharf, and on the wharf itself. I have given them the same right throughout the town.[15]

This important stipulation reflects a group of immigrant Jews involved primarily in buying and selling, and the impression created by Rudiger's charter finds echoes in the extant responsa literature from early northern European Jewry.

Responsa are answers to troubling questions of Jewish law raised throughout the ages. The questions – even more than the answers – regularly reflect socioeconomic circumstances of Jewish life. The early responsa from northern Europe, written by respected rabbinic authorities and hence deemed worthy of preservation, date from the eleventh

---

[14] Note the valuable essays on medieval Jewish economic activity in Europe in Michael Toch, ed., *Wirtschaftsgeschichte der mittelalterlichen Juden*. These essays cover a wide range of issues and are extremely useful. Note especially Toch's own essay, "Economic Activities of German Jews in the Middle Ages," and that of Giacomo Todeschini, "Christian Perceptions of Jewish Economic Activity in the Middle Ages." Toch has contributed an important chapter on Jewish economic activity in the period between 1000 and 1500 to the forthcoming volume 6 of the *Cambridge History of Judaism*.

[15] Chazan, *Church, State, and Jew*, 58.

century. They show a set of Jews involved primarily in trade, buying and selling goods locally or over an extended area. To be sure, there are occasional references to Jewish agriculture and viticulture, but the sense of these references is that these activities were very much secondary to trade.[16] Indeed, a very interesting responsum raises the question of whether Jewish taxes should be levied on agricultural activity along with Jewish business revenue or whether they should be levied on business profit only. The question emerges from the difficulties encountered in agriculture, for example, the unpredictability of seasons and weather. Clearly, however, a community in which agriculture was a major economic activity could not afford to contemplate removal of agricultural profits from the tax system.[17]

As the northern economy matured, Jews seem to have drifted increasingly toward moneylending. This transition in one sense took place in a fairly natural way. Merchants buying and selling occasionally sold on credit, and thus some drift toward lending without the selling was perhaps inevitable. However, the Jewish move into moneylending involved other factors as well. Both Jews and Christians read Deuteronomy 23:20 as a religious injunction with significant implications: "You shall not take interest from loans to your brother, whether in money or food or anything else that can be taken as interest. You may take interest from loans to the outsider, but you may not take interest from loans to your brother."[18] From this seminal verse emerged two major conclusions – the impropriety of lending at interest to members of one's own community and the propriety of lending at interest to members of outsider communities. Medieval Jews and Christians felt themselves bound by this important biblical law. To be sure, important issues required clarification. How precisely was interest to be defined? Who exactly constituted a brother, and who was the outsider? The basics, however, seemed clear enough, at least early on.

One result of the vitalization referred to recurrently was a far more powerful and aggressive Church. By the end of the eleventh century,

---

[16] For English translations of some of these responsa that deal with business matters, see Irving A. Agus, ed. and trans., *Urban Civilization in Pre-Crusade Europe.*

[17] Ibid., 2:439–40.

[18] I have deviated from the JPS translation in order to highlight the issues that emerged in medieval understandings of this important verse.

the Church was increasingly well organized, with the papacy serving as an ever more authoritative and active center. There was an accelerating commitment to defining the demands of Christian belief and practice and to insuring that the Christian population of western Christendom be encouraged or perhaps even forced when necessary toward fulfillment of these demands. The twelfth-century Church embarked on a number of major reforming campaigns, insisting for example on the need for clerical celibacy and attacking the sins of prostitution and moneylending at interest. Some of these battles were won; others were not. The struggle against moneylending at interest was relatively successful, but at a price.

While the twelfth century saw an increasingly powerful and militant Church and a relatively successful campaign against Christian usury, it was at the same time the scene of a rapidly expanding economy throughout Christian Europe. New and larger projects were undertaken all across western Christendom, projects that required considerable capital. The combination of expanding business needs and an ecclesiastical campaign to suppress lending at interest created a significant new outlet for Jewish business acumen. Both in a theoretical sense and in popular perception, Jews were outsiders to the community of believing and practicing Christians. Thus, ecclesiastical leaders – initially at least – deemed Jews to fit perfectly the "outsiders" from whom it was permitted to take interest and concomitantly to whom it was permitted to pay interest. Out of this concatenation of factors, moneylending became a Jewish specialty in the twelfth century, especially in northern France and England.[19]

As was the case with the Jewish immigration into northern Europe altogether, Jewish moneylending – as natural a development as it might have been – needed the support of the secular authorities of northern Europe. Never a popular economic activity, successful moneylending required first of all relative security. Lenders had to be relatively certain that their demands for repayment would not be met with violent refusal. As the political units of twelfth-century northern Europe matured, such elemental security was increasingly in evidence. Jewish moneylenders could ply their trade with growing confidence.

---

[19] The sense that Jewish lending at interest was ultimately illegitimate evolved toward the end of the twelfth century and entailed a reconsideration of Jewish otherness.

In fact, the role of the authorities went well beyond providing basic security. Moneylending takes a number of forms. The most rudimentary of these is pawnbroking, which insures return of the money extended by the lender through deposit of an object equal to or greater than the principal of the loan and the anticipated interest. Pawnbroking is a simple and effective technique for lending money with a high level of confidence. While on occasion large sums could be lent against extremely valuable objects, pawnbroking generally involved lesser loans against modest pledges. A second liability of pawnbroking involved the amassing of goods, which required careful protection and not infrequently the difficulties of disposing of objects that the lenders proved incapable of redeeming.

The more advanced polities of northern Europe – especially the English and French monarchies – led the way toward more sophisticated forms of Jewish moneylending. In both kingdoms, the monarchs developed increasingly effective bureaucracies capable of – for example – levying and collecting taxes more efficiently or of supporting Jewish lending more effectively. Governmental documents assuring the return of moneys disbursed by Jewish lenders created entirely new possibilities for the Jewish lending business. Jews could lend very large sums of money, with a high level of certainty of return. Lending against land, the most important collateral possessed by medieval northern Europeans, now became possible, prominent, and lucrative.

Just as we have earlier asked the question of the motivation of the rulers of eleventh-century northern Europe in supporting Jewish immigration, so too must we now inquire as to the motivations of the ruling class of twelfth-century northern Europe in its backing of Jewish moneylending. Not surprisingly, the answers to the two questions are broadly parallel. On the one hand, the rulers of twelfth-century northern Europe were genuinely and properly concerned with the economic well-being of their domains. Given the need for exchange of capital and the limitations on Christian lending demanded by the leadership of the Church, far-sighted rulers concerned with the economy of the territories over which they presided thought it essential to find ways of enhancing the flow of capital, and Jewish businessmen provided a means for so doing. Support for this useful economic activity seemed appropriate and essential.

Beyond simply providing the needed flow of capital, Jewish businessmen offered the possibility of assisting in the rationalization of the economy. H. G. Richardson has shown, for example, the ways in which the Jews of twelfth-century England played a central role in elimination of barons out of step with the times and transfer of their lands to the rising English business class. The English monarchs of the twelfth century rightly perceived this rebalancing of the economy as a useful Jewish contribution to societal progress.[20]

At the same time, as had been true for their predecessors who had supported Jewish immigration, the twelfth-century rulers of England and northern France saw in their Jewish clients valuable assets to the expanding powers of the monarchies. Having useful clients was in and of itself a benefit for the kings of England and France. In the same way that a growing bureaucracy staffed by the king's Christian protégés meant enhanced royal power and control, the emergence of a class of Jewish moneylending protégés achieved the same purposes as well.

In the case of the Jewish bankers, there was immediate financial benefit as well. Revenue-starved royal treasuries could levy heavy taxes on the significant profits of governmentally backed Jewish moneylending. Taxation was an ongoing problem for the increasingly puissant monarchies of northwestern Europe. Enhanced revenues were a necessity, but access to such revenues was extremely difficult. New notions of legislated taxation gained ground only very slowly. Many Europeans of this era strongly believed that only those taxes that had long been customary were legitimate – innovative taxes were not. In the drive toward enhanced royal revenue, Jewish moneylending offered a useful tool. Rulers could tax their Jewish clients more or less at will; these Jews were in no position to resist governmental demands. Jews depended totally on the backing of the secular authorities. More specifically, the hefty profits accruing from governmentally backed Jewish loans were even more obviously dependent on the ongoing support of the authorities.

By the end of the twelfth century, another factor heightened the availability of Jewish lenders to government taxation/exploitation. Well-kept records of indebtedness to Jews became increasingly more prominent.

[20] H. G. Richardson, *The English Jewry under Angevin Kings*, chapter 5. Recall the complaints noted earlier over Christians being forced to abandon ancestral holdings. From a personal perspective, this was disastrous; from a societal perspective, this was progress.

On the one hand, these carefully archived documents served to heighten Jewish security. Avoidance of loan repayment became ever more difficult in the face of the new archiving regulations, which for example in England stipulated loan documents filled out in triplicate – one copy for the lender, one for the borrower, and one for the governmental record office. At the same time, these carefully controlled records served a second purpose as well. They made available to the government full information on Jewish loans and hence Jewish wealth. By the early thirteenth century in England, where this record keeping was most advanced, every tax levy on the Jews was preceded by the closing of the *archae* – the governmental record centers spread all across the country – and the compilation of accurate evidence on Jewish holdings and thus the available Jewish wealth that might be subjected to taxation. Enhanced royal support for Jewish lending was a two-edged sword, partially beneficial and partially detrimental.

Jewish specialization in moneylending, with attendant advantages and liabilities, became a feature of Jewish life in the most advanced areas of northern Europe – the kingdoms of England and France. Clearly, not all northwestern European Jews became moneylenders during the twelfth and thirteenth centuries, just as earlier not all northern European Jews had been merchants. However, just as trade formed the backbone of the Jewish economy in the earlier phase of northern European Jewish history, so too did moneylending become the backbone of the Jewish economy in twelfth- and early-thirteenth-century northern Europe.

Very wealthy Jews became central to their co-religionists. They were the Jews with access to the halls of power; they were the economic supports of their fellow Jews; they were the mainstays of the Jewish community, bearing the heaviest burden of financing the necessary institutions of communal life and culture. The advantages of Jewish moneylending resided in the wealth and the political leverage it conferred. While this wealth and political leverage were restricted to a relatively small coterie of successful financiers, the benefits extended into the Jewish communities in which these wealthy and powerful Jews were embedded and which they tended to lead.

At the same time, the new economic specialization entailed serious liabilities as well. In the first place, the new Jewish moneylending generated substantial hostility among the Christian masses, especially among those who perceived themselves to be harmed in one way or another by it. We have noted earlier multiple expressions of animosity toward Jewish lending. The York massacre of 1190 reveals dramatically the intensification of this animosity. Ostensibly, the attack on the Jewish community of York was simply another instance of crusading sentiment spilling over against Jews, a phenomenon that can be traced back to the very beginning of the crusading enterprise.[21] However, the York attack shows unique characteristics. Some of the Jews sequestered in Clifford's Tower declared themselves prepared to accept baptism, as happened regularly during crusade-related violence. In the normal course of events, this willingness would have generated great enthusiasm on the part of the Christian attackers, and such Jews would have been hastened to the nearest church for their induction into the Christian faith. In York, however, the attackers slaughtered these Jews, indicating that factors other than normal crusading fervor were at work. The next step on the part of the attackers was to proceed into York itself, invade the cathedral, take possession of the Jewish loan documents held for safekeeping in the cathedral basement, and destroy all these documents. Clearly, intense resentment of Jewish lending accounts for the unusual features of the York incidents.[22]

A second liability of the new Jewish specialization involved arousal of ecclesiastical opposition. Ecclesiastical pressure against Christian moneylending at interest had paved the way for the emergence of this new Jewish specialty. Thus, Church leaders had to be and in fact were especially sensitive to the development of this Jewish specialization and its impact on Christian society. The first concern of the ecclesiastical leadership was the adverse effects of Jewish moneylending, especially on the vulnerable in Christian society. Church leaders lobbied strongly for safeguards that would protect Christian borrowers deemed especially at risk. These safeguards included limitations on the rate of interest Jews could charge, prohibition of compounded interest, limitation on the range of goods that could be accepted as pawns, and removal of certain classes of Christians from the ranks of potential borrowers. Slowly but surely, ecclesiastical pressure resulted in the enactment of many of these safeguards in royal and baronial legislation, especially in Capetian France.

---

[21] See Chapter 8.
[22] For a full study of these events, see R. B. Dobson, *The Jews of York and the Massacre of 1190*.

A more far-reaching target of Church pressure involved governmental support for the more advanced forms of Jewish moneylending. Ecclesiastical leaders often interpreted such governmental support as a partnership with Jewish lenders, in which the Jews supplied the capital and the authorities supplied the muscle. In the eyes of many observers, this arrangement in fact constituted genuine collusion and meant that the authorities were actually involved directly in collecting usury from their Christian subjects. Ecclesiastical pressures resulted – again especially in royal France – in a slow process of withdrawal of governmental support for Jewish lending that by 1223 resulted in the dismantling of the elaborate system of sealing, enrolling, and enforcing Jewish loans.[23]

The most radical step in ecclesiastical concern over Jewish moneylending involved a reexamination of the very legitimacy of these Jewish transactions. The Jewish right to take interest from Christian borrowers was grounded in an understanding of Deuteronomy 23:20 and its distinction between "brother," from whom it was forbidden to take interest (or to whom it was forbidden to give interest) and "outsider," from whom it was permissible to take interest (or to whom it was permissible to give interest). Early on in our period, understanding of this distinction for both medieval Christians and Jews involved a sense that the two communities were estranged from one another, meaning that the giving and taking of interest on loans was entirely permissible. As Jewish involvement in moneylending deepened, however, some Christian authorities began to question this view of Deuteronomy 23:20, suggesting that – disagreements and tensions notwithstanding – Christians and Jews were brethren to one another in important ways, meaning that Jewish acceptance of interest from Christians was prohibited. This view gained increasing currency in thirteenth-century northern Europe, eventuating in the most radical ecclesiastical pressure vis-à-vis Jewish lending, the pressure to outlaw it altogether. This led, in royal France, for example, to a governmental ban on Jewish usury.[24]

Church leadership took a series of positions on Jewish moneylending, beginning with demands intended to ameliorate negative impacts,

---

[23] See the documents in Chazan, *Church, State, and Jew*, 205–15, and the analysis in Jordan, *The French Monarchy and the Jews*, chapter 6.

[24] Chazan, *Church, State, and Jew*, 216–17.

proceeding to attacks on governmental collusion in the Jewish moneylending business, and concluding with an assertion of the illegitimacy of Jewish interest-taking from Christians altogether. The pressures
exerted on the authorities of northwestern Europe were intense and ultimately successful. The lucrative kind of moneylending that developed in
northwestern Europe during the twelfth century and enriched both Jews
and governments ground to a halt during the course of the thirteenth
century, in considerable measure as a result of ecclesiastical lobbying
efforts. There was, however, yet one more factor in the extinction of governmentally sponsored Jewish moneylending in northwestern Europe,
and that involved the dangers emanating from government knowledge
of Jewish financial resources, governmental latitude in levying taxes on
Jews, and the dynamic of governmental need and cupidity.

Erection of a sophisticated system for enrolling Jewish loans reinforced
the security of the Jewish lenders in their business affairs. At the same
time, it also enhanced governmental knowledge of Jewish business and
business assets, thus paving the way for more accurate and effective tax
levying and collection. The danger in all this was governmental need and
cupidity. Under constant fiscal pressure, the royal authorities in England
faced the constant temptation of exploiting or over-exploiting available
Jewish wealth. According to Robert Stacey, by the 1240s the English
authorities in fact went too far. They exploited Jewish wealth to the point
of bankrupting the leadership of English Jewry. Governmental exactions
took from the Jews the capital upon which their lending business was
based, thereby in effect bringing to a close this business with its steady
revenue for the Jewish lenders and their royal collaborators.[25]

Jewish moneylending with governmental support resulted in a brief
period of remarkable business success for the Jews of England and
northern France. These successes could not, however, be sustained. The
combination of ecclesiastical opposition and governmental exploitation
brought this brief period of success to a close. Interestingly, pious royal
pronouncements of moving the Jews into "normal" economic chan-
nels proved unavailing. Jews were not able to integrate into the general
economy. Whether this was the result of ongoing anti-Jewish pressures
or Jewish perceptions that it would be better to relocate geographically

[25] Robert C. Stacey, *Politics, Policy, and Finance.*

rather than retool economically cannot be clarified at this point. In any case, the elimination of this useful Jewish economic niche was a prelude to royal decisions in England and France to banish the Jews completely. Just as they had been invited to service the needs of a developing economy, loss of their economic *raison d'etre* in northwestern Europe meant the end of Jewish settlement in an area whose economic development made them dispensable.

Farther eastward, however, less impressive economic and political development meant that Jews did not enjoy the striking economic achievements of their more westerly co-religionists; at the same time, they did not suffer the same liabilities. Over the long haul, the Jews of the Germanic territories managed to create their own special niche economy, still rooted in the opportunities fostered by early readings of Deuteronomy 23:20 that permitted Jewish interest-taking from Christians. The important charter enacted for the Jews of Austria by Duke Frederick in 1244 conveys a sense of Jewish moneylending in the Germanic territories. This charter illuminates, on the one hand, the circumstances of mid-thirteenth-century Austrian Jews; at the same time, it served as a model for subsequent charters enacted for Jews farther eastward and thus provides a sense of the initial economic profile of the developing Jewries of eastern Europe as well.[26]

The Austrian charter consists of thirty provisions, equally divided among three broad topics – assurance of safety and security for Jews; protective judicial arrangements for Jews; stipulations governing Jewish business. In many instances, an individual provision relates to two of these three board concerns.[27] The entire thrust is toward protection of Jewish interests, with the obvious goals of reassuring Jews and encouraging their immigration into the duchy. The safeguards for Jewish security are considerable, with very high penalties for harming Jews physically or economically. The judicial arrangements are most generous to Jewish litigants, assuring fair treatment in cases that might be brought against Jews by Christians or that Jews might bring against Christian neighbors.

---

[26] Chazan, *Church, State, and Jew*, 84–88. Note the obvious relationship of the 1244 charter to that issued by Duke Boleslav of Greater Poland twenty years later – see Chazan, *Church, State, and Jew*, 89–93.

[27] Broadly, the charter provides ten provisions for Jewish safety and security, nine relating to judicial arrangements, and eleven involving business affairs. Again, some provisions serve double duty.

For our purposes at this point, the economic provisions are of primary interest. Because we have already encountered differing Jewish economic specializations, it is worth beginning by looking for hints of Jewish trade and governmentally backed Jewish lending. Of the first, there is no mention at all in the 1244 charter. Whereas Jewish mercantile activities had dominated the early German charters, such as that of Bishop Rudiger of Speyer, Duke Frederick's grant includes no reference whatsoever to trade. This of course does not mean that no Austrian Jew was involved in trade; it does mean that trade was no longer the dominant economic activity among these Jews.

Likewise, we have noted the emergence – alongside pawnbroking – of governmentally enforced and quite lucrative forms of lending among the Jews of England and France. Of this special kind of lending, there is only one mention in the Austrian charter: "If a Jew has lent money to a magnate of the country on his possessions or on a note and proves this through documents, we will assign the pledged possession to the Jew and defend them for him against violence."[28] This is – as is normal for the 1244 charter – a ringing protection of Jewish interests. However, the difference between this provision and what we have learned of earlier arrangements in England and France is striking. There is no evidence here of a governmental bureaucracy created and designed to enroll and enforce Jewish lending. Rather, this is simply an ad hoc arrangement for those instances in which Jews might lend funds against a documented baronial promise of land or goods in case of failure to repay an obligation. The contrast between this provision and the arrangements in the northwestern monarchies is stark.

Equally noteworthy is the absence of the ecclesiastical concerns that loomed so large farther westward. Thirteenth-century Church leadership expressed itself strongly with respect to the harm wrought in Christian society by Jewish lending, the collusion between government and the Jews, and the fundamental right of Jews to take interest from Christians. The 1244 charter contains no hint of the last two ecclesiastical stances. The duke of Austria obviously was unconcerned with the basic right of Jews to lend at interest, and – since there was no governmental bureaucracy for enrolling, enforcing, and exploiting Jewish lending – that issue as well is not mentioned.

[28] Chazan, *Church, State, and Jew*, 87.

There is only one acknowledgment of ecclesiastical concerns vis-à-vis Jewish lending in the entire document, and that comes in the very last clause, which in effect recognizes the Fourth Lateran Council's prohibition in 1215 of "heavy and immoderate" Jewish usury by setting an annual level of 33 percent as the maximum Jewish interest rate. At the same time, there is mention of another Church concern, the compounding of interest, with a somewhat curious stance toward this issue. The 1244 charter stipulates that: "If a Christian has redeemed his pledge from a Jew but has not paid the interest, the interest due shall be compounded if it is not paid within a month."[29] It is unclear precisely how this clause is to be understood. It certainly supports the practice of compounded interest, to which the Church was militantly opposed. However, by allowing the compounding of interest under the very specific circumstances of a pledge redeemed without payment of interest, Duke Frederick may be indicating that, under normal conditions, compounding of interest – like excessive interest – was not to be permitted.

Of the ten clauses involving Jewish moneylending, nine have to do with pawnbroking and essentially offer wide-ranging protection to Jews lending against pledges. Jewish lenders are offered a panoply of safeguards, for example in instances of dispute over the size of the loan, of disagreement as to whether the pawn has been returned or not, of pawns claimed to have been obtained illegally, and of loss of the pawn by the Jewish lender through robbery or fire. In all these instances and more, the duke forcefully supports the interests of Jewish lenders. The impression created by all these stipulations is that Jewish pawnbroking became in the Germanic territories and subsequently in eastern Europe as well the dominant form of the Jewish niche economy. Once again, this does not mean that all Jews were pawnbrokers; rather, this means that pawnbroking became the most significant Jewish economic outlet, the means through which a majority of Jews made their livings, and the occupation that won for the Jews the protection and support of the political authorities.

Finally, there is considerable evidence that the Jewish specialization in moneylending slowly made its way down into the older and more diversified Jewish economies of southern Europe. These older Jewish communities, which predated the emergence and development of the

---

[29] Ibid., 88 (33% interest) and 87 (compounded interest).

new Jewries of northern Europe, had exhibited throughout their earlier history the characteristic economic diversity of pre-1000 Jewries worldwide. This diversity did not entirely disappear. Thus, when the twelfth- and thirteenth-century Christian re-conquest of the Iberian peninsula occasioned a spate of charters intended to encourage the Jews of the newly conquered areas to remain in place and to contribute to the maintenance of the Iberian economy and political culture, these documents show no traces of the economic specialization we have noted in northern Europe.[30]

Nonetheless, numerous studies have suggested that, even in the south, there was a growing propensity for Jews to be attracted to moneylending, for all the reasons already indicated. While the specialization was less extreme, it is significant nonetheless. Let us note three indices of this accelerating specialization. The first comes from a relatively late blooming Jewish community in southwestern France, the Jewry of Perpignan. Attracted to a town that began to develop toward the end of the twelfth century, the Perpignan Jews were carefully studied by Richard Emery in a pathbreaking analysis of medieval Jewish economic activity grounded in surviving notarial records.[31] Emery's study of Perpignan Jews during the quarter century from 1261 through 1287 showed much the same scenario as we have elicited from northern Europe. These Jews involved themselves to a limited extent in business; however, the notarial registers show overwhelming Jewish involvement in moneylending. According to Emery: "Of the 228 adult Perpignan Jews mentioned in the registers 178 (almost 80 percent) appear as lenders in one or more of these 1,643 cases [the 1,643 debts owed to Jews in the registers]. Of the 149 adult male Jews mentioned more than twice, 139 (93 percent) were involved in such loans."[32] For Emery, the evidence for Jewish specialization in moneylending in Perpignan was incontrovertible.

Mark Meyerson has studied carefully the evidence for Jewish life in the Valencian town of Morvedre from the middle of the thirteenth century down until the eruption of the anti-Jewish riots of 1391 that swept all across the Iberian peninsula. The portrait that emerges once more shows Jewish specialization in moneylending, ecclesiastical concern and

---

[30] For a selection of these charters, see Chazan, *Church, State, and Jew*, 69–75.
[31] Richard Emery, *The Jews of Perpignan*.
[32] Ibid., 26.

pressures, broad royal backing for the Jewish loan business, and substantial tax revenues flowing from Jewish moneylending.[33] Once again, this did not mean that all Morvedre Jews were moneylenders; it did mean that moneylending was the backbone of Jewish economic life and the grounding for governmental profit and support.

What Meyerson projects on the micro-level of Morvedre was suggested in the fullest large-scale analysis of Jewish economic activity in medieval Spain, Yom Tov Assis's study of the Jewish economy in thirteenth- and early-fourteenth-century Aragon. Not surprisingly, Assis focuses on both Jewish economic activity and royal revenue from this Jewish economic activity, with the latter actually dominating.[34] The picture sketched by Assis is consonant with that projected by both Meyerson and Emery. Once again, Jews involved themselves heavily in the lending business, and that lending business was the economic contribution that won governmental support and served as the basis for governmental exactions and profit.

While moneylending as a Jewish specialization seems to have emerged in the northern sectors of Europe, where Jewish presence was new and where a diversified Jewish economy never developed, by the thirteenth century this specialization – perhaps in somewhat attenuated form – made its way southward into the older and originally more economically diversified Jewries of southern Europe. Here too the pattern of tensions discernible in the north was manifest as well. Jewish moneylending was clearly a useful economic activity in terms of the needs of society in general and in terms of its usefulness to the governing authorities in particular. Despite this usefulness, Jewish moneylending aroused considerable popular hostility and evoked significant ecclesiastical opposition. In most areas outside northwestern Europe, that opposition was largely focused on limiting the negative impact of Jewish lending on the Christian populace, rather than attacking the fundamental propriety of Jewish lending itself. Jews in southern Europe – like their brethren in the north – thus found themselves regularly caught in the crossfire among the interests of the authorities who were the guarantors of their basic safety and security, the Church, and the masses.[35] So long as these forces remained in relative equilibrium, Jewish life was maintained. When the equilibrium broke

[33] Mark D. Meyerson, *Jews in an Iberian Kingdom*, especially pp. 176–209.
[34] Yom Tov Assis, *Jewish Economy in the Medieval Crown of Aragon 1213–1327*.
[35] Meyerson, *Jews in an Iberian Kingdom*, chapter 5.

down, as happened on the Iberian peninsula in 1391, the Jews suffered disastrously. In 1391, popular and ecclesiastical animosity shattered this equilibrium and brought about ruinous violence.

In general then, the Jewish niche economy proved workable for the Jews of northern Europe and the Jews of the south as well. In the case of the former, the niche occupied by early immigrant Jews was developmental. Political leaders who recognized the need for capable urban businesspeople and saw Jews as potentially useful in filling the economic gap in their developing polities were strongly supportive. A more long-lasting niche evolved out of the Church's campaign against Christian usury. In this instance, the niche filled by the Jews was more systemic and more durable. While the special circumstances of the advanced monarchies of northwestern Europe brought Jewish moneylending and Jewish life to a close by the end of the thirteenth and beginning of the fourteenth centuries, moneylending continued to serve as the mainstay of the Jewish economy in north-central and northeastern Europe. Likewise, the systemic need for Jewish moneylending in western Christendom opened opportunities in the south, where Jewish life was better rooted and where the Jews had a tradition of economic diversification. Even in these areas, moneylending slowly became a Jewish specialty.

Thus, the imagery of Jews as limited in economic outlets and focused heavily in the area of moneylending is hardly chimerical. As noted, this imagery was the result of Jewish experience in medieval western Christendom, as that civilization began to mature during the period between 1000 and 1500. It is, however, necessary to examine carefully the corollary conclusions that this economic specialization was harmful to the majority societies within which Jews lived and was – at the same time – detrimental to the Jews themselves.

ECONOMIC PIONEERS

While the reality of a specialized Jewish economy has been fully acknowledged throughout this chapter, it is important to stress that this specialization was not total. I have regularly insisted that the Jewish niche economy – whether in trade or subsequently in moneylending – did not mean that every Jew in medieval Christendom was a trader or a lender. Throughout, I have urged that it was trade and subsequently moneylending that formed the backbone but not the totality of Jewish economic activity. Forming the backbone of the Jewish economy meant securing the support of the authorities and amassing the wealth and power that propelled Jewish traders and moneylenders into positions of contact with these non-Jewish authorities and that made them leaders within the Jewish community. Some Jews – who make far less of an appearance in the sources available to us – made their livings and supported their families in alternative ways.

Nonetheless, trade and then moneylending did constitute the backbone of the Jewish economy, and in all likelihood a more diversified Jewish economy would have been preferable in the long run for Jewish circumstances in medieval western Christendom. In general, a specialized economy creates the possibility of making individuals or groups dispensable, which happened to a significant extent in the more advanced areas of thirteenth- and fourteenth-century medieval northwestern Europe, that is, in England and France.

More specifically, the eventual Jewish economic specialty – moneylending – was especially problematic, arousing keen opposition in the Church and in the majority populace in general. The Church's opposition to Jewish lending was grounded in awareness that its own policies had in fact paved the way for this Jewish specialization. On the broader popular level, Jewish moneylending bore the potential for reinforcing and being reinforced by the broad themes of Jewish enmity and Jewish harmfulness. Having noted all these deleterious aspects of Jewish specialization in general and Jewish moneylending in particular, we might propose that Jewish specialization in both mercantile activity and the money trade was by no means entirely negative, when viewed from both the majority Christian perspective and the minority Jewish perspective.

We recall that medieval western Christendom was a peripheral area of Jewish settlement prior to the year 1000 and that Jewish settlement in the northern sectors of Europe was virtually nonexistent prior to the year 1000. The Jewish niche economy – specifically trade – opened the areas of the north to Jewish settlement altogether. While it may well be argued that such grounding for Jewish settlement was lamentable, establishing a Jewish foothold in this area was of great significance. Indeed, it is difficult to imagine the contours of Jewish history without that breakthrough.

Thus, for the Jews themselves the medieval niche economy as a general phenomenon was hardly an unmitigated disaster.

The same may be said of the particular Jewish specialization in moneylending that emerged during the twelfth century. To be sure, this specialization was costly in multiple ways, as we have had occasion to note. On the other hand, the moneylending specialty did permit the eventual growth of the Jewish population of medieval western Christendom, which was a major positive development in medieval Jewish history. Indeed, the more general capacity to assess societal needs and to serve those needs effectively was a significant Jewish skill honed in medieval western Christendom as a result of the resistances that Jews encountered. Jewish ability to assess emergent but important needs accounted for much Jewish economic success in medieval Christian Europe.

The more baneful economic imagery has involved the negative impact of the eventual Jewish specialization in moneylending on majority society – the Shylock imagery. There is, however, much in medieval Jewish experience that calls into question the negative Shylock imagery. In the first place, Jewish moneylending clearly played a positive role in the economic dynamism of medieval western Christendom and was appreciated by the ruling class for its beneficial impact.

An interesting reflection of this reality is reflected in a recollection of the expulsion of Jewish lenders enacted by Saint Louis in the mid-1250s. According to the royal biographer William of Chartres, when the pious king announced his intention to banish Jews unwilling to abandon their moneylending, he encountered the objections of a number of major barons and advisors. They argued that moneylending was obviously a requirement of every human society and that in fact the king himself had been constrained to borrow funds on occasion. Thus, the issue, these advisors urged, was not moneylending versus elimination of moneylending, but rather who would do the lending – Jews or Christians. If the Jewish lenders were expelled, as the king intended, then he would in effect be creating a class of Christian moneylenders. Better – they concluded – to let the Jews, who are damned in any case, carry on the nefarious business of moneylending. This argument posits the absolute necessity of moneylending for medieval French society, as well as for all other societies. Interestingly, Saint Louis's biographer does not show the monarch disputing this assumption at all. Rather, the king's (somewhat self-centered) defense is simply that the Jews are his religious responsibility, since it is through his support that they are present in France, and thus the stain of their sinfulness in taking usury rests on his soul.[36]

Jewish moneylending contributed significantly to the economic maturation of western Christendom. At the same time, it also contributed to political maturation. The wealth Jewish moneylending generated and the taxes it made possible constituted a factor in the accelerating power of the monarchies of northwestern Europe. Many in society recognized that the Jews served as a conduit for major rulers to access funds from the Christian population that would have otherwise been inaccessible to them. This medieval insight was often couched as moral criticism of the royal patrons of the Jewish lenders or as a complaint of the baronial forces opposed to the augmentation of royal power. To the extent that this augmentation of royal power forms an important element in the political maturation of medieval western Christendom, the Jews emerge as significant contributors to political maturation as well as economic progress.

Finally, the fascinating research of Joseph Shatzmiller in the archives of Marseilles has revealed that Jewish moneylenders could be warm and humane neighbors, whose decency and generosity were on occasion acknowledged by Christian clients and friends. Shatzmiller discovered in the archives at Marseilles protocols of the trial held in 1317 of a prominent Jewish moneylender named Bondavid. As part of his defense, Bondavid brought to court a sequence of Christian witnesses to attest to his good character in general and to his generosity in lending transactions in particular. These defense witnesses offered two types of testimony. Some related specific events to underscore Bondavid's probity and generosity; others made broad assertions about his character. Both types of testimony create a striking portrait of a Jewish moneylender that contrasts markedly with the earlier claims we have encountered of rapacious and malevolent Jewish usurers. One of the broad testimonials offers a flavor of this unusual portrait: "And actually [Bondavid] is more righteous than anyone he [the witness, Guillelmus Gasqueti, a cleric] ever met in his life.

---

[36] William of Chartres, "De vita et miraculis sancti Ludovici," 20:34.

He does not believe that there is [one] more righteous than he in the whole world. For, if one may say so, he never met or saw a Christian more righteous than he."[37]

Moneylending and banking adversely affect many people in society, yet at the same time they are indispensable. We recall the widespread imagery of moneylending and banking as sterile functions that are essentially parasitic and thus destructive in nature. As suggested, this perception permeated medieval western Christendom with the sense that Jewish moneylending was a vehicle through which Jews carried on their never-ending struggle against Christianity and Christians. Such imagery notwithstanding, societies cannot function without the flow of capital. When the flow of capital is impeded for some reason, the unsympathetic image of the banker-lender regularly gives way to a powerful sense of the indispensable role such figures play in all societies.[38] It was precisely this sense that the courtiers of Saint Louis expressed to their sovereign.

JEWISH ECONOMIC SPECIALIZATION IN GENERAL AND JEWISH SPECIALization in the money trade in particular were – despite the negative imagery – by no means thoroughly harmful to the Jews themselves or to their Christian neighbors. In effect, Jews served as economic pioneers, bringing new patterns of trade to northern Europe and subsequently innovating in the exchange of capital in the north and eventually in the south as well. Large and in fact growing numbers of Jews were able to support themselves through the Jewish niche economy we have identified, while at the same time enriching the milieu in which they lived.

This suggests that economic limitations need not have been utterly destructive. Creative exploitation by medieval European Jews of the limited economic options available to them could insure Jewish stability and success – at least for a time. The Jews of medieval Europe seem to have been capable of such creative exploitation.

---

[37] Joseph Shatzmiller, *Shylock Reconsidered*, 118.
[38] As this chapter was being written, American society lurched into a financial crisis that on the one hand activated negative perceptions of banking and bankers, while at the same time proved that banking and bankers are indispensable to the well-being of society.

7

~

Status

J EWISH STATUS IN MEDIEVAL WESTERN CHRISTENDOM WAS COM-
plex, to put it mildly. Key to this status was the traditional stance
of Christianity toward Judaism and Jews, as interpreted by the Church.
This stance contained multiple elements, often existing in considerable
tension with one another.[1] Moreover, as western Christendom evolved
from the eleventh through the fifteenth centuries, much changed in the
Church in general, and as a result new ecclesiastical views of the Jewish
place in Christian society emerged. To be sure, there were factors beyond
the Church in shaping the status of Jews. Governmental authorities –
ostensibly devoted to the dictates of the Church and committed to serving as the practical support toward implementation of its policies – often
had views of their own on the place of their Jewish clients in Christian
society. Finally, Church leadership and lower-level Church officials, governmental authorities at all levels, and the populace at large responded
to the evolving realities of Jewish existence with a more immediate sense
of what Jewish status in actuality was and what it should be.

We shall again begin by examining traditional imageries of Jewish
status, proceed to a close look at the detrimental aspects of Jewish status in
medieval western Christendom in actuality, and then note more positive
facets of the status of medieval European Jews.

THE ELDER SHALL SERVE THE YOUNGER

For both Jews and Christians, the biblical predictions of exilic conditions
we have earlier examined and analyzed ultimately shaped the Jewish place

---

[1] Recall the Baron observations, cited in Chapter 4.

in medieval Christian society. This biblical imagery stressed the horrors, the subjugation, and the humiliation that were to be the lot of the Jewish people during the period of exilic punishment.[2] We recall the striking note on which the warnings of Deuteronomy 28 end:

The Lord will send you back to Egypt in galleys, by a route I told you that you should not see again. There you shall offer yourselves for sale to your enemies as male and female slaves, but none will buy.

Divine punishment was to involve something even worse than enslavement – being sold into slavery with no one interested in buying.

Jews accepted the notion of degraded status in the Jewish "middle age" as they defined it, that is, the period between Jewish well-being in the Land of Israel prior to exile and the eventual restoration of Jewish fortunes that would accompany messianic redemption. Jews had well-developed views regarding the nature of this exilic suffering that was to be their lot. While humiliation and suffering were certainly key motifs in Jewish conceptions of exilic status, servitude reflecting divine rejection was not. Since Jewish suffering and divine rejection were central elements in Christian thinking in general and in Christian missionizing among medieval Europe's Jews in particular, there was full Jewish awareness of these Christian views and extensive Jewish wrestling with these Christian claims. For this reason, we shall engage majority thinking first and then examine the Jewish counterviews.

The Christian view of Jewish status was central to Christian self-perception. Christian accession to religious primacy emerged – in the Christian view – from Jewish sin and God's rejection of his original people. As a result, Christian conceptualization and imagery of purported Jewish punishment was ubiquitous, rich, and complex. Traditional Christian imagery projected Judaism as a superannuated religion that had lost its valued place in the cosmos with the advent of Jesus as Messiah and viewed Jews as misguided adherents of this superannuated religion. In terms of Jewish status, this basic view led in contradictory directions.

On the one hand, it suggested that Jews deserve respect as descendants of the initial believers in the one true God and the recipients of his original

---

[2] See Chapters 1 and 2.

blessings. Although Jews had erred in their failure to acknowledge Jesus as Messiah, their ancestors had nonetheless been the first to recognize the one true God and thus to bring him into the world, and that recognition entitled them to a distinguished place on the human scene. Excluding Christians to whom they were of course inferior, Jews constituted in effect the most distinguished branch of humanity.

On the other hand, the imagery of Jewish failure and sinfulness suggested – in opposite fashion – that Jews were the very worst of the human species. To fail in recognition of the one true God – as was projected initially for all of humanity other than Christians and Jews – is a lamentable but understandable shortcoming; to have been vouchsafed the truth by God and to fail to recognize that truth is a far more serious and damning shortcoming. Of these two diametrically opposed possibilities, it was the latter that tended to dominate, although the former by no means disappeared.

Christian thinking about Jewish status began along the same lines as Jewish thinking. Jews had sinned grievously and had thus opened themselves to the panoply of punishments predicted throughout the biblical corpus. Christian views diverged from those of the Jews in two decisive ways – the nature of the sinning, which Christians identified as rejection of Jesus, and the ultimate reconciliation with God, which in the Christian view would mean Jews joining the Christian community and accepting the Christian religious vision.

We have already seen the impact of key biblical images on Christian thinking vis-à-vis Jews. In our discussion of Jewish demography, we cited the considerable impact of the biblical image of the fratricide Cain. The saga of the patriarchs includes two instances of brothers whose relationship was contentious, and both episodes eventually played a major role in Christian conceptualization of the place of Jews in Christian society and of Jewish status. The first of these instances is presented in Genesis 16–21. In this set of events, the barren Sarah requested that her husband Abraham sire a child through her Egyptian maidservant Hagar, a request that she subsequently regretted, leading to maltreatment of the maidservant.[3] The situation became yet more complicated with the unexpected birth of a child – Isaac – to the aged Sarah. The relationship of the two half

---

[3] Gen. 16.

brothers led Sarah to insist on the banishment of Hagar and her son Ishmael, a demand that distressed Abraham greatly. God reassured Abraham in the following terms:

Do not be distressed over the son of your slave; whatever Sarah tells you, do as she says, for it is through Isaac that offspring will be realized for you. As for the son of the slave-woman, I will make a nation of him too, for he is your seed.[4]

Jews over the ages viewed themselves as the obvious heirs to the legacy of Isaac and projected other peoples – especially the Arab peoples in the wake of the remarkable Muslim conquests – as the heirs of Ishmael. Christians in turn made themselves the heirs of Isaac and thus the bearers of the covenant, projecting Jews as the offspring of Ishmael, the son of the serving woman, and thus consigned to the fate of slaves.

There was a second major account of brothers in conflict that played more extensively and decisively into subsequent imagery of Christian-Jewish relations and Jewish status. Genesis 25–27 details the tortured relationship between the twin brothers Jacob and Esau, sons of Isaac and Rebecca and thus heirs through Isaac to the legacy of Abraham, to whom the divine promise of fathering God's chosen people had been given. Technically, Esau was the older of the two and, as first-born, should have been the legitimate heir to the line. Matters were hardly that simple, however. Two specific incidents put the normal line of succession into question.

In the first place, there was already intra-uterine conflict between the two brothers. In her anguish, Rebecca complained of her pain, which elicited a divine response:

> Two nations are in your womb,
> Two separate peoples shall issue from your body.
> One people shall be mightier than the other,
> And the older shall serve the younger.[5]

---

[4] Gen. 21:12–13.
[5] Gen. 25:23. Israel J. Yuval has taken the citation "two nations are in your womb" as the title for his study of Christian-Jewish relations – *Two Nations in Your Womb: Perceptions of Jews and Christians in Late Antiquity and the Middle Ages*.

Thus, God seemed to predict a reversal of the normal course of things, with the younger son taking precedence over the older. Given the significance of the succession to the legacy of Abraham through Isaac, this shift in the normal course of things was of monumental importance.

The second incident occurred toward the end of the lifetime of Isaac, who had determined to confer his blessing on his older son, which would have been the customary procedure. Rebecca opposed this plan, however, and plotted to foil it. She arranged for Jacob to disguise himself as Esau in order to mislead the elderly and nearly blind Isaac, and the ruse was successful. In error, Isaac pronounced the following blessing upon his younger son:

> Let peoples serve you,
> And nations bow to you.
> Be master over your brothers,
> And let your mother's sons bow to you.
> Cursed be those who curse you,
> Blessed be those who bless you.[6]

This misdirected blessing thus fulfilled the earlier prediction of the elder serving the younger.

The subsequent biblical narrative follows the fate of Jacob, whose offspring became the tribes of Israel. Jews over the ages saw themselves simply and directly as the descendants of Jacob. Indeed, the very name taken by Jews as *benei yisrael* – children of Israel – attests to the Jewish perception of lineage rooted in the Jacob branch of the family, Jacob having won the name Israel in a later biblical incident. Once more, Jews identified others as the rejected son, in this case identifying for a variety of reasons Esau with Christians.

Christians read this biblical narrative quite differently. For them, the twin brothers were a clear foreshadowing of the linked religious communities of Jews and Christians, with the Jews obviously preceding in time and thus the elder. For Christians, the prediction of elder serving younger reflected the incontrovertible reality of the new and younger Christian community displacing the older and failed community of the Jews. We recall the distinction drawn by Christian thinkers between

---

[6] Gen. 27:29.

physical Israel and spiritual Israel and their insistence that the latter constitutes *Verus Israel*, the true Israel, meaning the genuine offspring and
heirs of the biblical Jacob/Israel. Furthermore, Isaac's blessing that Jacob
would become master over his brothers was – in the Christian view –
reflected in the reality of Christian dominance and Jewish subjugation.
Thus, both these sets of images served Christians as decisive indicators of
divinely predicted Christian succession to the blessings of the patriarchs,
to Christian domination of the Jewish people, and to the degraded status
of the Jews, successors to the delegitimized brothers Ishmael and Esau.

This imagery appears strikingly in the evocative opening to a letter of
complaint addressed by the powerful Pope Innocent III to the important
King Philip Augustus of France.

It does not displease God, but is even acceptable to him that the Jewish
dispersion should live and serve under Catholic kings and Christian princes
until such time as their remnant should be saved, in those days when "Judah
will be saved and Israel will dwell securely."[7] Nevertheless, such [kings and
princes] are exceedingly offensive in the sight of the divine majesty when
they prefer the sons of the crucifiers – against whom the blood cries to the
Father's ears – to the heirs of the crucified Christ and when they prefer
the Jewish slavery to the freedom of those whom the Son freed, as though
the son of a servant could and should be an heir along with the son of the
free woman.[8]

This contrast highlights Jewish sinfulness and Christian succession to the
covenantal promises. The distinction between sons of the servant and
sons of the free woman is an obvious allusion to the biblical contrasts
between Sarah and Hagar and their sons Isaac and Ishmael.[9]

Thus, there was considerable emphasis in medieval Church thinking on the necessarily degraded status of the Jews. This degraded status flowed from Jewish sinfulness and divine punishment, as predicted
widely throughout the Hebrew Bible; it was buttressed in Christian eyes
by the sibling imageries of Isaac and Ishmael and Jacob and Esau, with
Christians projecting themselves as the favored sons and identifying the

---

[7] Jer. 23:6.
[8] Grayzel, *The Church and the Jews in the XIIIth Century*, 1:104–7, #14.
[9] Further invocation of the contrast can be found in the letters of Pope Innocent III in
   ibid., #13 and #18.

Jews as the rejected sons. All this meant that, while Jews enjoyed legitimate rights of existence in Christian society, including the right to remain Jews and fulfill the dictates of their religious faith, Christians viewed the Jews of medieval western Christendom as living in subjugated status as a reflection of the theological disparity between the two faiths, in fulfillment of biblical prediction, and in consonance with biblical imagery.

Christian conceptualization of Jewish servitude went beyond official and theoretical pronouncements. Because of the importance of Jewish servitude to Christian self-perception, it was important that Christians of all levels and all capacities grasp this key teaching. Thus, imagery of Jewish servitude pervaded medieval Christian society. The most striking example of such imagery purveyed throughout Christian society was the ubiquitous contrast of the reigning Ecclesia/Church and the humiliated Synagoga/Synagogue. These contrastive figures were regularly etched in stone for all – Christians and Jews alike – to see and grasp, for they required no literacy to understand. Ecclesia was regularly projected as a regal figure – serene, crowned, and grasping in her hand a symbol of authority. The contrastive Synagoga figure was shown in a posture of humiliation, with crown slipping off her head, and with a broken staff of authority held in her hand. The message was clear and unequivocal, and it was broadly disseminated, available to the Christian majority as reinforcement for its sense of superiority and to the Jewish minority to reinforce the message of its failure and divinely imposed subjugation and servitude.[10]

How then did the Jews of medieval western Christendom react to this imagery of Jewish servitude and degradation? Did they create a counter-imagery for themselves, and if so, what was it? To an extent, Jews agreed with the imagery of Jewish servitude. Overall, Jews did not challenge the empirical reality of their inferior position. They acknowledged it readily, in part because the small size of the Jewish community and its position as a tiny minority in medieval western Christendom were too obvious to challenge. Moreover, the reality of dependence on the authorities of church and – to an even greater extent – of state was likewise too obvious to deny. More important yet, the realities of inferiority and dependence – perhaps even degradation – conformed to internal conceptions of the

[10] Note the essays collected in Mitchell B. Merback, ed., *Beyond the Yellow Badge.*

Jewish "middle age." Jews shared fully with their Christian neighbors the sense of Jewish sinfulness and divine punishment. That combination had – from the Jewish perspective – brought them into exile and exilic status, and exilic status featured degradation and humiliation.

What Jews were utterly unwilling to accept was the corollary that Jewish degradation and servitude also served as proof of Christian truth. Degradation – yes, for in fact it had been biblically predicted; servitude of some kind – yes, for the same reason; servitude to the true religious faith and to the heirs to the mantle of the True Israel – resoundingly no.

In order to rebut for themselves Christian contentions of Jewish servitude to the true faith and divinely chosen community, often advanced in polemical argumentation, medieval Jews took a number of tacks. The first was to deny any genuine truth to the new masters of Jewish fate. In the view of medieval Jews, God had ordained a number of powerful but religiously meaningless empires as overlords and oppressors of the Jewish people. Christianity was simply one of these materially powerful but spiritually vacuous oppressors. Key to this perception was the prediction of four empires in Daniel 2 and 7, especially the latter. For medieval Jews, the fourth beast of the Daniel imagery represented Christianity. Jews insisted that the power of these four beasts reflected no religious truth whatsoever; their power was worldly only and would eventually be superseded by the dawning of the messianic era, when the true faith community would finally enjoy hegemony. Christian worldly power was thus no more a religious challenge than that of their predecessors – the Babylonians, Persians, and Greeks; in religious terms, it meant nothing.[11]

Additionally, medieval Jews contested vigorously the notion of themselves as heirs of Ishmael and Esau. They did so in a double sense. On the one hand, they affirmed constantly their own role as the children of Israel, that is, the offspring of Abraham, Isaac, and Jacob – the genuine line of succession. For medieval Jews no matter the difficulties of their circumstances, there was never any doubt raised as to their bearing the designation Israel in every sense. There was no acknowledgment of any potential bifurcation of the title Israel into a material and spiritual duality. Jews viewed themselves regularly and insistently as simply and fully the children of Israel.

[11] See more fully in Chapter 9.

At the same time, medieval Jews identified the Muslim world as the offspring of Ishmael and the Christian world as the descendants of Esau. The biblical term *Edom*, the designation often used in the biblical narrative for Esau, was regularly invoked as the nomenclature for Christianity. Medieval Christendom – along with serving as the fourth oppressor-empire – was heir to the characteristics of Isaac's son Esau. Medieval Christendom was indeed powerful in material terms, overwhelmingly oriented toward the physical and military, and utterly devoid of spiritual sensitivity. The contrast with the thoughtful and spiritual Jacob and with his thoughtful and spiritual descendants – the medieval Jews – could hardly have been sharper in the eyes of the latter.

Beyond this generic and symbolic dismissal of Christian claims to religious truth and the title of True Israel, there was intense and focused rebuttal of the rich proofs of Christianity to ascendancy that claimed selection by God as the result of Christian acceptance of Jesus and Jewish failure to do so. Jewish polemicists and thinkers examined carefully (and polemically of course) the messianic claims associated with Jesus and dismissed them systematically. Christian ascendancy did not mean Christian truth; the appearance of Jesus was by no means the promised messianic denouement of human history. Jewish spokesmen pointed relentlessly to the alleged disparities between the messianic realities projected in Scripture and the substantially lesser achievements of the contemporary Christian world. For all its impressive power, of which medieval Jews were hardly unaware, Christian achievements did not reach the level predicted for the true faith community of the messianic era.[12]

Medieval Jews living in western Christendom were keenly aware of the Christian imagery of Jewish degradation and humiliation, which pointed above all else to the truth of the Christian faith. They were familiar with the theory, with the imagery, and with the extended arguments. These medieval Jews understood well the extent to which the perspective on their faith community was essential to the self-image of the Christian majority. They also knew that, of all the arguments directed by Christians at them, the argument from Jewish suffering and humiliation was in many ways the most disturbing, since it was simultaneously an intellectual and emotional thrust. Thus, these Jews created their own

---

[12] Chazan, *Fashioning Jewish Identity*, chapter 10, and Chapter 9 in this book.

version of Jewish servitude that stripped it of any implied Christian advantage and restricted its meaning to Jewish fate alone. Jewish servitude was a reflection of the relationship between God and his everlastingly chosen people and no more. Indeed, the majority population of medieval Christendom, which claimed to be the True Israel, could not have been more misguided in its assertions. Christians – for these medieval Jews – were in fact the offspring of the displaced son Esau and exhibited precisely his rough and unruly characteristics.

JEWISH SERVITUDE AND SERFDOM

The year 1000 – the point generally advanced as the onset of the vitalization of medieval western Christendom and simultaneously the point at which Jewish presence began to proliferate in this rapidly developing society – does not constitute the beginning of Jewish living under Christian rule. From the fourth century on, the Roman Empire had been by and large controlled by emperors who were adherents of Christianity and who ceded increasing power to the ecclesiastical leadership of the Roman Church. Nonetheless, the Christianized Roman Empire was quite different from medieval western Christendom. While notions of Christian truth and Jewish error and of Christian accession to the covenantal responsibility and honor once borne by the Jews were well worked out, society was far too variegated and loose to admit of the kind of theorizing about Jewish subjugation and degradation that was the norm in medieval Christian Europe.

In fact, the center of gravity in the Jewish world of late antiquity lay farther eastward, in Byzantine Palestine and – even more so – in Sassanian Mesopotamia. The largest Jewry of the fourth through seventh centuries was that of Mesopotamia, inhabited by a multiplicity of peoples and beliefs, in which the Jews constituted but one of a number of important elements. While Jews may have to an extent viewed themselves as living under the rigors of exilic status, there is no sense from the limited sources available of a central image – held by either the non-Jewish majority or the Jewish minority – of Jews as a minority people living in servitude.

During the seventh century, large portions of the Roman Catholic Western Roman Empire and the Greek Orthodox Eastern Roman Empire fell under Muslim domination. More striking yet, the venerable Sassanian

Empire succumbed to the conquering Islamic armies. As a result, the overwhelming majority of the world's Jews fell into the orbit of Islam. In the highly variegated Islamic world, there was a carefully articulated hierarchical theory of human groupings. At the apex of the hierarchy stood the community of Muslims, envisioned as the recipients of the third and full divine revelation. For the ruling Muslim majority, Islam was the ultimate divine dispensation and thus superior to all competing faiths. At the bottom of the hierarchy stood the polytheistic peoples, devoid of any genuine religious truth and thus stripped of any legitimacy in the Islamic scheme of things. Between these two poles were the *dhimmi* peoples, religious communities that acknowledged the one true God and had been blessed by that God with divine revelations, which were, to be sure, deficient. The capacity of these peoples to recognize the one true God in the universe and God's reward for this recognition in the form of revealed truths meant that these peoples were worthy of legitimacy and at least secondary status in the Islamic environment.

For our purposes, the important point is that the Jews of the medieval Islamic world were part of a class of religious communities, rather than a unique religious entity. As a *dhimmi* people, Jews were not singled out for special status or a special relationship to their Muslim rulers.[13] Demographic realities reinforced this theological status. Jews in the medieval Islamic world constituted one of a number of diverse human communities within society and in no way enjoyed or suffered unique status in theoretical or practical terms.

Thus, as regards Jewish status, medieval western Christendom was a wholly new environment, in which the Jews constituted a very special element in society and in many areas a new element at that. This was a milieu in which the Church exercised great influence, in which the theory of subjugated Jewish status seemed close to reality, and in which reality might be manipulated to correspond to the theory. Christian rhetoric and imagery projected the notion of Jewish servitude throughout medieval western Christendom. We have noted the widespread representations of *Ecclesia* and *Synagoga* as effective purveyors of the notion of Jewish servitude. We might also recall the fearsome depiction by Petrus Alfonsi

---

[13] Note the well-known Pact of Umar – available in Norman A. Stillman, *The Jews of Arab Lands*, 157–58 – which applied equally to Jews and Christians.

of Jewish subjugation and humiliation.[14] These perspectives permeated medieval Latin Christendom and created a sense of the Jews as a unique human community, designated by God for suffering and servitude.

To be sure, legislating degradation – of the Jews or of anyone else – is no easy matter. For the Church, the problem was especially acute, in that the Church rarely exercised direct control over the Jews of medieval western Christendom. By and large, the Church impacted Jewish life by exerting pressure on the secular authorities of Christian Europe, under whose protection and jurisdiction the Jews normally lived. Some expedients in order to bring the theory of Jewish servitude into consonance with the realities of Jewish life were fairly simple. The Church demanded that Jews might under no circumstances criticize Christianity or dispute Christian truth. Jewish public spaces had to be necessarily inferior to Christian public spaces. No synagogue could be higher or more lavish than neighboring churches. Occasionally, legislation prohibited the construction of new synagogues altogether. By the middle of the thirteenth century, Jews were regularly forced to attend missionizing sermons delivered by Christian clergymen. All these Church demands highlighted the inferiority of the Jews and served to buttress the sense of their servitude.

One of the common techniques for degrading groups within society has historically been to isolate them through segregative legislation. Being segregated legally has usually implied separate and inferior. Segregation of Jews became a staple of ecclesiastical legislation in medieval western Christendom from the thirteenth century on. Segregation required convincing the secular authorities to prohibit Jewish settlement in villages where considerable social contact was inevitable, to restrict Jews to certain sectors of towns, and – the most extreme expedient – to force Jews to wear identifying garb. The ostensible reason advanced for this legislation was the need to proscribe potentially dangerous contact – sexual or religious – between Jews and their Christian neighbors. Whether the Church intended the segregative legislation to humiliate, as such legislation usually does, is open to question; that it had that effect is not open to question. Jews as the segregated minority group felt keenly the degradation and humiliation that the segregative legislation entailed.

---

[14] See Chapter 2.

In theory, Church doctrine and practice should have determined Jewish status decisively in medieval Christian Europe, but in fact they did not. To a significant extent, the secular authorities of medieval western Christendom – who should have been wholly committed to enforcement of ecclesiastical policy and practice – exercised considerable independence. These secular authorities often had reasons of their own for protecting and supporting their Jewish clients. To be sure, secular authorities could ill afford to dismiss entirely Church demands. The Church exercised potent leverage on the rulers of medieval western Christendom through its control of the sacraments and religious life in general. In addition, it exercised further leverage through its hold on popular opinion. The rulers of medieval Christian Europe had to balance deftly the demands of the Church against their own perspectives and interests.

Given this tension, it is hardly surprising that the secular authorities eventually generated a theory of their own as regards Jewish status – so-called Jewish serfdom. The roots of this Jewish serfdom lay in the broad realities of the feudal system. With the breakdown of governing structures during the ninth and tenth centuries, which constituted the nadir of western Christendom's fortunes, societies restructured themselves on the more limited basis of bonds between powerful figures and those whom they protected. Within the feudal structure, there was a hierarchy of status, ranging from slaves and serfs at the bottom to kings and emperors at the top. In between the extremes, there were many intermediate positions, including high-ranking barons, petty nobles, Christian burghers, small Christian landholders, and anomalous groupings like the Jews.

Jews fit comfortably into the feudal system, with its emphasis on protector and protected. We have seen repeatedly the reality of special protections extended to Jews, in return for Jewish allegiance and heavy fiscal obligations owed to the governing authorities. This relationship gave rise to distinctly feudal terminology. Terms such as *Judeus meus* (my Jew) or *Judei nostri* (our Jews) were widely used throughout medieval western Christendom, pointing to the reciprocal relationship between the secular authorities, which provided protection and support, and "their" Jews, who contributed in return to general economic development and more specifically to royal and baronial coffers. We recall once again the sense attributed to the pious King Louis IX of France that the Jews of his kingdom were his personal responsibility, because he provided the ultimate grounding for their presence.[15]

Given the reality of this special relationship and of the ecclesiastical doctrine of Jewish servitude, it was a short leap from *Judeus meus* and *Judei nostri* to the locution of Jewish serfdom. David Abulafia has shown the widespread use of the terminology of Jewish serfdom as early as the late twelfth century on the Iberian peninsula. More important, Abulafia insists on the multiple meanings of the terminology, with these multiple meanings by no means entirely pejorative or demeaning.[16] Salo Baron suggested some time ago that the adoption of the terminology of serfdom represented – more than anything else – an assertion by the secular authorities of their rights over Jews, as opposed to the claims advanced by the Church, and that suggestion has seemed reasonable to many observers.[17]

Perhaps the most wide-ranging and well-known assertion of Jewish serfdom is that enunciated by Emperor Frederick II in 1236. In the wake of growing insecurity for Jews in general in the Holy Roman Empire and more specifically of the appearance of the accusation of Jewish use of Christian blood, Emperor Frederick II confirmed for all the Jews of Germany the charter granted by his grandfather for the Jews of Worms, to which he added specific reference to the blood libel and its inadmissibility in court. Frederick prefaced this protective proclamation by noting his special responsibility "to rule non-believers properly and protect them justly, as a special group committed to our care." This of course is yet another articulation of the special relationship between Jews and their governmental protectors. More specifically, in this protective edict the emperor referred to all the Jews of his empire as "serfs of our court in Germany."[18]

Generally, the terminology of Jewish serfdom did not involve specific and onerous restrictions on Jewish life. In many instances, such as the proclamation of Emperor Frederick II, the emphasis was on protection, rather than limitation. To be sure, at some points the language of

---

[15] See Chapter 5.
[16] David Abulafia, "The King and the Jews," 43–54, and his further studies cited therein.
[17] Salo W. Baron, "Medieval Nationalism and Jewish Serfdom," 17–48. Baron pursued these issues subsequently in *A Social and Religious History of the Jews*, 9: chapter 40.
[18] Chazan, *Church, State, and Jew*, 124–26.

serfdom served to underline rights over the Jews and limitations of Jewish freedom. These efforts at "enserfing" the Jews were mainly limited to the special circumstances of twelfth- and thirteenth-century northern France. Northern France was, in the first place, a center of development, on both the economic and governmental fronts. As a result, the rapidly developing governments of the area came to recognize the value of Jewish moneylending and supported it, partly for the good of society as a whole and partly because of substantial revenue flowing from the Jewish lenders whom the authorities supported.[19] At the same time, toward the end of the twelfth century northern France remained a patchwork of baronies, with the royal domain relatively modest. Thus, enjoyment of considerable revenue from Jews by numerous rulers led in the direction of safeguarding such revenue, with the royal authority at the forefront of these efforts. Concern for safeguarding revenues derived from Jews meant limiting the considerable Jewish mobility noted earlier.[20] Jews on the move from domain to domain translated in governmental eyes to lost revenue.

Governmental expedients aimed at control of Jewish movement begin to appear in northern France toward the end of the twelfth century. The reality of neighboring baronies that might entice Jewish businessmen by offering better circumstances and fuller support alerted the northern French authorities to the need for limiting Jewish mobility and thus maintaining control of Jewish taxation. These authorities took a number of steps in order to limit Jewish movement. The simplest was to deal with the Jews directly. Thus, for example, when King Philip Augustus conquered the wealthy principality of Normandy, which housed an affluent Jewry, he had Norman Jews coming under his jurisdiction swear an oath and deposit pledges as surety that they would not leave his land.[21]

On the other hand, at about the same time King Philip Augustus exploited the demographic instability stirred up by the preaching of Fulk of Neuilly and the displacement of Jews from a number of baronies in order to settle many of these displaced Jews in the royal domain. Once again, he hoped to ensure that these newly acquired Jews remain in place

---

[19] See Chapter 6.
[20] See Chapter 5.
[21] For a full description of this document, see Jordan, *The French Monarchy and the Jews*, 57.

and that the revenue they represented not be lost. In order to do so, the wily monarch drew up treaties with neighboring barons, recognizing mutual rights over Jews. The king would not assert control of Jews belonging to his baron, and the baron would not take possession of Jews newly acquired by the king.[22] These treaties protected the investment of each side. The losers of course were the Jews themselves, since the mobility that was so meaningful to them as businessmen ever on the lookout for better circumstances disappeared.

As the French authorities increasingly felt the pressure of ecclesiastical opposition to aspects of Jewish moneylending, they – under the leadership of the kings – determined to take requisite steps to meet Church demands. These steps began with limiting harmful aspects of Jewish lending, such as excessive usury, and proceeded to withdrawal of the governmental authorities from support of Jewish lending altogether. This was a radical step, extraordinarily harmful to the Jewish business success that had developed in northern France. Out of an understanding that this new legislation – so inimical to Jewish business interests – might well lead to massive relocation of Jews from principalities in which the legislation was in force into principalities where it was not, the kings of France led the way in enactment of innovative legislation limiting more broadly Jewish population movement.

The landmark legislation of 1223, enacted through the leadership of the newly installed King Louis VIII, dismantled the system of governmental enrollment of Jewish loans. This legislation was signed by a bevy of northern European barons, most of whom were holders of Jews. Strikingly, the law includes the following:

It is to be known that we and our barons have decreed and ordained concerning the status of the Jews that none of us may receive or retain the Jewish of another. This is to be understood both for those who have sworn to the ordinance as well as for those who have not.[23]

To an extent, this is merely an extension of the non-retention treaties noted previously. In two senses, however, it goes well beyond those

---

[22] For one such treaty document, see Chazan, *Medieval Jewry in Northern France*, 75.

[23] Chazan, *Church, State, and Jew*, 212. See the landmark study of Gavin I. Langmuir, "'Judei Nostri' and the Beginning of Capetian Legislation," 203–69.

treaties. In the first place, it obligated large numbers of barons simul-taneously, rather than merely two signatories. More important yet, it obligated those who signed the ordinance and those who did not. Thus, in effect the Jews of northern France – adversely affected by the new leg-islation – could not escape it through relocation to a neighboring barony in northern France. They had to remain in the domain of the ruler under whom they had been living.

The ordinance of 1230, enacted early in the reign of King Louis IX and under the direction of those exercising regency on his behalf, represented yet a further step in extricating the governments of northern France from involvement in Jewish moneylending. It proclaimed that "we and our barons shall henceforth cause no contracted debts to be repaid to the Jews." All governmental support for Jewish lending was to come to an end. Once again, the severity of the blow led the authorities to envision a Jewish desire for relocation, which necessitated the broad commitment to non-retention of Jews included in the 1223 ordinance. The language, however, is a bit sharper and harsher.

Nor shall anyone in our kingdom be permitted to retain the Jew of another lord. Wherever anyone shall find his Jew, he may legally seize him as his serf, whatever the custom the Jews might enjoy under the rule of another or in another kingdom.[24]

Here the language of serfdom is advanced directly. The combination of ecclesiastical theory, the realities of the relationship between Jews and their lords, and the new restrictions of Jewish movement combined to make the language of Jewish serfdom seem utterly appropriate.

To be sure, the ordinance of 1230 itself makes it clear that this "serf-dom," that is, wide-ranging restriction on Jewish movement, was highly innovative. Reference is made to the prior custom of free movement, to which Jews cannot appeal. To be sure, the kind of limitation on Jewish movement that developed in northern France hardly became the norm for subsequent Jewish life throughout medieval western Christendom. The norm remained the special relationship between Jews and their pro-tective/exploitative lords, but without the radical implications of that

---

[24] Ibid., 231–14.

relationship drawn in the advanced and complicated area of northern France.

Jewish subjugation to the secular authorities was realized in practice in two prominent ways. The first was through exorbitant financial exactions. The potential for governmental exploitation of Jewish clients was an ever-present threat in medieval Christian Europe. In many instances – especially in the most advanced monarchies of northwestern Europe – governments did exploit their Jews in a way that concretized the subjugation of their Jewish subjects. Yet more significant as realization of the imagery of Jewish servitude and Jewish serfdom was the power of the authorities to banish their Jews. Banishment was a widespread phenomenon, initially in the more advanced areas of thirteenth- and fourteenth-century northwestern Europe and spreading during the fifteenth century to the Iberian peninsula in the southwest and all across central Europe, both south and north. Rulers could not expel Jews capriciously; in all cases, they had to justify banishment by identifying Jewish misdeeds, although these claims obviously could be manipulated by adroit rulers and in fact were regularly exploited.[25] In any case, expulsion represented the most painful and tangible index of Jewish subjugation in medieval western Christendom.

JEWISH RIGHTS AND UTILITY

Overall, the ecclesiastical and secular imageries of medieval Jewish servitude and serfdom and the policies generated by these imageries were surely harmful to Jewish life, but should not be exaggerated. The rhetoric and practice of Jewish subjugation were extremely important to the medieval Church, and it promoted them ceaselessly. Yet the Church did have an alternative rhetoric and a protective policy. The alternative rhetoric emphasized in Pauline fashion the original dignity of biblical Israel, the physical progenitor of the medieval Jews. The protective policy posited the fundamental rights of Jews to live in physical security and in accordance with Judaism within Christian society. These rights were grounded in the conviction of Jewish utility to Christianity and in the assumption of the eventual conversion of Jews. This protective policy

[25] See Chapter 5.

played a far more significant role in Jewish fate than did the alternative and more positive rhetoric. Church leadership intervened regularly on behalf of Jews who were judged to be in jeopardy of losing these basic rights – through misinterpretation of ecclesiastical policies, as a result of the depredations of the secular authorities, or through the misguided thinking of the populace.

While much of Church activity related to the Jews involved efforts at limitation and even humiliation, the ecclesiastical authorities regularly took a protective stance as well. To an extent, this involved protection against threats to basic Jewish rights emanating from the policies of the Church itself. Two of the most important innovations in the increasingly aggressive twelfth- and thirteenth-century Church stance toward Judaism and Jews were the imposition of distinguishing garb and condemnation of the Talmud. Strikingly, however, Church leaders were willing to hear Jewish and Christian complaints about the problems flowing from the imposition of distinguishing garb and to countenance a relaxation of such garb under given circumstances, as indicated in the following letter of Pope Honorius III to the archbishop of Tarragona.

Our dearest son in Christ, James, king of Aragon, called the following to our attention. Although in his land the difference of the clothes of either sex has from ancient times set apart and distinguished and still distinguishes Jews from Christians, so that it is impossible for Jews to have relations with Christian women or Christians with Jewish women, nevertheless under the pretext of the General Council certain ones among you try to force them [the Jews] to wear a new sign, not so much in order that such crimes should be avoided, as because they have the chance to extort money. For this reason, many Jews withdraw from his land, much to his loss and the loss of his kingdom, and he fears that still others have by this time departed. Wherefore not wishing that you should convert to this end that which was established in order to prevent the danger of wicked intercourse under the cloak of error, we command you by apostolic writings to the effect that you no longer trouble them about the wearing of a new sign.[26]

The anti-Talmud campaign of the 1230s and 1240s provides a yet more prominent example of Church willingness to rethink policies and restrain extreme anti-Jewish positions. The anti-Talmud campaign, unleashed by

---

[26] Grayzel, *The Church and the Jews in the XIIIth Century*, 1:156–67, #44.

Pope Gregory IX in the mid-1230s, proved deeply harmful to Jewish academic and religious life and elicited strenuous Jewish objections. Jews argued before Gregory's successor, Pope Innocent IV, that stripping the Jews of the Talmud was tantamount to prohibiting Judaism altogether, since Jews could not follow the dictates of their faith without the guidance of the Talmud. Thus, in effect the ban on the Talmud constituted nullification of the basic right of Jews to live as Jews in Christian society. These Jewish objections gained a sympathetic hearing on the part of Pope Innocent IV. He insisted that the Paris ecclesiastical court – which had examined the Talmud, had found it utterly unacceptable in Christian society, and had ordered its destruction – reconsider its conclusions. He urged the Paris tribunal to overturn its total condemnation of the Talmud, to excise offensive passages, and to return the rest of the Talmudic corpus to the Jews. Although the Paris court ultimately rejected the papal suggestion, the policy advanced by Pope Innocent IV became the norm for most of medieval western Christendom. Censorship of the Talmud – while onerous for the Jews – was far preferable to its wholesale destruction and prohibition.[27]

More common was ecclesiastical condemnation of what were viewed as excesses on the part of the secular authorities. Church leaders were especially sensitive when such excesses were rooted in campaigns initiated by the Church itself. We have noted at a number of points the anti-usury initiative launched by Church leadership toward the end of the twelfth century. Not surprisingly, certain secular authorities turned this initiative to their own purposes, utilizing the ecclesiastical campaign as a pretext for extortion of Jewish wealth. In a remarkably sympathetic letter, Pope Gregory IX, who initiated the damaging assault on the Talmud in the late 1230s, railed a few years earlier against the injustices suffered by Jews in the course of the anti-usury campaign that had been initiated by the Church. Gregory depicts in horrifying and empathetic terms the anguish of these Jews, noting that they have "fled to the protection of the Apostolic Throne, begging us humbly to deign to take them under apostolic supervision." Pope Gregory responded to these Jewish entreaties and ordered the archbishops and bishops of France "to warn all the faithful Christians in your dioceses and to induce them not to

---

[27] Ibid., 274–81, #119.

harm the Jews in their persons nor to dare to rob them of their property nor – for the sake of plunder – to drive them from their lands, without some reasonable cause or clear guilt on their part, but rather to permit them to live in pursuance of their laws and their former status, as long as they do not presume to insult the Christian faith."[28]

Similarly, in reporting a discussion between himself and the archbishop of Narbonne, Rabbi Meir ben Simon has the archbishop asserting that Jews should not take usury from Christians, because Christians are brethren and not strangers. The prelate based his claim on the reality of governmental exploitation of the anti-usury campaign and episcopal protection against that exploitation:

Now consider well. Do you have a brother or sister among your co-religionists who could rescue you from the despoliation of the seneschal and his officers, who just this year sought to drive you from your spacious homes and to send you forth naked and unclothed into the cold? [Indeed, the seneschal sought] to hold your wealthy men in prison until they would redeem themselves with what they were thought to have safeguarded elsewhere or until they would circulate through the villages and towns at the doorsteps of Jews or of those you deem strangers [i.e., Christians] so that they [the Christians] would release to them [the beleaguered Jews] their funds – illegitimately in fact as regards usury. Indeed, they [Christians like the archbishop] were better than brothers, standing by you in your hour of trial.[29]

The most energetic ecclesiastical interventions on behalf of medieval European Jews involved correction and restraint of misguided popular actions and perceptions. When Pope Urban II set the First Crusade in motion in 1095, he almost certainly had no sense that the call to arms against the Muslims would move a small number of Christian warriors and burghers to a cry for vengeance against Jewish neighbors. While this deflection of crusading ardor occurred in only very limited circumstances, especially in the major towns of the Rhineland, the results in those towns were devastating. Thus, as the Second Crusade began in the mid-1140s, the spiritual leader of the new venture – Bernard of Clairvaux – was aware of the potential for misinterpretation of the renewed call to arms. As the anti-Jewish potential showed signs of actualizing, he

---

[28] Ibid., 202–3, #70.
[29] This letter is cited in Robert Chazan, "Anti–Usury Efforts in Thirteenth–Century Narbonne," 53.

appended to his crusading letter explicit identification and denunciation of what he perceived as a misinterpretation of the crusading effort.

For the rest, not I but the Apostle warns you, brethren, not to believe every spirit. I have heard with great joy of the zeal for God's glory that burns in your midst, but your zeal needs the timely restraint of knowledge. The Jews are not to be persecuted, killed, or even put to flight.[30]

Bernard grounds this prohibition of anti-Jewish violence in a variety of considerations, some quite negative with regard to Jews and others relatively positive. In any case, Bernard was extremely serious in his commitment to squelching anti-Jewish violence. When it became clear that the potential for such violence was mounting once again in the Rhineland, he journeyed to the area and warned in person against killing Jews. His warnings seem to have been quite effective. Bernard's intervention – combined with parallel determination on the part of the secular authorities and cautious steps taken by the Jews themselves – averted a repetition of the 1096 tragedy.[31]

Similarly, as increasingly irrational and harmful stereotypes of Jewish malevolence began to circulate during the second half of the twelfth century and on into the first half of the thirteenth, ecclesiastical leadership was fairly consistent in examining the allegations carefully, rejecting them, and urging Europe's Christians to disavow these claims. While Church dismissal of the allegations seems to have had little impact on popular thinking, the ecclesiastical stance was clear and consistent.[32]

Jewish circumstances in medieval Europe suffered as a result of the ecclesiastical doctrine of Jewish servitude, demeaning ecclesiastical imagery of Jews and Judaism, and ecclesiastical policies aimed at limiting Jewish life; Jewish circumstances benefited from the Church's more positive doctrines, imagery, and policies. The impact of ecclesiastical

---

[30] Chazan, *Church, State, and Jew*, 103–4.

[31] Likewise, there were careful preventive measures by Church leadership in conjunction with parallel efforts by the secular authorities during the early stages of the Third Crusade as well. See Robert Chazan, "Emperor Frederick I, the Third Crusade, and the Jews," 83–93.

[32] Note for example the letter of Pope Innocent IV of 1247 dismissing the burgeoning accusation that Jews utilize Christian blood for their Passover ritual – Grayzel, *The Church and the Jews in the XIIIth Century*, 1:268–71, #116. Shortly thereafter, the same pope added a clause to the *Constituio pro Judaeis* dismissing the blood libel allegation; ibid., 274–75, #118.

doctrine, imagery, and policy was, however, equaled in importance by the stances of the secular authorities of medieval Europe. Ultimately, the key to Jewish circumstances generally lay with these secular authorities. When these authorities were well disposed to their Jewish clients, Jews were hardly a subjugated minority group in medieval western Christendom; often, they could even be called a privileged urban community. When for a host of reasons the authorities turned against their Jewish clients, then the Jews did suffer badly and looked much more like what the Church claimed them to be – subjugated and humiliated adherents of an outmoded religious vision.

In the face of ecclesiastical doctrine and imagery of Jewish servitude, the secular authorities emphasized Jewish serfdom. However, this imagery generally had very few harmful overtones. Most often, the language of Jewish serfdom was invoked to highlight the responsibility of the authorities to their Jewish clients. Only in a very limited set of circumstances were the implications of Jewish serfdom negative, with for example an emphasis on the limitation of Jewish freedom of movement. Governmental policies toward Jewish life were basically free of pre-existent constraints. Rulers in theory governed in accordance with the demands of Church theory and practice, and ecclesiastical pressures did influence governmental postures toward Jews. Nonetheless, Europe's rulers generally enjoyed considerable latitude and treated Jews as they deemed appropriate and useful to the circumstances of their domains.

In examining the outlines of Jewish demography and Jewish economic activities, we have noted recurrently the support and protection offered to Jews by the authorities and we have seen that, without such support, Jewish life was impossible in medieval western Christendom. Time and again, we have encountered European rulers seeking to maintain Jewish presence in their domains in the face of change or to attract Jews to locales they had not previously inhabited. The attempt to woo Jews could not be grounded in projecting Jews as an enslaved and humiliated group. Instead, all the charters cited emphasized the boons that the authorities were prepared to offer Jews whom they wished to entice to stay or to immigrate. We have examined the reasons for this support, noting the broad advantages to the general economy expected from the Jews and the more specific advantages to the coffers of the rulers anticipated as well. All this conveys no sense of Jewish servitude and humiliation. To the contrary, the charters project the Jews as highly useful, worthy of serious support and encouragement.

In this complex of ecclesiastical and secular imageries and policies, the Jews of medieval western Christendom were a small, weak group, but they were hardly powerless. They enjoyed a set of fundamental rights guaranteed by the Church and the protection of supportive rulers. Although the Jewish negotiating position was limited, it did exist. It was up to the Jews themselves to recognize the forces arrayed against them, to identify the supportive allies to whom they might turn, and to present clear and compelling arguments to these supportive forces.

In order for the Jews of medieval Christian Europe to maximize their negotiating options, they had to create effective internal governance of Jewish life. That Jews would run their own affairs was an assumption of the diverse premodern contexts within which Jews lived. In the monotheistic environments of Muslim and Christian civilizations, this assumption was especially strong. The Jews themselves shared the majority desire that Jews govern their own affairs, partly out of suspicion of the non-Jewish majority and partly out of a sense that Jewish religious tradition required Jewish self-governance. While self-governance was thus a reality, the important issue for Jewish status and well-being was the effectiveness of the Jewish self-governing agencies. The sense from medieval western Christendom is that the Jews of this period and area were successful in fashioning highly effective agencies of Jewish self-government, capable of negotiating adroitly – albeit not always successfully – with the authorities of both Church and state.

The second avenue into the halls of power involved unusually successful Jews, whose business achievements brought them into contact with the ruling class, whose financial resources made them important to the authorities, and whose influence within the Jewish community was pervasive. These leading Jews became a second and often dominant channel for Jewish negotiation. In southern Europe, the position and power of the courtier class was a legacy from the period of Islamic rule that was well maintained subsequent to the Christian conquest. In the newer Jewish communities of the north, the efficacy of the elite of wealth was quickly manifest. Such Jews in both the southern and northern sectors of Europe helped Jews maximize their negotiating power. Jewish negotiations were by no means always successful. Nonetheless, Jewish successes once again indicate the extent to which the ecclesiastical theory of Jewish servitude was belied by the real circumstances of Jewish life in medieval Christian Europe.

DESPITE THE JEWISH SENSE OF EXILIC DEGRADATION AND HUMILIATION and despite the important ecclesiastical imagery of Jewish servitude, Jewish status in medieval Christian Europe was in fact complex and diversified. Jewish status was influenced by ecclesiastical imagery and policy, by secular support or rejection, and by popular acceptance or animosity. There were periods of high status and periods of low status. Jewish status, however, does not distill into a neat and negative package.

Relations with the Christian Populace

*A*SSUMPTIONS OF INCESSANT JEWISH WANDERING, LIMITED Jewish economic outlets, and debased Jewish status are important elements in the prevailing sense of the horrors of Jewish experience in medieval western Christendom. Overshadowing these negative images is the conviction that the Jews of medieval Christian Europe were the victims of unrelenting violence, grounded in historical hatred of and irrational fantasies about Judaism and Jews. For many modern observers, Jews were unceasingly the objects of assault, from the First Crusade at the end of the eleventh century and down through the close of the Middle Ages toward the end of the fifteenth century.[1] The regular violence Jews suffered was purportedly the most devastatingly negative aspect of Jewish life in medieval western Christendom.

To be sure, it is immediately puzzling that the Jewish population of medieval Christian Europe – allegedly the most hostile of all the environments Jews have encountered – should have grown steadily throughout the period between 1000 and 1500, laying the foundation for what became the largest Jewish community in the world.[2] Were the Christian population of medieval Europe implacably hostile to Jews and were violence in fact a constant of Jewish life, it would be difficult indeed to account for the ongoing Jewish population growth. A community exposed to unceasing hostility and violence would not have opted to remain in such a destructive environment and would not have enjoyed the demographic

---

[1] Scholarly views have changed, as indicated in Chapter 4. However, these evolving scholarly views have made little headway against popular stereotypes.

[2] Recall Baron's emphasis on Jewish population growth in his 1928 article, as noted in the Prologue.

growth that eventually produced the world's largest Jewry. Steady Jewish population growth should at least raise some doubts about the widely purveyed sense of intense and constant anti-Jewish violence during the course of the European Middle Ages.

Again, we shall begin by examining prevailing assumptions about the animosity and violence supposedly endemic to Jewish history, looking at both Jewish and Christian stereotypes concerning this animosity and violence. We shall proceed to study the reality of popular fear and hatred of Jews in medieval western Christendom and the ways in which fear and hatred exploded periodically into anti-Jewish assaults. We shall close with evidence of more normal relations between Jews and their Christian neighbors. While evidence for everyday relations between Jews and their Christian neighbors in medieval Europe is sparse, enough remains to balance the one-sided picture of hatred and violence widely projected. This evidence – sparse though it is – enables us to see that the Jews of medieval Christian Europe generally led normal lives, that they opted reasonably to remain in the challenging but dynamic environment of Christian Europe, and that they continued to grow and expand as a vibrant Jewish community.

YOU SHALL BE CONSTANTLY ABUSED AND ROBBED

Our review of traditional Jewish views about exilic circumstances revealed wide-ranging convictions as to the punishments Jews would endure in the period between banishment from the Holy Land and divinely ordained redemption. A key element in these punishments was to be the animosity of non-Jews and the violence such animosity would spawn. Jews were to be the targets of regular hostility and ill-treatment, which would make their lives unendingly bitter.

To return once more to the dire Mosaic predictions of Jewish sufferings found in Deuteronomy 28:

> You shall not prosper in your ventures,
> But you shall be constantly abused and robbed,
> With none to give heed.
> If you pay the bride-price for a wife,
> Another man will enjoy her.
> If you build a house,

You shall not live in it.
If you plant a vineyard,
You shall not harvest it.
Your ox shall be slaughtered before your eyes,
But you shall not eat of it.
Your ass shall be seized in front of you,
And it will not be returned to you.
Your flock will be delivered to your enemies,
With none to help you.
Your sons and daughters shall be delivered to another people,
While you look on.
Your eyes will strain after them constantly,
But you shall be helpless.[3]

In fact, much of the subsequent biblical narrative is devoted to instances of such oppression, all of it preceding the onset of the lengthiest exile. Following their entry into the Promised Land, the Israelites were subjected to recurrent conflict with their Canaanite neighbors. During the eighth pre-Christian century, the conflict no longer involved local forces, but rather the imperial power of Assyria. This new-style conflict ended with the destruction and exile of the northern kingdom. A century and a half later, the southern kingdom confronted the Babylonian Empire, resulting once again in defeat and banishment. In Babylonian-Persian exile, the biblical books of Daniel and Esther portray the exiled Judeans as creating effective alliances with the Persian authorities, but beset with the enmity of elements in the Persian population. In the later strands of biblical narrative, Jews returning from exile encountered the hostility of the local population of the Land of Israel and – in the very last layers of biblical material – suffered persecution at the hands of their second-century Greek overlords.[4] The history of the Israelites/Jews depicted in the biblical corpus could easily be and has often been construed as a lengthy sequence of persecutions.

Moving beyond the biblical corpus and toward what is viewed as the post-70 exile (generally projected as *the* exile), the next stage of Jewish life in Palestine took place under Roman domination, with tensions

---

[3] Deut. 28:29–32.
[4] Modern scholars generally date the closing six chapters of the book of Daniel to the period of Greek persecution.

building up to the point of Jewish rebellion and Roman suppression of the uprising, resulting in massive destruction and dislocation.[5] Even then, the embers of Jewish rebelliousness remained and were fanned into one more unsuccessful effort to overthrow Roman rule. The Bar-Kokhba revolt ended again in defeat and persecution, eventuating in harsh restrictions on Jewish religious practice and the martyrdom of major Jewish spiritual leaders.

While there was much that was positive in this lengthy period that stretched over more than a millennium, the recurrence of physical violence sufficed to reinforce the biblical imagery of Israelite-Jewish life as beset by oppression and to confirm the biblical predictions that exilic fate would involve unending persecution. The popular Passover service richly captures and conveys this overarching sense of unending persecution. The Passover *Haggadah* text includes serious wrestling with dolorous Jewish fate, but projects the firm conviction of ongoing divine support and eventual redemption. The holiday itself is an uplifting commemoration of Egyptian bondage and divinely orchestrated liberation from that bondage, viewed as paradigmatic for subsequent Jewish history. The happy part of the saga is projected divine intervention, but the prelude to such divine intervention is the ongoing reality of oppression. This sense is captured in the well-known observation that:

Not one [enemy] only stood up against us to destroy us. Rather, in every generation [enemies] stand up against us to destroy us. But the Holy One, blessed be he, saves us from their hands.[6]

In this view, Jewish history is a never-ending sequence of oppression and divine assistance in the face of inevitable hostility.

Given this broad sense of Jewish history and the reality of significant anti-Jewish sentiment and action in medieval western Christendom, it is not difficult to see how persecution and suffering became the core impressions expressed during the period itself and subsequently. We recall the histories of Joseph *ha-kohen* and Samuel Usque, written during the sixteenth century and projecting persecution as the *leitmotif* of the Jewish past. Both early-modern histories center on oppression as the core

---

[5] Recall the caveat indicated at the beginning of Chapter 1 as to the actual significance of the year 70.

[6] E. D. Goldschmidt, *The Passover Haggadah*, 79.

feature of exilic Jewish history, with Usque extending the theme of persecution backward beyond the onset of the longest of the exiles. Heinrich
Graetz, poised at the juncture of premodern and modern Jewish sensibility, absorbed much of the premodern focus on persecution. Abandoning
the traditional emphasis on divine intervention, Graetz suggested that
the Jewish capacity to overcome oppression through intellectual and
spiritual achievement constituted the uplifting element in the Jewish
saga.[7]

Christians shared much of the Jewish sense of ongoing oppression
as divinely ordained punishment. Christians thus agreed that the persecution endured by Jews was merited, although they differed in their
assessment of the sinfulness that had aroused divine wrath. The Christian
sense was that Jews suffered oppression as punishment for their failure to
acknowledge the Messiah promised by the biblical prophets and – what
is more – for their persecution of this blameless figure sent to redeem
them. As a result, the Christian conviction of ongoing oppression of the
Jews was – if anything – more intense than that of the Jews themselves.
For Christians, Jewish suffering was proportional to the pain they had
inflicted on Jesus. Since the suffering of Jesus was a key religious theme
among Christians, the focus on the related and merited pain of the Jews
was strong and continuous.

In addition, for Christians there was a personal sense of grievance
associated with Jewish sinfulness. For Christians, purported Jewish persecution of the messianic and divine figure central to the Christian faith
was responsible for the subsequent suffering of the Jews. This alleged sinfulness evoked bitterness within Christian ranks, as Christians identified
with their persecuted Messiah. To be sure, this bitterness was to occasion
no human retribution against Jews. Nonetheless, Christian emphasis on
the fully merited suffering of post-Crucifixion Jews led to the highlighting of physical violence against Jews in general and projected this violence
as a central feature of Jewish life in medieval Christendom in particular.

We noted early on that there has been a remarkable reversal in Christian
emphasis on physical violence against Jews in medieval Christian Europe.
Whereas medieval Christian observers highlighted the persecution of
Jews as warranted punishment – an index of the sin-punishment dynamic

[7] See Chapters 1 and 4.

in general and of the truth of Christianity in particular – some Christian views in the wake of the Holocaust have shifted dramatically. For certain groups of recent Christian observers, oppression of the Jews in medieval Christian Europe serves as an index not of Jewish malfeasance and guilt, but rather as an index of Christian malfeasance and guilt. For these Christian observers, medieval persecution of Jews constitutes one of the major historic sins of Christianity. Repentance for this sinfulness must begin with acknowledgment of the shortcoming, resulting in an altered emphasis on the physical violence perpetrated against Jews in medieval western Christendom. For entirely new and different reasons, the suffering of Jews in medieval western Christendom has come to the forefront of Christian consciousness.[8]

The stereotypes of physical violence and suffering have been potent. I have no intention of arguing that Jewish life in medieval western Christendom was devoid of persecution and suffering. I will argue, however, that physical violence was by no means the whole of the story. Alongside the outbreaks of violence were periods of tranquility, which enabled Jews to live normally, to develop their communal existence, to commit themselves to the Christian environment in which they lived, and to expand and mature as a community.

POPULAR ANIMOSITY AND VIOLENCE

Looking back at the two thousand years of anti-Jewish persecution chronicled by Samuel Usque, we note that governmental authorities inflicted the bulk of the early violence. Governmentally generated violence derived largely from political conflicts between Jews and their self-governing neighbors or – more often – between Jews and their imperial overlords. The tragedies of persecution and destruction at the hands of the Assyrians, Babylonians, Seleucids, and Romans all fall into this latter category. Imperial rulers attacked Jews perceived as fomenting rebellion or actually in a state of rebellion. Popular hatred of Jews and violence emanating from such popular hatred were relatively rare. To the extent that there were instances of simple friction between Jews and their neighbors, this friction seems to have derived from immediate and local issues such as

[8] See Chapter 2.

competition for status and economic advantage in a given environment. Missing in the early episodes of popular anti-Jewish violence is any coherent and long-term grounding for a popular anti-Jewish ideology.

From the seventh century well down into the second half of the Middle Ages, the largest number of Jews lived within the orbit of Islam, in settings that ranged from the Middle East across into Asia Minor and around much of the circumference of the Mediterranean Sea. These Jewish communities constituted part of the segment of the population identified by Islam as *dhimmi* peoples, peoples that had come to recognition of the one true God in the world and had been vouchsafed divine revelation. As a *dhimmi* people, Jews were not a unique grouping, but were absorbed into a larger category. They were deemed religiously inferior, were constrained in some of their activities, but enjoyed important rights and protections – all as a result of their categorization as a *dhimmi* community. Thus, there is no evidence of specially directed governmental concern or popular hostility toward Jews.

In fact, since the two major groupings of *dhimmis* were Christians and Jews, Jews were by and large the preferred *dhimmi* grouping. Because Christians living under Islam were part of a global Christian community locked in strife with the Islamic world, Jews seemed to their Muslim overlords more trustworthy than their Christian contemporaries. To the extent that Jews fell victim to persecution, their suffering was the result of generalized anti-outsider governmental actions, as happened for example under the Almohades of North Africa and the Iberian peninsula. To an even lesser extent, there were occasional outbreaks of popular violence. Such outbreaks were not endemic to the Islamic world and reflect unusual circumstances, such as the remarkable power exercised by Samuel ibn Nagrela and his son Joseph, which resulted in a bloodbath in Malaga in 1066.[9] Neither governmental persecution nor popular violence characterized Jewish life in the Muslim sphere.

Medieval Christian Europe represented a totally new and different environment for Jewish life. The kind of governmental violence that had afflicted Israelite and Judean life during the biblical period or the Jews under Roman rule is nowhere in evidence in medieval western

---

[9] For full treatment of the rise and fall of Joseph ibn Nagrela, see Elihyahu Ashtor, *The Jews of Moslem Spain*, 2:158–89.

Christendom. Jews of course were no longer living as an independent polity or even as a self-governing entity with aspirations to resume independent status. Thus, perceptions of actual or potential Jewish rebellion disappeared and with them the bases for the kinds of actions taken by the Assyrian, Babylonian, Greek, or Roman authorities. The governing powers of medieval Christian Europe could and did mistreat Jews, both through radical exploitation of Jewish wealth and through banishment. Physical assault on Jews by the governing authorities was not, however, a normal factor on the medieval scene.[10] The prevailing sense of Jews as exposed to constant attack is the result of a new dynamic. In medieval western Christendom, Jews were the victims of popular violence, sparked by a potent set of anti-Jewish motifs grounded in traditional Christian thinking and thus widely shared within the Christian populace.

In much of Christian Europe, with the major exception of Spain, Jews were the single significant non-Christian group, which in and of itself constituted a new and problematic situation. Living as a unique out-group is fraught with danger. Beyond this simple demographic reality, the highly charged history of Christian-Jewish relations made Jews an especially problematic group in the strongly Christian environment of medieval Europe. As the group whose purported hostility constituted the sole opposition to Jesus in the moving and always fresh Gospels, medieval Jews were constantly identified with the hostile questioning of the Pharisees and the priests and – yet more damagingly – with the cruelty of the Crucifixion. With the Crucifixion as a central moment in Christian history, as the core of the annual celebration of Easter, and as a dominant theme in medieval Christian art, Jewish malfeasance inevitably played a front-and-center role in the consciousness of medieval European Christians.

The Church, as it advanced to a position of power in the Roman world, adumbrated a complex – and thus necessarily unstable – stance toward Jews and their place in Christian society. The Church highlighted Jewish shortcoming and failure for important internal reasons. These failures were the basis for Christian replacement of the Jews as God's favored people, and the Jews' crime and its aftermath served as important

---

[10] There were inevitably occasional exceptions. We shall deal with one such incident – the violence perpetrated against the Jews of Blois by the local count in 1171 – at a later point in this chapter.

indices of the truth of Christianity and were thus highlighted. For those who might question the errors of Judaism and the corresponding truth of Christianity, Jewish post-Crucifixion fate served as tangible proof of Christian truth and Jewish error. Church leaders urged their followers to ponder continually the misdeeds of the Jews, the results of these misdeeds, and the truth of the Messiah whom the Jews rejected.

However – and this was no simple matter – the outrage that Christians might feel when contemplating historical Jewish animosity and cruelty was not to occasion human vengeance and/or to engender anti-Jewish actions. The theory was that Jews had sinned and that God had provided the requisite punishment, clearly visible to the naked eye in Jewish exile and degradation. Human action was superfluous, illegitimate, and therefore prohibited. Ecclesiastical law stipulated that Jews enjoy the right to safety and security within Christian society.

While Church leadership regularly articulated and assiduously promoted this complex theory, it was in fact an extremely difficult combination for the common mind to absorb. Christians were to recall constantly and ponder Jewish malevolence and cruelty and were to be strengthened in their Christian identity thereby. They were not, however, to take action on feelings of outrage and anger. The theory makes sense, but it asks a great deal of the Christian populace. This theory demands that Christians recall the horrifying sins of the ancestors of Jewish neighbors, absorb and ponder the depth of that sinfulness and its meaning, be moved by the spectacle of the crucified Christ, but create a barrier between the feelings of counter-hatred and any behavioral outcomes. To absorb such intense feelings but restrain from action is a tall order for any community, but this is what the Church demanded. Little wonder that the populace of medieval Europe failed repeatedly in meeting this demand.

In fact, as western Christendom began its process of vitalization and went on the offensive against its enemies, the inherent instability of Church policy immediately became manifest. During the first half of the Middle Ages, western Christendom lay very much at the mercy of the forces surrounding it from every direction. What military power could be organized was channeled toward defensive actions against the incursions of the Muslims, the Byzantines, and the Norsemen. New-found strength from the late tenth century onward enabled European Christians to transition from a defensive to an offensive posture and to sally forth against neighboring enemies. The initial offensive thrusts took place on European soil itself, in areas that the Muslims had conquered on the Italian and Iberian peninsulas. The process of pushing the Muslims back on both peninsulas began in the middle of the eleventh century and resulted in slow but steady and irreversible progress.

As Christian forces began their push southward on the Iberian peninsula, we hear almost immediately of anti-Jewish violence associated with this initiative. The sources are minimal, limited to a fascinating letter from Pope Alexander II commending the bishops of Spain for their assiduous protection of Jews in the face of violence perpetrated by Christian warriors battling the Muslim foe.[11] The letter gives us little sense of the thinking that animated these Christian warriors, since it focuses rather on the Church policy that the warriors were contravening. With regard to the thinking of the Christian warriors, Alexander tells only that they were "moved surely by foolish ignorance and strongly by blind cupidity."

However, his recapitulation of Church policy suggests alternative motivations. Pope Alexander II describes the Jews as

those whom divine charity has perhaps predestined for salvation [an echo of Paul]. In the same manner, Saint Gregory also admonished those agitating to annihilate them, indicating that it is impious to wish to annihilate those who are protected by the mercy of God, so that – with homeland and liberty lost, in everlasting penitence, damned by the guilt of their ancestors for spilling the blood of the Savior – they live dispersed throughout the various areas of the world.[12]

The "foolish ignorance" of the Christian warriors lay in their inability to balance the complexities of the policy that Alexander sketches. In all likelihood, these warriors absorbed recurrent emphasis on "the guilt of their [the Jews'] ancestors for spilling the blood of the Savior," failing to understand that they were to recall this guilt but to refrain from acting on it. In the heat of battle against Muslim enemies, it was clearly difficult to maintain the restraint the Church demanded.

We are far better informed with regard to the next stage in the offensive military activities of Christian Europe. In 1095, Pope Urban II announced

---

[11] Chazan, *Church, State, and Jew*, 99–100.
[12] Ibid., 100. Recall the Cain imagery discussed in Chapter 5, with its notion that Jews – like Cain – were promised protection by God from the wrath of those who might encounter them.

an armed campaign to liberate the sacred sites of Christianity from the Muslims, who were allegedly abusing them. The call to what has subsequently become known as the First Crusade recapitulated the emphasis on reclaiming from the Muslim enemy territory that had been removed from Christian control, but it was far more radical. In the call to the crusade, the objective was no longer European land that had fallen into Muslim hands and that was immediately contiguous with Christian territory. The audacious call to the crusade involved conquest deep in Muslim territory, with Christian warriors urged to make a lengthy and perilous journey far from their home base. Moving spiritual stimulation was added as well. The spiritually laden symbols of Jerusalem and the Holy Sepulcher intensified and enriched the sense of religious obligation associated with what was at its core a military undertaking.

So far as is known, Urban included in his message no mention of Jews whatsoever, neither in the form of identifying Jews with the Muslim enemy nor with reasserting the protective theory adduced by his predecessor Alexander II some decades earlier. Indeed, the organized military bands that embarked on the perilous journey and in fact achieved their objective of conquest of Jerusalem and its sacred shrine have left no evidence of anti-Jewish sentiment or behavior. To be sure, upon the conquest of this sacred site these bands inflicted a massive bloodbath on the local inhabitants, including Jews. This bloodbath does not reflect, however, specifically anti-Jewish sentiment, for it was indiscriminate, taking the lives of Jerusalem Muslims, Jews, and even Christians. It seems to have been an emotional catharsis that obliterated distinctions among the various groupings of victims.[13]

The call to crusade assumed that an ecclesiastically led and controlled army would carry out the sacred mission. In fact, such an army never materialized. Rather, a set of militias – poorly coordinated, but highly effective – constituted the Christian fighting force that made its way against remarkable odds to the Holy Land and achieved the goal of the mission, conquering Jerusalem in the summer of 1099. However, the European response to the papal call went far beyond the organized clergy and the warrior class for which it was initially intended. Popular preachers

---

[13] The most basic depiction of the bloodbath in Jerusalem is that of the *Gesta Francorum*, which speaks of "such a massacre that our men were wading up to their ankles in blood" – *Gesta Francorum et Aliorum Hierosolimitanorum*.

absorbed and distorted the papal call and disseminated it in ways that can no longer be reconstructed, but that were clearly potent. Through these preachers, a wide swath of the European population embraced with intense enthusiasm the spiritual-military undertaking. The thinking of the audiences influenced by this preaching is extremely difficult to reconstruct and obviously included elements that would have been utterly unacceptable to Pope Urban II and his court.

In the Rhineland area, where in any case papal influence was weak, a range of anti-Jewish behaviors emerged. These behaviors included exploiting Jewish fears to extort funds, despoiling Jewish property, blaspheming and destroying Jewish *sancta*, randomly assaulting individual Jews, and attacking in organized fashion Jewish communities in their entirety. Those responsible for these behaviors included individual crusaders, individual burghers, ad hoc coalitions of crusaders and burghers, and organized crusader militias. Organized forces perpetrated the most serious violence, which resulted in the nearly total destruction of three major Rhineland Jewish communities, those of Worms, Mainz, and Cologne, during the spring months of 1096.[14]

For these organized assaults, sources emanating from both the Jewish and Christian sides provide invaluable information. The Christian sources tell us briefly but directly that the popular crusading militias saw the elimination of Jews as a religious obligation, directly linked to the crusading enterprise itself.[15] The Jewish chroniclers corroborate this information. The earliest of the Jewish narratives informs us in fuller form that, as the German crusading bands began to coalesce, "they circulated a report [indicating] that anyone who kills a single Jew will have all his sins absolved."[16] Now, absolution of sin was in fact a reward for participation in the sacred endeavor. The ecclesiastical leadership never suggested, however, that killing Jews would entail such a reward, but the popular militias adumbrated such an illegitimate view, making killing Jews an integral element in the enterprise.

Both the Jewish and Christian narratives give us a sense of the underlying thinking that animated this anti-Jewish turn in the thinking of the popular bands. A number of the narratives report a recurrent anti-Jewish

---

[14] For full treatment, see Chazan, *European Jewry and the First Crusade*.
[15] See the discussion of these Christian sources in ibid., 65–66.
[16] Ibid., 226.

slogan invoked by the popular crusaders. The version recounted in the oldest of the Jewish narratives goes as follows:

We take our lives in our hands in order to kill and to subjugate all those kingdoms that do not believe in the Crucified. How much more so [should we kill and subjugate] the Jews, who murdered and crucified him.[17]

This reported slogan diverged from the official call to the crusade in numerous ways. The pope clearly did not set in motion a campaign to "to kill and to subjugate all those kingdoms that do not believe in the Crucified." The crusade was a far more focused undertaking, aimed at conquering Jerusalem and the Holy Sepulcher. More pertinent to our interests, it is likewise obvious that the *a fortiori* argument moving from those who do not believe in Jesus to the more heinous Jews who were responsible for his death would have been resolutely rejected by the papal court and the established Church leadership. The illegitimacy of the slogan is patent, but its emotional impact was powerful.

It seems clear that there was more stimulating the anti-Jewish thinking than the simple and direct notion of taking vengeance on enemies – general and Jewish – as potent as that might have been. Since the enterprise centered on imagery of Jerusalem and the Holy Sepulcher, these powerful symbols brought to the fore recollections of the Crucifixion, which further heightened the focus on Jews, who in the Christian view had made the Holy Sepulcher the sacred shrine that it was. The combination of the notion of crusading as warfare against Christianity's diverse enemies and the recollections of the Holy Sepulcher and thus the Crucifixion stirred the exhilarated popular crusaders to acts that would have been condemned by the official Church and that were generally criticized by the Christian chroniclers who depicted them.

In fact, there was yet one more factor at play, a factor that is exceedingly difficult to track. While we have not a shred of evidence from the exhilarated popular militias themselves, the evidence provided by their detractors – both Jewish and Christian – suggests that there was considerable millennial hysteria among these bands. This millenarianism seems to have resulted in the desire to wipe out the Jewish communities encountered in their entirety. The earliest of the Hebrew narratives

[17] Ibid., 225.

describes the thinking that set in motion the assault on Worms Jewry in the following terms: "Behold the time has come to avenge him who was crucified, whom their ancestor slew. Now let not a remnant or a residue escape, even an infant or a suckling in the cradle."[18] Indeed, what is striking in the assaults of 1096 is the thoroughness of the effort to destroy the Jewish communities of Worms, Mainz, and Cologne and the success of that effort.[19]

While the destruction of these Jewish communities is lamentable, the violence associated with the First Crusade was limited in its geographic and temporal dimensions. There is no real evidence of anti-Jewish violence all across southern Europe, which then housed the largest Jewish communities in western Christendom. In the north, the serious outbreaks were limited to the Rhineland only.[20] While some modern observers have projected 1096 as a wide-ranging calamity and as a decisive turning point in the history of medieval Jewry, such a perception is highly exaggerated. The tragedy was localized, and those communities destroyed in 1096 quickly rebuilt themselves. Even in northern Europe where the massacres took place, 1096 did not slow the trajectory of ongoing Jewish growth and development, which was maintained at a rapid pace all through the succeeding century and a half and in fact continued down through the end of the medieval period.

Once the leaders of the Church recognized that crusading might generate anti-Jewish thinking and illegitimate anti-Jewish violence, they took energetic steps to obviate repetition of the 1096 slaughter. Aided by concerned secular authorities and the Jews themselves, Church leaders were successful in forestalling serious anti-Jewish outbreaks during the major crusades of the twelfth and thirteenth centuries. To be sure, Jewish observers maintained the rhetoric of disaster, which has been regularly repeated by modern historians as well, but the reality of disaster did not recur. Ephraim of Bonn, eyewitness as a youngster to the events of the Second Crusade, penned a narrative account of the events of the 1140s, utilizing much the same rhetoric employed by the Jewish chroniclers of 1096. What Ephraim depicts, however, is by no means a repetition of the destruction associated with the First Crusade in the Rhineland; rather,

---

[18] Ibid., 228.
[19] Ibid., chapter 3, and idem, "'Let Not a Residue nor a Remnant," 289–313.
[20] There were only minor incidents elsewhere.

he portrays only sporadic and random loss of Jewish life. A coalition of ecclesiastical leaders, secular authorities, and Jews took vigorous steps to forestall anything like the 1096 loss of Jewish life in the major Rhineland cities.[21]

More realistically, what crusading did was to heighten the sense of the coherence of medieval western Christendom. Pope Urban II intended his focus on external danger to bring together the diverse and fractious elements of the Christian population within western Christendom, and crusading against the Muslim foe certainly did that. This achievement, so positive from the Christian perspective, augmented the perception of the Jews as a non-Christian element – often the only non-Christian element – in the population. Even more so, the focus on a world full of foes reinforced the sense of Jews as enemies, traditionally viewed as historical enemies but with the potential to be perceived as contemporary enemies as well.[22]

Pope Alexander II back in the middle of the eleventh century drew an important distinction between the Saracens, whose contemporary enmity allegedly necessitated a Christian military offensive against them, and the Jews who purportedly evinced no such contemporary enmity. As the Second Crusade began to organize and the first signs of anti-Jewish agitation appeared, the chief spiritual leader of the new enterprise – Bernard of Clairvaux – appended to his regular crusading epistle a paragraph on anti-Jewish violence, which he vigorously denounced and categorically prohibited. Bernard set forth an array of arguments to make his point. His closing claim drew a distinction similar to that drawn by Pope Alexander II between Muslims and Jews. Bernard argued that the former have "begun to attack us" and thus had to be met with force. The Jews, on the other hand, were according to Bernard living peacefully, which meant to him that they must be spared from any Christian aggression.[23]

The important abbot of Cluny, Peter the Venerable, challenged the view set forth by Pope Alexander II and Bernard of Clairvaux in a well-known letter written to the king of France on the eve of the Second

---

[21] For an English translation of Ephraim of Bonn's narrative, see Shlomo Eidelberg, trans., *The Jews and the Crusaders*, 121–33.

[22] See Jonathan Riley-Smith, *The Crusades, Christianity, and Islam*, 25–27.

[23] Chazan, *Church, State, and Jew*, 101–4.

Crusade. Peter began by clearly disavowing anti-Jewish violence, adducing the traditional arguments we have already seen. He did not, however, agree with the assessment of Pope Alexander II and Bernard of Clairvaux that Jews in medieval western Christendom were living quietly as docile subjects. According to Peter the Venerable, the Jews of ancient Jerusalem exhibited profound opposition to Jesus, and the descendants of these Jerusalem Jews maintained that virulent opposition, for example through ongoing blasphemy of Christianity and its *sancta*. At every turn, according to Peter, Jews took advantage of opportunities to curse and mistreat the sacred symbols of the majority faith.[24]

Peter the Venerable was by no means alone in his perception of contemporary Jewish opposition to Christianity – allegedly expressed vigorously and viciously – and this perception was undoubtedly true to a significant extent. The medieval centuries were a period of intense religiosity and religious particularism. The Church strove energetically to foster the religious identity of the Christian majority, and it did so in positive terms on the one hand and by attacking the alternatives – Judaism and Islam – on the other. Ecclesiastical leaders vilified Judaism and Islam at every turn and in the most abusive terms. Jews were, as we have seen, prohibited from public disparagement of the ruling faith, and to do so would have been to court serious danger. Nonetheless, within the confines of their own community medieval Jews expressed their contempt for the Christian alternative with considerable vehemence. The polemical literature of the Jews of medieval Christian Europe – intended for internal Jewish consumption only – is replete with slashing critiques of Christianity.[25] Clearly, however, Jewish indictments of Christianity went far beyond the intellectual thrusts of medieval Jewish polemicists and involved passionately held convictions and occasional radical behaviors.[26]

---

[24] For a translation of the critical section of this important letter, see Robert Chazan, *Medieval Stereotypes and Modern Antisemitism*, 49. For incisive discussion of Peter the Venerable and his views of the Jews, see Iogna-Prat, *Order and Exclusion*, chapter 10. For a contrast of Bernard of Clairvaux and Peter the Venerable, see Chazan, *Medieval Stereotypes and Modern Antisemitism*, 41–52.

[25] For the intellectual critiques, see Chazan, *Fashioning Jewish Identity in Medieval Western Christendom*, chaps. 13 and 14.

[26] The research of Elliott Horowitz shows that the Jewish opposition occasionally expressed itself in radical behaviors. See his "The Jews and the Cross in the Middle Ages," 114–31, and his *Reckless Rites: Purim and the Legacy of Jewish Violence*.

To this extent, Peter the Venerable was in all likelihood correct in his assessment of active but internally directed Jewish opposition to Christianity. Almost a century after he leveled his charge of ongoing Jewish blasphemy, a convert from Judaism to Christianity named Nicholas Donin argued before the court of Pope Gregory IX that the authoritative rabbinic literature of the Jews included blasphemous statements about Jesus and Mary and that this literature condoned, indeed demanded hostile behaviors toward Christians. The allegations were serious and received an attentive hearing at the papal court.

The testing of Donin's allegations took place in the great ecclesiastical and academic center of Paris. There, Nicholas Donin led a team that translated the Hebrew and Aramaic of the Talmud into Latin and organized the translated segments of the Talmud into a series of damning indictments. The Paris court condemned the Talmud, which resulted in a massive burning of Talmud manuscripts and prohibition of the Talmud text in its entirety. Jewish intercession with Pope Innocent IV resulted in an alternative stance toward the Talmud text, which was censorship.[27] For our purposes, what is key is reinforcement of the perception advanced by Peter the Venerable that the Jews of Christian Europe were intense and vocal in their denigration of Christianity.

For popular thinking, this broad perception of Jewish hostility toward Christianity and Christians did not require the mid-thirteenth-century translation of rabbinic materials into Latin. Long before the appearance of Nicholas Donin, segments of the broad Christian populace had concluded that Jews were implacably hostile to Christianity and Christians. This conclusion involved projection of Jewish contempt for Christianity and its symbols; it also involved projection of Jewish hatred for Christians as well. This latter projection transformed Jews – in the eyes of some – into an immediate danger on the European scene.

In the mid-1140s – precisely the point at which the Second Crusade was being generated, Christian burghers in the German town of Wurzburg and in the English town of Norwich became convinced that a corpse discovered in their vicinity reflected Jewish murder of a Christian neighbor – in the former case an adult male and in the latter case a beloved youngster. In both cases, those convinced of Jewish culpability assumed that

---

[27] See Chapter 7.

the motivation for murder lay simply with Jewish hatred of Christians. This conclusion transformed the two from unfortunate victims of random violence into targets of Jewish religious hatred and thus Christian martyrs. To be sure, there was considerable discord over these murders. Not all Christians in Wurzburg and Norwich believed that Jews were the culprits in these crimes. The bishop of Wurzburg opposed vigorously the notion of Jewish culpability and Christian martyrdom. In Norwich, there was considerable disagreement over the crime, with some burghers assuming Jewish guilt and Christian martyrdom and others ranged in opposition.[28]

As the Norwich cult of the purported Saint William developed, a late-arriving cleric – Thomas of Monmouth – undertook to articulate the case for the sainthood of William. He did so by pointing in three directions: the sweet childhood of the lad, the miracles produced at his grave, and – most important of all – his death at the hands of Jews moved simply by hatred of him as a Christian. In order to drive home his point most effectively, Thomas of Monmouth alleged that there was eyewitness testimony to the details of the death of the young lad. The Jews of Norwich – Thomas claimed – viciously crucified the sweet youngster William. This culminating embellishment to the case for sainthood laid out by Thomas served to identify William with his Savior in an immediate way. It also served to link the purported Jewish behaviors in ancient Jerusalem with Jewish behaviors in twelfth-century Norwich.[29] In this view, Jews were – as suggested by Peter the Venerable – far more than simply ancient foes of Christianity and Christians; they were in fact lethal contemporary enemies of the Christian population of medieval Europe.

The allegation of ritual murder via crucifixion represented a major deterioration in the imagery of the Jews of medieval western Christendom, centering around the Easter period and celebration. Before long, the Easter-related allegation gave way to a Passover-related charge as well. By the 1230s, European Christians advanced the claim that Jews murder Christian youngsters in a different way and for alternative

---

[28] On both these incidents, see Chazan, *Medieval Stereotypes and Modern Antisemitism*, 58–70.

[29] Note the classic article by Gavin I. Langmuir, "Thomas of Monmouth: Detector of Ritual Murder," 822–46.

purposes. No longer did the Crucifixion occupy center stage; rather, it was alleged that the ritual needs of the holiday of Passover involved Christian blood. Jews purportedly killed Christian youngsters in order to provide the Christian blood necessary for fulfillment of these ritual obligations. For reasons that are not all that clear, the blood libel outlasted the ritual murder allegation in time and exceeded it in intensity.[30]

By the end of the thirteenth century, yet another variant on the theme of Jewish malevolence and criminality surfaced. In this new charge, Christians alleged that Jews vented their historic and contemporary hostility on Christianity via assaults on the host wafer, believed to be transubstantiated into the body of Christ. This charge first surfaced in Paris in 1290, where – it was claimed – a Jewish moneylender obtained a host wafer by bribing a Christian client and then subjected the wafer to all manner of violent mistreatment. Miraculously, the wafer survived the violence. Through a statement by the Jew's son to a passerby, the incident became known, and the authorities arrested the Jew and his family. While the rest of the family converted, convinced by the miracle of the host, the authorities condemned and burned the Jew himself. With papal blessing, a Parisian burgher transformed the site of the atrocity *cum* miracle into a shrine. Paris thus added yet another potent stereotype of Jewish hatred and malevolence to the expanding European repertoire.[31]

The last of the major motifs of Jewish hatred and malevolence involved the perception that Jewish enmity led to the poisoning of the wells of Europe and thus to the spread of the bubonic plague. While this motif made a brief appearance in 1096, it burst into prominence during the mid-fourteenth-century crisis of the Black Death.[32] The horrendous nature of the plague, which carried away somewhere between one-quarter and one-third of the population of western Christendom, occasioned a frantic effort at comprehension and self-protection, which necessarily included a search for culprits. Given the backdrop of two centuries of widespread perception of Jews as steeped in hatred of Christianity and Christians that was so intense as to occasion the taking of Christian lives, it is hardly surprising that many all across Europe identified Jews as those

[30] Chazan, *Medieval Stereotypes and Modern Antisemitism*, 70–73.
[31] See the full study of Miri Rubin, *Gentile Tales*.
[32] For the 1096 allegation, see Chazan, *European Jewry and the First Crusade*, 228.

responsible for the disaster that was costing the lives of so many European Christians.[33]

Thus, from the twelfth through the fourteenth centuries, the populace of Christian Europe adumbrated a series of allegations of Jewish hatred and Jewish malevolence. The spectrum of victims of this purported hatred was broad, ranging from the *sancta* of Christianity – especially the host wafer – through individual Christians – especially youngsters – and on to masses of Christians dying of the bubonic plague. These perceptions transformed the Jews from a theologically significant minority into a mortal danger, against which the Christian majority had to organize itself in self-defense.

The Christian populace of Europe was divided in its absorption of these stereotypes. Obviously, many medieval Christians accepted them; equally obviously, many medieval Christians did not. By and large, the duly constituted authorities of church and state were among the rejecters. The ecclesiastical leadership of medieval western Christendom regularly and authoritatively dismissed the allegations in specific cases and more broadly in vigorous general papal statements. Papal disavowal of the allegation of Jewish use of Christian blood for Passover ritual was especially strong, as was rejection of the notion that Jewish well-poisoning was at the core of the loss of life from the bubonic plague.[34] To be sure, papal support for the Parisian shrine dedicated to the desecration and miraculous survival of the 1290 host wafer did much to enhance the hold of that particular allegation on the popular imagination.[35]

The secular authorities were no less assiduous in rejecting the proliferating allegations. Perhaps the most dramatic instance of dismissal of the blood libel was that of Emperor Frederick II. Frederick did more than simply proclaim his disbelief. He empaneled an expert commission composed of converts from Judaism to Christianity, who had intimate knowledge of Jewish belief and practice and could by no means be suspected of sympathy for the faith and community they had abandoned.

---

[33] On the Black Death, see Philip Ziegler, *The Black Death*, and John Kelly, *The Great Mortality*. Both books treat at length the persecution of Jews. For useful collections of documents on the Black Death, see Rosemary Horrox, ed. and trans., *The Black Death*, and John Aberth, *The Black Death*.

[34] For the former, see Grayzel, *The Church and the Jews*, 1:268–71, #116; for the latter, see Horrox, *The Black Death*, 221–22, #73, and Aberth, *The Black Death*, 158–59, #40.

[35] Grayzel, *The Church and the Jews*, 2:196–97, #71.

When this commission concluded that Jewish use of Christian blood was utterly unthinkable, Frederick was able to announce conclusively that the charge was baseless and that, in practice, it would never gain a hearing in the imperial courts.[36]

The pronouncements of the ecclesiastical and secular authorities carried some weight with elements in the Christian populace. However – not surprisingly – many dismissed the rejections, convinced that historic Jewish enmity, which was a core teaching of Christianity, readily transformed into contemporary Jewish hatred of Christians and into unspeakable anti-Christian behaviors. More important than pronouncements were the actual behaviors of the authorities of church and state, especially the latter. In fact, the record of the authorities, at least during the twelfth and most of the thirteenth centuries, was regularly protective. The initial incidents of projection of Jews as contemporary enemies during the mid-1140s were immediately indicative. In Wurzburg, the bishop – in an unpopular move – rejected publicly the allegation and assisted with the burial of the victims of the violence.[37] In Norwich, where the issue of Jewish guilt survived much more vigorously through the cult erected to the purportedly martyred lad William, the English authorities were resolute in their dismissal of all efforts to bring the Jews of Norwich to judgment. So far as is known, there was no physical violence perpetrated against these Jews in the wake of the allegation.

Especially instructive is the incident at Blois that took place in 1171. There, a major northern French baron for complex reasons supported the allegation that Jews murder Christian youngsters. Count Theobald of Blois subjected the Christian witness of the alleged Jewish crime to the outmoded judicial procedure of trial by ordeal. When the Christian witness survived the ordeal, the count pronounced the Jews guilty and had thirty or more executed. This was a breathtaking breach of the normally protective posture of the twelfth-century secular authorities. In the wake of this dangerous precedent, the Jews of northern France banded together and approached major ecclesiastical and secular figures, including the archbishop of Sens (a brother of Count Theobald), the count of Champagne (another brother), and King Louis VII (a brother-in-law).

36 Chazan, *Church, State, and Jew*, 124–26.
37 Eidelberg, *The Jews and the Crusaders*, 127–28.

All these important figures rejected the murder allegation and castigated their relative for his misdeed. The stance of the medieval authorities was generally that of the king of France, the count of Champagne, and the archbishop of Sens.[38]

Clearly, governmental weakness or breakdown posed significant danger to the Jews of medieval western Christendom. At points of governmental breakdown, the power to intercede effectively against popular passions was much reduced, and Jews thus lay exposed to outbreaks of popular violence. While governments were by and large augmenting their power all across Christian Europe during the twelfth and thirteenth centuries, the fourteenth century – it is widely agreed – constituted a period of general retrogression in western Christendom, with depopulation, economic downturn, and diminution of governmental authority observable everywhere. These were precisely the conditions that would foster augmented hostility toward the Jewish minority, as everyone in society felt threatened by the broad retrogression, and the authorities would be less effective or often ineffective in countering this augmented hostility. During the fourteenth century, the Jews of Europe lost the security that had essentially been their lot from the onset of European vitalization in the late tenth and early eleventh centuries.

Wide-ranging and massive Jewish loss of life took place all across western Christendom from the closing years of the thirteenth century down through the closing years of the fourteenth century. This loss of Jewish life is apparent all across the older areas of Jewish settlement in the south and the newer areas of Jewish settlement in the north. By this time, the Jews of England had been expelled, and the Jewish presence in northern France had been radically diminished. Thus, the center of Jewish population in the north was the German lands, where anti-Jewish violence became endemic, as societal animosity intensified and the power of the authorities to intercede diminished. Beginning in the 1290s and then in the 1330s and once more in the 1340s and 1350s, the Jews of the Germanic lands were subjected to waves of violence, which were wide-ranging and protracted.[39] These persecutions stimulated Jewish

---

[38] Chazan, "The Blois Incident of 1171."

[39] See the valuable survey by Muller, "*Erez gezerah* – 'Land of Persecution.'" Note especially Map 18, pp. 252–53, and the other maps cited, all of which give a graphic sense of the range of the persecutions.

population movement in the direction of the developing areas of eastern Europe.[40]

The same pattern of extensive and recurrent anti-Jewish violence is evident in the south as well. There were outbreaks in the 1320s and in the late 1340s and early 1350s as a result of the Black Death.[41] The culminating violence of this period in the south took place in 1391, when anti-Jewish assaults swept across the entire peninsula, with devastating results. However, just as the features of Jewish life in medieval western Christendom should not be projected as the fundamental characteristics of exilic Jewish existence over the ages, so too the realities of the grim fourteenth century should not be taken to characterize the entire experience of Jews in Europe from 1000 through 1500. Prior to the fourteenth century, Jews enjoyed a relatively high level of effective protection, and relative security was reestablished in the fifteenth century, especially on the Iberian peninsula, where such terrible destruction had taken place.[42]

Medieval western Christendom was a setting rife with anti-Jewish sentiment that had the potential to escalate into anti-Jewish violence. The anti-Jewish sentiment flowed from traditional Church teachings, although ecclesiastical leadership made strenuous efforts to keep the impact of these teachings within bounds. The Church demeaned Judaism and Jews, in order to protect its flock from any potential Jewish influence on Christian behavior and belief. Vilification of Judaism pointed inevitably back to first-century Jerusalem and the opposition of its leaders to Jesus. Christians were to be reinforced in their conviction of Jewish error and subsequent punishment; Christians were not to proceed beyond these convictions into anti-Jewish actions, based on the enmity of first-century Jewish leaders to Jesus. Ecclesiastical leaders were – in conjunction with their secular counterparts – quite successful in minimizing anti-Jewish violence flowing directly from these traditional teachings.

What the Church could not control was the projection of Jewish enmity from first-century Jerusalem into medieval Europe. To the extent that this occurred, the Jews shifted from a theologically errant people into an immediate societal and personal danger. Here, the Church notion of

[40] See Chapter 5.
[41] On the violence of the 1320s, see the important study of David Nirenberg, *Communities of Violence*. On the violence associated with the Back Death, see note 32.
[42] See Mark D. Meyerson, *A Jewish Renaissance in Fifteenth-Century Spain*.

divine punishment of Jews and the illegitimacy of human anti-Jewish activity fell by the wayside. Christians who felt threatened by what was projected as contemporary Jewish enmity and anti-Christian violence felt the need to defend themselves against the Jewish danger, and they did so.

Serious socioeconomic resentment and concern added to this fear of medieval Jews as a societal and personal danger. Since Jews were unable to achieve economic diversification in medieval Europe, they gravitated to economically useful pioneering roles, but these roles – as helpful as they might have been to the general economy – stirred deep resentments, both on the part of those adversely affected in a direct way and on the part of onlookers as well. In fact, many in European society perceived these pioneering roles as yet another vehicle utilized by the Jews in their hostility toward Christian society and their determination to inflict harm upon it.

These perceptions of contemporary physical and economic danger emanating from the Jews of Europe aroused deep fear and consequent hatred. At points of crisis, the fear and hatred of course intensified, while the power of the secular authorities to manage the heightened anxiety diminished. The result was the potential for considerable violence, and that potential was recurrently actualized, especially during the very late thirteenth century and the fourteenth century, a period widely acknowledged as an epoch of ongoing disasters natural and man-made, wide-ranging decline of political authority, and augmented popular violence in general. After more than three hundred years of steady demographic and economic expansion and enhanced political and cultural achievement, the fourteenth century constituted a major setback to European civilization.

Once again, however, it is important not to exaggerate the range of this fourteenth-century violence. Just as the crusade-related persecution was limited in scope, so too was the more potent violence associated with the sense of the contemporary dangers Jews presented to life and safety of their Christians neighbors. The devastation in the German lands during the closing decades of the thirteenth century and the opening decades of the fourteenth century was real and widespread, as was likewise true for the southern European violence of the 1320s. The violence of the 1340s was even more devastating in that it was pan-European, affecting Jews throughout Christian Europe. The culminating violence of the 1390s was again localized, but did enormous damage to the Jewish communities of the Iberian peninsula. These episodes of significant anti-Jewish violence should not, however, give rise to a pervasive sense of medieval European Jews living their lives under the threat of daily danger to life and limb. These periods of wide-ranging anti-Jewish violence represent the exception rather than the rule for medieval Jews. In between these explosions of violence, Jews could and did live normal lives. Only in this way can we understand the ongoing Jewish decisions to remain in western Christendom and the capacity to foster a burgeoning Jewish population and a rich Jewish culture in medieval Europe.

NORMAL HUMAN RELATIONS

The sources for everyday Jewish life in medieval western Christendom – sources that might include evidence of normal human relations between Jews and their non-Jewish neighbors – are relatively limited. During this period (as now), there was a strong human tendency to highlight the aberrant and the violent, rather than to depict the normal and placid. While the lack of sources and the tendency to highlight the violent make the portrayal of comfortable human relations between the Jews of medieval Christian Europe and their non-Jewish contemporaries difficult to achieve, it is nonetheless possible through careful reading to glean considerable evidence of peaceful interactions, along with the disruptive and destructive.

Prior to looking at this limited but significant evidence, it is important to note the extent to which Jews were integrated into medieval western Christendom. While there were strenuous efforts on the part of both the Christian and Jewish religious leadership to maintain strictly the boundaries between the two communities, there was much that brought Christians and Jews into intimate daily contact.[43] First of all, the Jews of medieval Christian Europe spoke the language of the majority environments in which they lived. While there is often a projection onto medieval western Christendom of the later linguistic realities in eastern Europe, where Jews developed their own language culture, in medieval Christian

---

[43] See the pathbreaking study of Jacob Katz, *Exclusiveness and Tolerance*.

Europe Jews regularly utilized the language of their surroundings for everyday communication.[44]

In fact, the rapid loss of prior language culture was a striking feature of Jewish life in eleventh- and twelfth-century Europe. In those areas of southern Europe conquered by the Christian forces descending from the north, the prior language culture of Arabic disappeared rather quickly, necessitating a massive translation effort to assure the availability of some of the Jewish masterpieces created in Arabic. By the thirteenth century, there was little command of Arabic among the Jews of the Iberian peninsula, even within the intelligentsia. Rather, the Jews adapted themselves to the dual language culture of their environment, speaking the local vernacular for oral communication and paralleling the majority use of Latin for literary purposes by using Hebrew for Jewish literary creativity.

The situation was much the same in the north. There, the immigrating Jews fairly quickly abandoned the languages with which they came to northern Europe in favor of a similar combination – the local vernacular for oral communication and Hebrew for written communication. The great eleventh-century Jewish exegete Solomon ben Isaac of Troyes (Rashi) employed the local northern French dialect for explicating difficult Hebrew and Aramaic terms in his monumental commentaries on both the Bible and the Talmud. Since Rashi represents a fairly early stage in the history of northern French Jewry, his absorption of the French dialect of his surroundings is especially telling. As a result of this linguistic integration, the Jews of medieval western Christendom could communicate easily and freely with their Christian neighbors.

Jews and their Christian neighbors lived contiguously as well. It is true that Jews tended to live in somewhat separate neighborhoods. In this, they were very much like many other subgroups on the medieval European scene, which clustered in their own neighborhoods. Jewish clustering in such neighborhoods is amply documented for all sectors of medieval Europe. However, the towns of medieval western Christendom were generally small, so that real isolation was simply not possible. Indeed, the limitations on Jewish economic activity forced restless movement

---

[44] For more on the imposition of late-medieval- and early-modern eastern European paradigms onto Jewish life in medieval western Christendom, see Chapter 9.

from the largest towns toward smaller urban areas. These smaller urban enclaves fostered enhanced contact between Jews and their Christian contemporaries. Moreover, the Jewish neighborhoods – like the parallel clusters of other groups – were by no means exclusively Jewish. The thirteenth-century Church's augmented insistence on segregation of Jews reflects nicely the reality of extensive and regular physical contact between Jews and their Christian neighbors in medieval Europe.

Beyond the physical contiguity, the economic circumstances of the Jews set the conditions for extensive contact as well. As noted by Jacob Katz, the limited economic repertoire of the Jews – particularly in the north but increasingly in the south as well – meant that Jews were not doing business with fellow-Jews in self-imposed economic segregation. Rather, Jews were providing economic services to the non-Jewish population and coming in regular contact with their non-Jewish clients. At the same time, since Jews were limited in their economic pursuits, they in turn depended on non-Jews for a host of services. The result of all this was constant contact in the economic sphere, with Jews serving as both purveyors of services and recipients of services at the same time, resulting once more in considerable Jewish–non-Jewish contact.[45]

Especially noteworthy is the constant Church concern with Christians working in Jewish homes from the late twelfth century on. Prohibited vigorously in the Second Lateran Council of 1179, Christians working in Jewish homes seems to have remained a reality during the ensuing centuries, as evidenced by the persistent ecclesiastical complaints on the subject. The fear of Church leaders was that intimate daily contact would lead to religious influence by the Jews on their Christian employees. For our purposes, the reality of ongoing Christian presence in Jewish homes suggests once more considerable daily contact, which would translate into normal and normally amicable contact between Jews and at least some Christian neighbors.

Finally, there is considerable evidence that Jews were greatly influenced by everyday styles in such matters as clothing, making them visually indistinguishable from their Christian neighbors. The artistic relics from our period – preeminently illuminated manuscripts – show Jews dressed no differently from their Christian neighbors, except of course for the

---

[45] Katz, *Exclusiveness and Tolerance*, chapter 3.

ecclesiastically mandated distinguishing garb, generally in the form of badges or hats. Beginning with the Fourth Lateran Council of 1215, the Church made strenuous efforts to create readily identifiable distinctions between the Jews and their Christian contemporaries. The language of the 1215 decree is noteworthy:

Whereas in certain provinces of the Church the difference in their clothes sets Jews and Saracens apart from Christians, in certain other lands there has arisen such confusion that no differences are noticeable. Thus it sometimes happens that, by mistake, Christians have intercourse with Jewish or Saracen women and Jews or Saracens with Christian women.[46]

The decree suggests that Jews in many sectors of medieval Europe were indistinguishable from their Christian neighbors, leading to the closest kind of intimacy. To focus for the moment on the first element, the fact that Jews were indistinguishable from Christians set the stage for considerable human contact. The specific focus of the decree on sexual intimacy suggests the most intense human contact.

Medieval literary sources – like modern literary sources – tended to highlight the disruptive and the violent and to disregard the normal and the peaceful. The kind of documentation that would provide evidence of the mundane is largely missing for our period. For most of the medieval centuries, we lack diaries and personal letters that would indicate a casual meeting or chat between Jews and Christians. Nonetheless, here and there the curtain is lifted on the everyday and the banal, both in the south and in the north. Once again, we might well anticipate that there would be more comfortable contact in the south – where Jewish settlement was old and well established – than in the north, where the sense of Jews as newcomers was strong. Nonetheless, evidence remains from both spheres of Jewish life.

From the south, we recall the case of the Jewish polemicist Jacob ben Reuben. Jacob suffered exile from his hometown, for reasons that are not clear. He found refuge in a town that may have been in a Christian area of Spain, where he developed a close relationship with a major figure, whom he describes as "one of the leading citizens of the town and one of the learned of the generation – he was a priest expert in logic and sophisticated in esoteric wisdom." It seems clear that Jacob

---

[46] Grayzel, *The Church and the Jews in the XIIIth Century*, 1:309, #X.

derived great benefit from this relationship. To be sure, Jacob responded to the challenge of the relationship to pen his important polemical work, *Milhamot ha-Shem*. Yet one of the striking characteristics of this early polemical tract is that the Christian protagonist is a clever and feisty figure, regularly accorded the opportunity to respond to Jewish claims and to rebut them. While the Jewish view always wins out in the end, the battle is a serious and protracted one, which seems to reflect the closeness and intensity of the relationship between Jacob and his mentor.[47]

The case of Bondavid of Marseilles, admirably reconstructed and analyzed by Joseph Shatzmiller, provides us from an entirely different domain with evidence of amicable relations between Jews and their Christian neighbors.[48] We have noted earlier the willingness of a number of Christian witnesses to appear in court and to testify to Bondavid's remarkable generosity. This willingness and this praise for the Jewish moneylender suggest from the Christian side extremely warm and positive feelings. We recall one testimony to Bondavid's generosity that concludes with the witness's sense that he did not believe "that there is [one] more righteous than he [than Bondavid] in the whole world."[49]

At the same time, the generosity attested by the Christian witnesses suggests parallel human feelings from the Jewish side as well. One of the witnesses told the story of a woman who came to Bondavid's house and repaid the loan she had taken. The witness then reported the following in the wake of the repayment:

Bondavid asked her: "Tell me, mother, how do you live, and what profession do you have?"

She answered" "Know, Sir, that I have nothing to live from if not the labor and toil of my husband."

When Bondavid heard it and considered her poverty, he gave back to the woman a large quantity of money.[50]

This and similar tales of Bondavid's generosity suggest from the side of the Jew a warm and caring relationship with Christian clients.

[47] Chazan, *Fashioning of Jewish Identity*, 98–103.
[48] Shatzmiller, *Shylock Reconsidered*.
[49] Ibid., 118.
[50] Ibid., 114.

While we lack this notarial evidence of everyday contact and warmth from the northern areas of Europe, precisely some of the narratives that detail persecution – when read carefully – offer telling evidence that, prior to the outbreak of violence, Jews and their Christian neighbors lived amicably with one another. Curiously, some of our best evidence of normal Christian-Jewish relations comes from the narratives that detail the first major outbreak of popular anti-Jewish violence in western Christendom in 1096.

The oldest of the Hebrew narratives, much concerned with depicting the early evolution of the crusade and its related anti-Jewish violence, tells the story of the arrival in Mainz of a band of French popular crusaders, led by a woman and her specially endowed goose. As they passed through town, these crusaders taunted the Jews. Pointing to their divine assistance in the form of the goose, this band and their burgher sympathizers challenged the Jews,

saying to us: "Where is your source of security?" How will you be saved? Behold the wonders that the Crucified does for us!"

Then all of them came with swords and spears to destroy us. Some of the burghers came and would not allow them [to do so]. At that time, they stood... and killed along the Rhine River, until they [the sympathetic burghers] killed one of the crusaders.[51]

This is rather remarkable testimony to the warm and caring relationships that existed in Mainz prior to the outbreak of the crusade-related hostilities.

The incident at Wurzburg in 1147 reveals Christian willingness to assist a particular Jewess in mortal distress. As noted earlier, the discovery of a corpse led to the allegation that Jews had murdered the victim out of their fundamental hatred of Christianity and Christians. This charge resulted in the killing of more than twenty Jews. Mentioned specifically is "a Jewish lad, a fine student, Simon ben Isaac," who was grievously wounded, but survived his wounds and lived for a year. The story of Simon's sister is told in greater detail.

They [the Christian attackers] took his sister to church in order to baptize her, but she sanctified the Name and spit on the cross. They then struck her

---

[51] Chazan, *European Jewry and the First Crusade*, 233.

with stones and fist, for they do not bring swords into church. However, she did not die – she fell down there among them and pretended to be dead. They continued to smite her and to burn her in order to know whether she was dead or not. They laid her out on a marble slab, but she did not awake or move a hand or a foot. Thus she deceived them until evening, until a Christian laundrywoman came and carried her home and hid her and saved her.[52]

In the hate-filled environment that spawned the attacks on Jews in Wurzburg, a Christian laundrywoman came and rescued the young Jewish girl, in testimony to warm and supportive human feelings.

These positive human feelings emerge even more strikingly in the patterns of Jewish behaviors in the face of the utterly unexpected anti-Jewish violence of 1096. Regularly, the Jewish chroniclers portray the Jews of the Rhineland turning in one of two directions. The first direction, which we would fully anticipate given the prior discussion of the role of the authorities of medieval Europe, was to the duly constituted authorities both ecclesiastical and secular. What is unexpected, however, is the extent to which Jews facing mortal danger fled to Christian neighbors in anticipation of genuine caring and effective protection. Thus, for example, the Jews of Worms, hearing of the incipient violence in nearby Speyer, split up into two cohorts, with one turning to the local bishop and the other seeking safety with Christian neighbors. These were Jews terrified for their lives and the lives of loved ones, and they had sufficient conviction of genuinely caring concern on the part of Christian neighbors to entrust their lives to these neighbors. To be sure, the burghers of Worms ultimately failed their Jewish friends.[53] On the other hand, the Jews of Cologne exhibited the same trust, and in this instance the confidence proved reasonable. The Jews of Cologne survived the initial threat of violence, until they could be moved out of town by the archbishop in what turned out to be a failed attempt to save them.[54] Crucial for our purposes is the Jewish assumption of genuine caring and protection on the part of Christian peers.

In fact, in a number of cases friendly Christian associates seem to have urged Jews – out of concern for Jewish safety, rather than out of

---

[52] Eidelberg, *The Jews and the Crusaders*, 127, with modifications.
[53] Chazan, *European Jewry and the First Crusade*, 228.
[54] Ibid., 273–75.

conversionist motivation – to be baptized. The cursory description of the fate of Regensburg Jewry seems to reflect such benevolent intentions. We are briefly told the following:

Indeed, those who were in the town [obviously the Christian burghers], when the crusaders and the common folk gathered against them [the Jews], pressed them against their will and brought them to a certain river. They made the evil sign on the water – the cross – and baptized them all simultaneously in the water.[55]

The report is not altogether clear, but it seems that sympathetic Christians forced their Jewish neighbors into a formal act of baptism in order to save their lives. In fact, the author of this sketchy report notes immediate return to Judaism, further strengthening the sense of an insincere act of baptism. Thus, even the accounts of anti-Jewish violence provide us with regular hints of warmth between Jews and their northern European Christian neighbors, acts of human kindness on the part of Christians during the violence itself, and Jewish expectations of assistance – sometimes fulfilled and sometimes disappointed.

THE BACKDROP TO JEWISH–NON-JEWISH RELATIONS IN MEDIEVAL western Christendom was hardly promising. In a society increasingly organized around the Christian religious vision, the anti-Jewish motifs embedded in the Gospels inevitably set the stage for negative perceptions of Jewish neighbors. As descendants of the Jews of Jerusalem who – according to the Gospel accounts – had been responsible for the Crucifixion, the Jews of medieval Christian Europe were stigmatized *ab initio*. In addition, the Jews of the northern sectors of Europe were recent immigrants and suffered the societal resentment that is the normal lot of newcomers. The resistance spawned by the combination of traditional Christian imagery and the reluctance to accept newcomers forced Jews into constricted patterns of economic activity. While these economic activities were in fact useful to the development of medieval Christian Europe, they aroused resentment on the part of significant portions of the Christian populace.

[55] Ibid., 293.

Surely the most significant negative imagery relative to Jews was their transformation by many medieval European Christians from the descendants of the supposedly hostile Jews of Jerusalem in the first century into immediate and threatening twelfth-, thirteenth-, fourteenth-, and fifteenth-century enemies. Jews – many European Christians firmly believed – blasphemed Christianity; abused the *sancta* of the Christian faith; surreptitiously murdered unsuspecting Christians, often in cultic fashion, either by crucifying the Christian victim or by utilizing his blood for Jewish ritual purposes; and attempted to kill large numbers of Christians through well-poisoning. These negative images were no longer theological; they became part and parcel of widely shared European folklore.

The Church purveyed the teaching that the Jews of first-century Jerusalem were responsible for the Crucifixion, but it also indicated clearly that this Jewish guilt should not occasion Christian vengeance against the descendants of the Jerusalem Jews. This ecclesiastical stance was deeply rooted in Church doctrine, was regularly articulated, and was insisted upon by major Church leaders. Early in the First Crusade, the notion of Jewish guilt for the Crucifixion did spark anti-Jewish violence in the Rhineland. It is not possible to gauge the extent to which the themes of Jewish newness and Jewish economic activity in trade may have played a role in that violence as well, but the sources focus on the recollection of Jewish responsibility for the death of Jesus. In any case, the Church – once alerted to the potential for crusade-related anti-Jewish outbursts – took careful steps to forestall repetition of such outbursts.

With respect to the other sources of anti-Jewish sentiment, there was little the Church could do. While ecclesiastical leaders regularly condemned such notions as Jewish use of Christian blood and Jewish well-poisoning, the foundation of these condemnations was empirical, not theological. When the Church insisted that Jews must not be assaulted as a result of their role in the Crucifixion, the Church stance was solid and unarguable. When the Church insisted that Jews do not utilize Christian blood or poison wells, it was making an empirical observation that could readily be contested. Thus, with respect to what were the most potent of the anti-Jewish perceptions, the Church could in fact do little.

Protection of the Jews of medieval Christian Europe from actions stemming from anti-Jewish perceptions – especially the perception that Jews do harm to their Christian neighbors – fell largely to the secular authorities. These secular authorities, like the Church, regularly denounced many of the anti-Jewish canards, but they did a great deal more as well. In the first place, powerful secular authorities could and did provide a sense that they were committed to the protection of all elements in society – protection of Jews from their attackers and protection of Christians from the purported dangers emanating from Jews. More important yet, when danger did threaten, well-established and potent secular authorities could and did protect their Jewish clients. Thus, in a real sense, the fortunes of the Jews of medieval western Christendom were intimately linked to the fortunes of strong governments. When governments were strong enough to maintain law and order, Jewish life was secure, although we have already noted the potential for damage inflicted by these authorities through unconscionable exploitation of Jewish wealth and through banishment of Jews.

From the early eleventh through the end of the thirteenth century, Jewish life was relatively secure. While there was an outbreak of anti-Jewish violence in 1096, it was on balance quite limited and did not resurface during the subsequent major crusades. Toward the end of the thirteenth century, as Europe slipped into a difficult period of decline, anti-Jewish violence became endemic, first in the northern areas of Europe and subsequently in the south as well. This violence should not, however, be generalized to the entirety of Jewish experience in medieval western Christendom.

In fact, the Jews of medieval Europe lived in relative security throughout much of the period between 1000 and 1500. Despite the lack of quotidian materials that would enable us to reconstruct the everyday life of these European Jews, substantial indications remain of normal, placid, and even warm relations between Jews and their Christian contemporaries. Christians treated Jews with respect and fraternal feelings, and Jews reciprocated. The reality of placid periods and of normal human relations enables us to account for the persistence of Jews in remaining within the borders of medieval western Christendom. Were Jewish life as relentlessly oppressive as often portrayed, it is difficult to understand why Jews should have opted to stay in a totally hostile environment. Finding a safer ambiance would surely have made sense to many Jews in medieval Europe, if relations had been as negative as often suggested. Indeed, these Jews did more than simply remain on the scene. During the period between 1000 and 1500, the Jewish population of Christian Europe expanded steadily, moving toward its eventual position as the dominant demographic element on the world Jewish scene.

9

Identity

*W*HEREAS JEWS AND NON-JEWS HAVE GENERALLY PORTRAYED Jewish material circumstances in medieval western Christendom in exceedingly somber terms, Jews and others have regularly depicted Jewish spiritual circumstances rather glowingly. We recall Heinrich Graetz's double-sided portrait of exilic Jewry as, on the one hand, mired in degradation and pain – "subjugated Judah with the pilgrim staff in hand, the pilgrim pack upon the back, with a mournful eye addressed toward heaven, surrounded by prison walls, implements of torture, and red-hot branding irons" – and on the other hand, rising above its suffering with a commitment to the life of the mind – "the same figure with the earnestness of the thinker upon his placid brow, with the air of a scholar in his bright features, seated in a hall of learning."[1]

While most observers have not gone to quite the extremes of Graetz, there has been a substantial consensus that the Jews of medieval Christian Europe led lives that were by and large spiritually unruffled or were at least relatively unfazed by challenges from the surrounding environment. The assumptions are that the cohesive Jewish communal organizational structure provided effectively for the educational and spiritual needs of its constituents and that these constituents were profoundly committed to their community and faith, in no way challenged by what is often projected as a backward medieval Christian society and civilization.

Two post-medieval developments have strengthened this consensus. In the first place, the removal of many northern European Jews to eastern Europe toward the end of the Middle Ages, where they did live in relative

---

[1] See Chapter 4.

isolation from the indigenous population, has created a broad and undifferentiated picture of premodern European Jews untroubled by spiritual
challenges from their neighbors – living in their own enclaves, speaking their own language, and spiritually unaffected by the world around
them. There is considerable accuracy in this portrait of late-medieval-
and early-modern-Jewish life in eastern Europe; this portrait, however, bears no relationship to the situation of Jews in medieval western
Christendom.

Subsequently, modern developments have led in the opposite direction, away from separation and toward integration into the larger cultural
ambiance. As modern European and Western states radically restructured themselves from the late eighteenth century on, Jews encountered
opportunity and often pressure to integrate more fully in all respects
into majority society. As a result, Jews have become far more intimately
engaged with their general environment, increasingly conversant with it,
and thus profoundly challenged by it. These developments have eventuated in considerable weakening of Jewish identity and significant defection from Jewish ranks. In the face of this weakening of Jewish identity
and these defections, the portrait of a prior idyllic age, in which Jews lived
autonomously, relatively removed from their ambiance, and in religious
security and comfort, has had beguiling appeal. Jewish religious leaders
during the modern period have often invoked this supposed premodern
Jewish spiritual security as a cudgel with which to berate their followers,
regularly accusing them of lacking the faith and commitment of their
pious ancestors.

The central argument of this closing chapter is that, just as the bleak
portrait of the material circumstances of the Jews of medieval western
Christendom is distorted, so too is the contrastive depiction of idyllic
spiritual conditions. Medieval western Christendom – contrary to popular imagery – was a dynamic and exciting civilization. Precisely this
dynamism and excitement moved southern European Jews to transfer
their political allegiance to the Christian conquerors rather than retreat
with their former Muslim overlords, attracted Jewish settlers to areas of
northern Europe previously devoid of Jewish population, and convinced
Jews who suffered banishment to remain within the borders of Christian
Europe rather than relocate elsewhere. The dynamism and creativity of
medieval western Christendom posed a serious challenge to the Jewish

psyche. Jews living in this exciting ambiance could hardly be oblivious to the material *and* spiritual achievements of their environment. To be sure, they erected defenses against these achievements. The immediate impact of the dynamic Christian milieu was nonetheless significant and potentially damaging.

Beyond the immediate impact of Christian material and spiritual achievement, the Jews of medieval western Christendom were also the targets of a well-funded and carefully orchestrated missionizing assault, led by energetic and capable Church spokesmen. Jews defended themselves vigorously against the proselytizing campaign, but the Church campaign was intense and protracted and occasionally produced results. Thus, to portray the Jews of medieval western Christendom as living in spiritual security, unfazed by their surroundings, is to misinterpret their experience. Profoundly challenged by their dynamic environment and by the militant Roman Church, the Jews of medieval western Christendom had to ponder their spiritual circumstances and to create effective defenses against the challenges with which they were regularly confronted. For the most part, they did so effectively.[2]

Once again, we shall follow a tripartite organizational pattern. We shall begin with the traditional thinking that has projected idyllic Jewish spiritual circumstances; we shall proceed to survey the evidence of serious and ongoing challenge to Jewish identity, both implicit and carefully orchestrated; we shall conclude with the ways in which the Jews of medieval Christian Europe met these challenges with relative success, which contributed notably to the demographic health and ongoing development of this rapidly expanding Jewry.

A PEOPLE DWELLING APART

Jews have often been perceived by others and especially perceived themselves as living outside the bounds of the societies within which they find themselves, as somehow disconnected from the larger environment surrounding them. This perception often begins with the curious prophecy of the biblical seer Balaam. According to the book of Numbers, as the Israelites reached the lowlands of Moab prior to their entry into Canaan,

---

[2] Chazan, *Fashioning Jewish Identity.*

the Moabite king Balak, purportedly fearful of the approaching Israelite horde, convinced the seer Balaam to curse these dangerous intruders. Recurrently, the seer was unable to do so, instead delivering at divine behest positive visions of the Jewish future. In one of these positive visions, Balaam says the following:

> As I see them from the mountain tops,
> Gaze on them from the heights,
> There is a people that dwells apart,
> Not reckoned among the nations.[3]

Jews have embraced this projection of themselves as a "people that dwells apart" over the ages and have viewed this separation as a badge of honor.

Proceeding further in the biblical account, the book of Deuteronomy consists of a set of lengthy addresses by Moses, prior to the conclusion of his role as leader of the Israelites and to their crossing the Jordan River into the Promised Land. One of the central themes in these addresses is the demand that the Israelites refrain from attraction to the beliefs and mores of the Canaanite peoples. Repeatedly, Moses admonishes the Israelites against learning the ways of the Canaanites and imitating them. To cite but one such passage,

When the Lord your God has cut down before you the nations that you are about to encounter and dispossess and you have dispossessed them and settled in their land, beware of being lured into their ways after they have been wiped out before you. Do not inquire about their gods, saying: "How did these nations worship their gods? I too will follow those practices." You shall not act thus toward the Lord your God.[4]

Moses enjoins utter separation from the beliefs and practices of the Canaanites, and throughout subsequent Jewish history Jewish leaders have echoed the call for distance from others. As just now noted, the Jewry of eastern Europe – the largest concentration of Jews during the early modern period – came rather close to achieving the ideal of distance from the surrounding environment, which has reconfirmed for many modern Jews the biblical ideal.

[3] Num. 23:9.
[4] Deut. 12:29–31.

Not surprisingly, since we have noted this confluence regularly, Christian views of Jewish separatism have to a significant extent paralleled the Jewish sense, with of course divergent assessment of this separatism. While Jews have seen it as a biblical mandate and highly laudable, Christians have perceived Jewish unwillingness to integrate into the Christian fold as evidence of Jewish blindness and spiritual obtuseness. Christians have historically been astonished by the failure of Jews to grasp the obvious truths of Christianity and to appreciate the equally obvious evidence of divine favor for Christianity and divine abandonment of Judaism. These Jewish failures have resulted – in the Christian view – from Jews sequestering themselves from the larger societies in which they have lived, as a way of blocking out the realities that would convince them to acknowledge Christian truth and abandon Jewish error.

Modern scholars have devoted considerable energy to studying the relationship of Jews over the ages to the environments in which they have found themselves. There is a considerable consensus on the significant impact of Hellenistic and Roman culture on the Jewish communities of late antiquity. This impact was by no means confined to figures like Josephus and Philo; there is growing recognition of the extent to which Greco-Roman culture deeply affected rabbinic Judaism. Elias Bickerman went so far as to argue that the Jews showed a unique capacity to adapt Hellenistic culture to their own indigenous civilization.[5] There has likewise been little argument over the embeddedness of the Jews in their medieval Muslim environment. Since these Jews were a long-settled element throughout the Near East and the Mediterranean basin, and since Arabic was the spoken and written language of the medieval Muslim ambiance, social and cultural factors conspired to make Jews fully conversant with and deeply influenced by their Islamic milieu.

The Jews of medieval western Christendom have been somewhat more puzzling with respect to their familiarity with and absorption of the culture of their environment. In general, the distinction often noted between Mediterranean and northern European Jewish communities has regularly resulted in a sense of the Mediterranean Jewish communities of Iberia,

---

[5] Elias J. Bickerman, "The Historical Foundations of Postbiblical Judaism," 1:70–114. At the very end of his essay, Bickerman asserted that "the Jews remained the only one people in antiquity which dealt effectively with Greek culture."

southern France, and the Italian peninsula as affected by their environment, while the Jews of the north have often been portrayed as divorced
from their surroundings. This latter sense has sometimes resulted in the
view that these northern European Jews were more "authentically" Jewish
than their southern co-religionists. Over the past few decades, however,
this perception of medieval northern European Jewry has begun to give
way. Research in such areas as education, mothering, and martyrdom
has suggested a far deeper immersion in the culture of northern Europe
than heretofore suspected.[6]

Study of the immersion of medieval European Jews in their environment to the point of loss of Jewish identity has been rather slow
to develop. The initial placement of modern Jewish studies within
Jewish institutions and the communal functions of much nineteenth-
and early-twentieth-century historical scholarship meant that serious
study of loss of Jewish identity would not have been welcome in those
educational contexts. To be sure, one major episode of loss of Jewish
identity has been inescapable, and that involves the massive conversions
attendant on the violence of 1391 on the Iberian peninsula, which we shall
examine shortly. Scholars have often contrasted these conversions with
the Jewish martyrdoms of 1096, reinforcing the perception of northern
European Jews as authentically Jewish, in contrast with their supposedly
inauthentic Iberian confreres.[7]

More recently, however, there has been a growing awareness that
the contrast should not be overdrawn. The Jewish communities of
both southern and northern Europe show evidence of conversions that
involved no duress.[8] All across medieval Christian Europe, Jews, attracted
in some way to Christianity, left their faith and faith community to join

---

[6] Ivan G. Marcus, *Rituals of Childhood*; Elisheva Baumgarten, *Mothers and Children*;
Chazan, *European Jewry and the First Crusade*; Eva Haverkamp, "Martyrs in Rivalry,"
319–42, has taken this argument to a new level by examining the Xanten segment of
the Solomon bar Simson 1096 chronicle against the immediate background of the
Christian institutions and traditions in Xanten itself, showing rich Jewish awareness of
local Christian thinking in that town.

[7] For the assaults of 1391, see Baer, *A History of the Jews in Christian Spain*, 2:95–169. Baer
noted recurrently, albeit briefly, the contrast between Jewish behaviors in 1096 and
1391. See ibid, 2:130–31, and his introduction to Habermann, *Sefer Gezerot Ashkenaz
ve-Zarfat*, 1.

[8] Note especially the work on peaceable Jewish conversion in the north in the work of
Robert C. Stacey, *The Conversion of Jews to Christianity in Thirteenth-Century England*,
263–83, and Chaviva Levin, *Jewish Conversion to Christianity*.

the Christian majority. This should occasion no surprise. Perhaps more striking is the fact that these losses did not slow the process of growth of the Jewish communities of medieval western Christendom.

Indeed, the contrast between the duress of 1096 and the duress of 1391 is misleading, since the circumstances were so thoroughly divergent. In 1096, Jews faced the alternatives of conversion or death as a result of militant distortion of the call to holy war by some of the fringe crusading bands. Thus, Jews attacked in the name of radical commitment to Christianity responded with a radical commitment to Judaism. On the other hand, the assaults of 1391, largely grounded in socioeconomic grievances, were unlikely to produce anything like the frenzied Jewish religious response of 1096. In addition, there is considerable evidence of millenarian enthusiasm among the 1096 attackers and thus among the Jewish victims as well, a sense that the confrontation between besiegers and besieged was apocalyptic and that the most radical Jewish responses were appropriate, indeed required.[9] The violence of 1391 shows no such religious extremism.

Both during the medieval period itself and in modern scholarship, the focus on duress has been only a first step. The real culprit – in many eyes – was precisely the embeddedness of the Jews of Spain in their hellenistically inflected society. Especially noteworthy in this view was the impact of the study of philosophy, which purportedly attenuated the genuine Jewishness and Jewish commitments of the Iberian Jews. The major modern proponent of this position has been the great historian of Iberian Jewry, Yitzhak Baer, in his monumental study of the history of Spanish Jewry under Christian rule. In Baer's view, philosophy eroded the authentic mythic foundations of Jewish life and thus dramatically weakened Jewish resolve in the face of threats. Only Jews who shared the northern European commitment to authentic mythic Judaism could encounter successfully the challenges posed by Christian violence.

To make the immersion in philosophy the "culprit" in the defections of 1391 is to overlook a far more obvious "culprit," namely the attractions of Christian society, culture, and spirituality. To the extent that modern students of Jewish life in medieval Christian Europe remain wedded to the superannuated view of medieval Christendom as barbaric and

---

[9] Chazan, "'Let Not a Residue nor a Remnant Escape.'"

primitive, such an alternative is unthinkable. To those who acknowledge the vigor, power, and creativity of medieval western Christendom, such an alternative makes eminent sense. Our next step is to examine the intrinsic appeal of medieval Christian society and culture and – beyond the intrinsic appeal – the powerful efforts of the Roman Catholic Church to entice Jews into its fold.

CHALLENGES TO JEWISH IDENTITY

Assessment of medieval western Christendom has become part and parcel of subsequent societal tensions and strains. Enlightenment thinkers tended to project the European Middle Ages in the darkest of colors, while the Romantics saw the period in a much more benign light. Eventually, a balanced portrait has emerged, which posits enormous achievement along with serious deficiencies.[10]

This more balanced picture involves of course full acknowledgment of the achievements of medieval western Christendom, which took place on the demographic, economic, military, political, cultural, intellectual, and spiritual planes. The major development of the period between 1000 and 1500 from the perspective of Jewish history was initiation of the momentous shift in worldwide Jewish population distribution that with the passage of further time made the Christian West the demographic center of the Jewish world. That shift in and of itself bears eloquent testimony to the dynamism and accomplishments of medieval western Christendom and to full Jewish awareness of this dynamism and these achievements.

I recall visiting the great cathedral city of Chartres many years ago. I was, first of all, interested in identifying the site of the medieval Jewish neighborhood of Chartres and found that site rather easily. Standing on this narrow street in the lower section of the town and gazing upward, it was impossible not to be awed by the sight of the splendid cathedral looming over the entire area. I could not help but wonder about the feelings of the members of the Jewish community of medieval Chartres, as they watched from their small street a rich and colorful procession wending its way up the hill toward the imposing cathedral. I was

[10] See Chapter 3.

already aware – and have become more fully aware over the subsequent decades – that these Jews developed defenses against the achievements of their Christian neighbors, but I realized the enormous importance of these defenses against the magnificence of such monuments as the Chartres cathedral. Likewise, I was already aware that Jews had defenses that would enable them to dismiss the achievements of the great learning centers of medieval western Christendom that evolved with the passage of time into the universities of the West, in which so much new knowledge of the medieval Jewish experience has of late been generated. The challenges to the Jewish psyche posed by the environment of medieval Christian Europe could easily have been overwhelming. That the Jews of medieval western Christendom were not overwhelmed constitutes a major achievement – an achievement realized through determined effort and intense creativity.

The Jews of medieval Christian Europe faced, in addition, a militantly missionizing Church. This missionizing commitment flowed from a number of disparate factors. In part, it was simply an age-old obligation. Jesus had commissioned his disciples to go forth and preach his message, and historically the Church has seen this commission as a cornerstone of its responsibilities.[11] While preaching Christian truth was a generalized obligation incumbent upon Christians, preaching to the Jews always had special resonance and significance. Jews were, after all, the people of Jesus and his initial audience. Jews should have been the first to accept the new message, since they were the recipients of the prophecies that Jesus had come to fulfill. Put negatively, Jewish failure to accept the Christian message was a constant reproach. While this failure was rationalized by the Church as grounded in Jewish shortcoming and while Christians were assured that at the end of days Jews would recognize and accept the truth of Christianity, the ongoing intransigence of contemporary Jews was continuously troublesome and distressing. Thus, missionizing among the Jews was a high Christian priority.

To be sure, proselytizing could not be and was not pursued zealously in every age. During the tenth and eleventh centuries, as western Christendom struggled to lift itself out of backwardness and weakness, there

---

[11] The preaching mission of the disciples is the note on which each of the three synoptic Gospels closes.

was little energy available for reaching out to others. By the end of the eleventh century, progress allowed the Church greater latitude for aggressive action, but that aggressive action was militaristic at the outset. As the crusading venture began to suffer setbacks, voices within the Church argued that military engagement with the non-Christian world was fundamentally misguided, that Christ's original call had been to preach and teach the truth of his vision.[12] As a broad commitment to missionizing began to take shape, the Jews emerged as a prime target, for two reasons. The first is simply the special valence of preaching to Jews already noted. In addition, from a tactical perspective preaching to Jews (or to Muslims for that matter) located within Christian society was far easier than preaching to non-Christians located outside the perimeters of Christendom.

Finally, there was a broad drive in medieval western Christendom toward homogeneity under the umbrella of the Church. Doctrinally, there was recognition that, in the pre-redemptive phase of human history, division among human groupings was an acceptable reality. More specifically, both the doctrines and policies of the medieval Church recognized the legitimacy of Jewish life in Christian society. Nonetheless, the yearning for something better – the desire for a society unified in its entirety around the Christian religious vision – was strong in medieval western Christendom, and successful proselytizing among the Jews was an entirely permissible, indeed laudable, way of moving toward such unity.

The Church, as it embraced an enhanced commitment to missionizing in general and to proselytizing among Jews in particular, carefully laid the groundwork for such efforts.[13] It identified a number of elements in effective missionizing, with special attention to the requirements for success with Jewish audiences. Important initial elements involved fuller knowledge of Jewish traditions and Jewish defenses and the creation of a cohort of carefully trained missionizers. These desiderata were achieved through absorption of Jewishly learned converts, who brought knowledge of the Hebrew language and Jewish tradition into their new faith community. In addition, the Church sponsored language schools in which Hebrew

---

[12] See Benjamin Z. Kedar, *Crusade and Mission.*
[13] Robert Chazan, *Daggers of Faith.*

and Arabic were taught. The result was the establishment of a cadre of learned and well-trained missionizers – especially within the Dominican and Franciscan Orders – who could persuasively bring the Christian message to Jewish audiences.

The next desideratum was the establishment of ready modes of confronting Jewish audiences with Christian argumentation. Here, the situation of the Jews within medieval western Christendom played a helpful role. Given the special relationship between Jews and their secular overlords, these secular authorities held the key to access to Jewish audiences. Were these authorities willing to force their Jewish clients to attend missionizing encounters, then access to Jewish audiences would be readily available. By the middle of the thirteenth century, many secular authorities had begun to be supportive, and forced sermons were on their way to becoming an established reality of Jewish life. These forced sermons, usually held in synagogues, required Jewish attendance and eventuated in extensive and direct Jewish exposure to Christian argumentation.

A spin-off of the forced sermon was the forced disputation. These disputations were by no means free and equal exchanges of religious views. They were, rather, carefully contrived extensions of the forced sermon. The rules of these engagements required Jewish protagonists to listen to Christian arguments and allowed them to attempt rebuttal. Christian protagonists then advanced responses to the Jewish rebuttals, hopefully from the Church perspective in decisive fashion. Under the rules of engagement, Jewish spokesmen could under no circumstances make observations that might be construed as derogatory to Christianity. Such statements were of course deemed illegitimate and illegal under the circumstances of Jewish life in medieval Christian Europe. In effect, the rules confined Jews to a reactive posture only, with no opportunity whatsoever to take a proactive stance.

Finally, Church leadership had to identify lines of argumentation that would be effective among medieval Jews. The oldest lines of Christian argumentation – central to the Gospels themselves – involved Jesus' miracles and his fulfillment of prior biblical prophecy. Clearly, Jesus' Jewish contemporaries had already rejected these lines of argumentation. Thus, arguments from Jesus' miracles almost never appear in medieval Christian preaching. Christian missionizers recognized that claims from Jesus' miracles would simply not resonate among medieval Jewish listeners, as frustrating and distressing as that recognition might be. Claims grounded in Jesus' fulfillment of biblical prophecy continued to appear, out of a sense that medieval western Christendom had made enormous strides in its understanding of the biblical legacy. As the perception of progress in biblical exegesis developed, it was believed that increasingly rigorous and objective readings of the biblical texts proved beyond doubt the confluence of the predictions and the realities of Jesus' lifetime. Christian missionizers thus hoped that these increasingly rigorous and objective readings might convince medieval Jews, long inured to this line of argumentation. Nonetheless, there is little evidence that this line of argumentation proved effective, given the lengthy and rich Jewish tradition of counter-exegesis of key biblical verses and passages.

The efflorescence of philosophic study in medieval western Christendom, eventually centered in the newly crystallizing universities, offered another traditional avenue of Christian argumentation that was seen as more fully developed and thus potentially useful. Indeed, the movement toward rational argumentation in the medieval universities was most impressive. A major figure like Thomas Aquinas could undertake proof of Christian truth without recourse to revelation, grounded in rational proofs only. This line of argumentation, with its utterly rational appeal, seemed quite promising. In fact, however, it appears in the actual medieval context in only the most limited fashion. The essential weakness of this approach is the same as its essential strength – the abstract and purportedly objective argumentation required an extremely high level of intellectual sophistication on the part of preacher and audience. For public preaching to a Jewish audience, arguments that required a high level of philosophic sophistication were essentially doomed to irrelevance.

Thirteenth-century western Christendom pioneered in a new line of missionizing argumentation to Jews, grounded somewhat surprisingly in rabbinic literature. This new line of missionizing argumentation seems to have begun with a shadowy convert from Judaism to Christianity. The innovator in this new missionizing argumentation seems to have been originally a Jew from southern France named Saul, who studied in the Jewish academies of his home area, left the Jewish fold, took the Christian name Paul, eventually joined the Dominican Order, and won from his Dominican associates support for his innovative proselytizing approach. Friar Paul argued before Jewish audiences that the rabbis of yore interpreted key biblical verses in ways that proved their recognition of Christian truth. In effect, he attempted to force medieval Jews to conclude that their traditional anti-Christian readings of such key biblical verses were in fact contradicted by the readings proposed by their own esteemed rabbinic authorities.

A simple example of this approach involves the well-known "Suffering Servant" pericope of Isaiah 52:13–53:12. Over the ages, Christian exegetes had pointed to this dramatic passage as obviously fulfilled by Jesus, who had suffered grievously for no sinfulness on his part and had subsequently been raised to great honor through the spread of the faith he founded. Jews had claimed just as adamantly that the referent in this passage was not the Messiah, but was rather the Jewish people, which had suffered grievously for no sinfulness of its own and would eventually be raised to great heights. Friar Paul pointed to numerous rabbinic texts that explained the "Suffering Servant" passage as pointing to the fate of the Messiah, arguing that in effect medieval Jews were denying their own religious authorities.

After extensive experience preaching in the synagogues of southern Europe, Friar Paul and his Dominican colleagues were successful in winning the support of King James the Conqueror of Aragon for a public disputation between Friar Paul and a leading figure in the Aragonese Jewish community, Rabbi Moses ben Nahman of Gerona.[14] In this engagement, Friar Paul's new missionizing argumentation underwent rigorous testing. The ground rules stipulated that the friar would advance rabbinic statements that purportedly proved Christian truths and that the rabbi was then free to rebut these claims. These ground rules assured that no anti-Christian statements might be advanced by the rabbi; they further assured that the outcome could only be Christian victory or non-victory. In the latter case, the rabbi might have destroyed the new line of missionizing argumentation, but in the process he would have in no way inflicted damage on the Christian belief system.

We do not know precisely what transpired over the four days of debate in Barcelona. A Christian source claims total Christian victory; Rabbi Moses ben Nahman himself penned a colorful account of the engagement that showed him consistently outwitting and out-debating his opponent.

---

[14] Idem, *Barcelona and Beyond.*

In fact, it seems likely that neither side actually won and neither side actually lost the debate. From the Christian perspective, the Barcelona engagement did not result in the victory of Jewish conversions, so far as we can tell. On the other hand, it did not discourage Friar Paul and his Dominican associates, who continued to refine and utilize the new approach for centuries. The Dominicans did appreciate the need for further work on the new approach, which was undertaken by another friar, Raymond Martin. Friar Raymond in his *Pugio Fidei* gathered many more Jewish sources and extended the approach to encompass all the major beliefs of the Christian theological system. From the Jewish side, Rabbi Moses could not savor the sense of defeating and dismantling the new line of argumentation. It was clear even to him that Dominican preachers would continue to make Friar Paul's arguments for the foreseeable future. On the other hand, the lack of immediate conversions was surely encouraging to the leadership of Aragonese Jewry.

The final line of Christian argumentation involved once again – like the direct biblical exegesis and the appeal to philosophy – a traditional Christian approach much reinforced by medieval developments. As we have seen repeatedly, Christians were convinced that alleged Jewish responsibility for the Crucifixion entailed almost immediately divinely imposed punishment. Christian successes and Jewish suffering served as indices of divine approbation and divine rejection and thus also as indices of Christian truth and Jewish error. Christian thinkers regularly addressed these claims at Christian audiences. With the efflorescence of medieval western Christendom, as Christian Europe rose to an increasingly dominant position in the Western world, the Christian conviction of divine support for the Christian camp and divine rejection of the Jews became increasingly intense and was utilized in argumentation with Jews as well.

We noted earlier the sense of the former Jew turned Christian polemicist Petrus Alfonsi that Jewish suffering was uniquely horrific, a sure sign of its divine origins and hence of Jewish error. Petrus advanced this claim to his twelfth-century Christian audience.[15] Increasingly however, Christian missionizers directed this argument at Jewish audiences. As a result, we see the argument from contrastive Christian and Jewish fate appearing more regularly and more prominently in Jewish polemical

---

[15] See Chapter 2.

sources, indicating that Jews were deeply aware of this line of Christian argumentation and were deeply concerned with it. In one of the earliest of the medieval Jewish polemical works composed in western Christendom, Jacob ben Reuben's *Milhamot ha-Shem*, the author describes himself as involved in a friendly and productive relationship with a learned Christian. At some point in this relationship, the friendly Christian challenged his Jewish friend with the argument of contrastive Christian and Jewish fates and urged Jacob to acknowledge the obvious and convert. This exchange, rooted in the issue of Christian successes and Jewish failures, purportedly stimulated the writing of *Milhamot ha-Shem*.

About half a century later, another learned Jew who seems to have enjoyed close relations with a Christian counterpart exhibits parallel awareness of the centrality of the argument from historical fates. At a major point in his sprawling polemical work, *Milhemet Mizvah*, Rabbi Meir bar Simon of Narbonne gathered together a wide range of Jewish polemical claims against Christianity. He introduced this extensive collection with the following:

A Christian sage asked a Jewish sage: "Why do you not leave the religion of the Jews? For you see that they have been in exile for a very long time and decline from day to day. Conversely, you see with regard to the faith of the Christians that they become greater from day to day. Their success has been great for a long time. Now, you will live among us in great honor and with high standing, instead of being in exile and fearfulness and accursedness."[16]

Jews were fully aware of this crucial thrust in Christian argumentation. They had no real option of denying the reality of Christian power and Jewish subjugation. Again, as the power of western Christendom increased, these claims had even greater salience. Jews had to interpret a reality they could not deny, and such interpretations abounded, as we shall see.[17] From many perspectives, this line of Christian missionizing focused on Christian successes and Jewish suffering constituted the most potent and threatening of the lines of argumentation utilized by the increasingly aggressive medieval Church.

Our final question concerns the evidence of success in the Christian missionizing campaign. In attempting to address this issue, it is useful

[16] Chazan, *Fashioning Jewish Identity*, 190.
[17] For the Jewish responses, see below.

to begin with two sets of distinctions, the first involving geography and the second involving classes within the Jewish community. We have noted recurrently the differences between the Jewish communities of the south and those of the north. There is a broad sense of the differences with respect to conversion between these two sets of Jewries. This is the result in part of the unique circumstances of 1391, which involved the Jewish communities of the Iberian peninsula. However, even beyond the events of 1391 there is ongoing evidence of defection from the Jewish communities of the south. At the same time, it is important to distinguish between conversion of peripheral and less educated members of the Jewish community and conversion of those at the center of Jewish life and equipped with deep knowledge of Jewish tradition. We shall utilize both sets of distinctions.

For Jews, a defense against the debilitating spectacle of conversion was to identify the converts as peripheral members of the Jewish community, attracted in large measure by the economic advantages of joining the Christian majority and unprotected by deep knowledge of their own tradition. It is clear that many of the converts did in fact come from the poor and unlettered in the Jewish world. Papal letters from the thirteenth century show ongoing concern for the financial well-being of converts.[18] Establishment of institutions for converts, such as the *domus conversorum*, was intended to afford assistance to converts in dire need and reflect the same aspect of the placement of converts within the Jewish world.[19] The reality of poor and less educated converts, while worth noting, cannot obscure the reality of accelerating conversion by members of the Jewish intellectual elite.

We have already cited the twelfth-century Petrus Alfonsi, who left the Jewish fold as a learned and well-trained intellectual and emerged eventually as a major figure in Christian intellectual life.[20] During the thirteenth century, such figures began to multiply. Prior chapters have highlighted Nicholas Donin, the obscure southern French Jew who converted and led the assault on the Talmud.[21] In the project of translating portions

---

[18] Grayzel, *The Church and the Jews in the XIIIth Century*, passim.
[19] See again Stacey, "The Conversion of Jews to Christianity in Thirteenth-Century England."
[20] For an overview of Petrus Alfonsi, see John Tolan, *Petrus Alfonsi and His Medieval Readers*.
[21] See Chapter 7.

of the Talmud, it is clear that Donin had the assistance of a number of similarly learned converts from Judaism. We have also noted Friar Paul Christian, who pioneered in the new line of missionizing argumentation based on utilization of rabbinic literature. While Rabbi Moses ben Nahman consistently portrays Friar Paul as only semi-learned and quite obtuse, it is obvious that the friar had enjoyed some significant level of Jewish learning prior to his conversion, and it is somewhat questionable that the Dominicans who were so supportive of him would have chosen to back the kind of dunce that the rabbi projects.

The latter decades of the thirteenth century saw the appearance of a remarkable convert from the Jewish community of Burgos. Abner of Burgos was a highly respected figure in his community, regularly sought out for religious guidance. For decades, he secretly harbored doubts about his religious faith, eventually succumbing to these doubts. His post-conversion literary corpus, which was broad and brilliant, suggests that it was ultimately the last of the lines of Christian argumentation – the claims rooted in the contrastive fates of Christians and Jews – that tipped the balance for him toward acceptance of the majority faith. Subsequent to his conversion, Abner wrote broadly, with a heavy emphasis on convincing his former co-religionists to join him in the Christian fold. Striking in his polemical writings are the breadth and depth of Abner's Jewish knowledge and the rabbinic style in which he wrote. Readers of his polemical epistles who block out the Christological content and focus merely on the literary style would think that they were reading the work of a learned expert in Jewish law and exegesis.[22] During the closing century of Jewish life on the Iberian peninsula, learned figures of this kind continued to appear on the scene.

All the figures cited thus far come from the southern sectors of medieval Europe, seemingly lending credence to the distinction noted between southern and northern Jewish conversion. It might be argued that conversion of peripheral elements in the Jewish world may well have taken place all throughout medieval Europe, but that conversion of the learned was a southern phenomenon only. Even this more restrained view, however, does not stand up to scrutiny. In the north as well, there is evidence that members of the Jewish elite on occasion made their way

[22] On Abner, see especially Baer, *A History of the Jews in Christian Spain*, 1:327–54.

into the Christian camp. There are, for example, obscure reports that the son of Rabbi Gershom of Mainz, who was the first giant figure in northern European Jewish intellectual life, defected from his father's faith community. Although the reality seems uncontestable, the details are exceedingly difficult to reconstruct.[23] An autobiographical memoir by a German Jew named Hermann purports to describe in some detail the lengthy process that led to the conversion of the writer, who came from the center of twelfth-century German Jewry and not from its peripheries.[24]

A fascinating twelfth-century incident in England shows a serious student from a distinguished family attracted to the symbols of Christianity.

Once in England there was a studious and wealthy student who sat in the academy. His name was Yom Tov, blessed be the memory of the righteous. On the eve of Shavu'ot [Feast of Weeks] he took his hanger and hanged himself.... [There follows an extensive description of the aftermath of the suicide, including the limited funeral arrangements.] That night [the night of the funeral], he [the deceased Yom Tov] appeared to me in a dream, and I saw that he was beautiful, more so than he had been while still alive. He also appeared to many others, as he had come into the Great Light and was assured of [reaching] that other world immediately. The rabbi [the father of the deceased] too saw this vision. On the eighth of Sivan, [they journeyed] to London and eulogized him greatly. He was a pious person and God-fearing. I have not seen his like in any of the [Jewish] communities. He was utterly straightforward, and I saw in him every measure of sanctity and purity. Subsequently, it became clear that he had judged himself extremely harshly. Indeed, he was afflicted with a demon.... He further indicated that the demon would show him the cross and would urge him to worship idolatrously.[25]

In northern Europe as well as in the south, Jews at the center of the community could be enticed by the majority environment.

[23] On Rabbi Gershom of Mainz, the fullest survey is that of Avraham Grossman, *The Early Sages of Ashkenaz,* 106–74. The murky episode of the conversion of his son can be found there, 112–13.

[24] *Hermannus quondam Judaeus.* This account has given rise to considerable controversy. For an overview of the controversy and many reasonable suggestions toward resolution, see Jean-Claude Schmitt, *La Conversion d'Hermann le Juif.*

[25] This text was published by Ephraim Kupfer, "Towards the History of the Family of R. Moses b. Yom Tov," 385–87. I have used with some modifications the translation of Yechiel Y. Schur, *Care for the Dead in Medieval Ashkenaz,* 148. Schur used this important text for the light it shed on funeral practices. For a discussion of the tempting of Yom Tov, see Horowitz, "The Jews and the Cross in the Middle Ages."

The pressures brought to bear on Jewish identity were real, persistent, and intense. Jews did succumb to these pressures and leave their minority community for the majority faith. As we shall see now, the leadership of the Jewish communities of medieval western Christendom was fully cognizant of the ongoing threat and mobilized resources to counter the ever-present dangers. Ultimately, the losses – as distressing as they might have been to the Jews directly affected by them – were not sufficient to impede the steady expansion of Jewish numbers in medieval Christian Europe or to destabilize the Jewish communities of the area.

REINFORCEMENT OF JEWISH IDENTITY

The intellectual and spiritual challenges posed to the Jews of medieval western Christendom were ongoing and threatening. They required diversified and thoughtful intellectual responses, which were in fact forthcoming, and a variety of emotional reinforcements of these intellectual responses as well. We shall begin with the lines of intellectual rejoinder and then proceed to the arguably more important emotional reinforcements, which are far more difficult to track.

We have identified four major lines of Christian intellectual assault. Some of these thrusts were easier to reject than others. We shall proceed from the easier of the thrusts to the more difficult. We shall also note that the intellectual leaders of the Jewish communities of medieval western Christendom did not content themselves with simply parrying the Christian thrusts; they also went on the offensive and attacked central aspects of Christian religious belief and societal life. To be sure, Jewish leaders could not air these attacks publicly, since giving voice to such anti-Christian views ran afoul of the basic rules of Jewish behavior in Christian society. Within the Jewish community, however, Jews could and did express such anti-Christian views regularly and powerfully.

Perhaps the simplest of the Christian thrusts to counter involved the introduction of philosophic considerations. Philosophic speculation was one of the intellectual glories of medieval western Christendom, but we have already noted the limitations of this philosophic erudition for the missionizing campaign. Jewish audiences were unlikely to muster the requisite sophistication to follow a philosophic presentation. In fact, the liabilities of the philosophic approach ran deeper. Jews had long been inured to see key Christian teachings as utterly irrational and intellectually indefensible. The key Christian doctrine of Incarnation inspired many of the most penetrating insights of medieval Christian philosophers, but for medieval Jews the notion was intellectually absurd and morally obnoxious. Likewise, the notion of the Trinity, which vigorously exercised the ingenuity of medieval Christian thinkers, could not attract serious attention on the part of medieval Jews, who perceived this doctrine to be polytheism pure and simple. Philosophic issues – rather than serving as arguments for the Christian side – were a source of considerable Jewish attack on Christianity and were perceived as Christian weaknesses.[26]

The Gospels present Jesus' miracles as key proofs of his divine mission. However, medieval Christians almost never argued with medieval Jews on the grounds of these miracles, since they were fully aware that Jesus' Jewish contemporaries had already rejected this line of argumentation. Thus, claims grounded in Gospel and subsequent assertions of Jesus' fulfillment of biblical predictions were the oldest of the lines of medieval Christian argumentation. To an extent, the antiquity of this line of argumentation suggested a lack of efficacy. If Jews had heard these claims from the very inception of Christianity and had not accepted them, then the likelihood that these thrusts would now be effective should have seemed minimal. As noted, however, Christian readiness to maintain usage of these traditional claims was rooted in the conviction of medieval progress in biblical exegesis. While such progress was a reality, it did not result in significant breakthroughs with Jewish audiences. Jews also felt pride in the progress they had made in understanding biblical texts and were extremely comfortable in engaging the Christian claims drawn from well-known biblical verses or passages.

Jews battled each and every biblical citation adduced in support of Christian claims. More broadly, they advanced two sets of general considerations in their engagement with this line of Christian missionizing argumentation. In the first place, Jews insisted that they and they alone were engaging the biblical text in its original Hebrew. While they were reading and interpreting the text in its original form, their

---

[26] Daniel J. Lasker, *Jewish Philosophical Polemics.* See especially chapter 4 (Trinity) and chapter 5 (Incarnation).

Christian opponents by contrast were dependent on the Latin translation of Jerome. In Jewish eyes, such dependence was an inherent shortcoming, and in addition – medieval Jews argued – Jerome's translation was seriously flawed. Jews argued that many Christian proselytizing arguments evolved from Jerome's egregious errors. Moreover, medieval Jews insisted that Christian preference for allegorical explanation of biblical texts constituted yet a second generic weakness in the Christian approach to the Hebrew Bible. In contrast, medieval Jews prided themselves on strict fidelity to the straightforward meaning of the biblical corpus.

Christian utilization of rabbinic exegesis had a number of major advantages. In the first place, there was the simple advantage of newness. This was an innovative line of argumentation, and innovation itself was useful. In addition, there was surely something disconcerting for medieval Jews in hearing Christian preachers cite rabbinic texts – a sense of Christian power in appropriation of Jewish treasures. Nonetheless, Jews generally felt comfortable in combating this new thrust as well. Again, each rabbinic passage adduced by Christian missionizers like Friar Paul met careful scrutiny on the part of Jewish spokesmen in search of flaws in citation and argumentation.

Once again, there were generic Jewish claims as well. In the first place, there was a broad sense of superior Jewish mastery of the rabbinic corpus. Moses ben Nahman's account of the Barcelona disputation is dotted with dismissive comments about Friar Paul's failure to understand properly the texts he was introducing. In addition, Jewish spokesmen like Moses ben Nahman argued that the notion of rabbinic awareness of Christian truth is inherently unthinkable, since there is no evidence of rabbis of antiquity acting on such purported insights. As insisted for example by Moses ben Nahman, these rabbis lived and died as Jews, which made the claims of their acknowledgment of Christian truth absurd.

In many ways, the argument from contrastive fates – Christian successes and Jewish suffering – was the most difficult for medieval Jews to engage. It spoke equally to the minds and the hearts of medieval Jews. It was obviously painful for medieval Jews to contemplate this combination of success and suffering. Moreover, although the reality of Christian success could be and was attacked, the reality of inferior Jewish status could not be disputed. Jews had to acknowledge their secondary circumstances in medieval western Christendom. The key Jewish responses to this painful line of Christian argumentation lay in assessment and interpretation of Christian achievement and interpretation of Jewish secondary status.

Jewish responses focused heavily on the first half of the contrast, on the Christian successes. Interestingly, with the passage of time and growing awareness of the realities of Muslim political and military power, Jewish polemicists began to argue that Christianity was not actually as successful as it claimed, that it constituted only one of the world's two religious superpowers or even perhaps the second and not the first of the world's religious superpowers. If might was suggested as reflecting right, then perhaps – it was suggested in tongue-in-cheek fashion – both Christians and Jews should convert to Islam. As the tide of fortunes shifted in the Near East and Christian forces began to lose their grip on the Holy Land, this thrust became even more prominent in Jewish polemical argumentation.

More broadly, Jewish thinkers argued that, even allowing for considerable Christian achievement, these accomplishments fell far short of the level established by the prophets of Israel for messianic redemption. Since the Christian case revolved around Jesus as the promised Messiah and the remarkable spread of the faith he founded, then – Jews argued – this spread of Christianity must be measured against the standards established by the prophets for messianic delivery. When these standards were imposed, it became clear – in the Jewish view – that Christian achievements were deficient. Messianic redemption was supposed to involve, *inter alia*, the peace promised in Isaiah 2, but that peace was nowhere in evidence. To the contrary, one of the major achievements of medieval Christian Europe – as we have seen – was its successes in warfare and not in peace-making. Another major feature of the redemptive era was to be worldwide unity in worship of the one true God, and that too was nowhere in evidence. The world was divided into competing religious blocs, and even within Christendom discord and diversity of views abounded. It should be obvious to any observer – argued Jews – that the total acknowledgment of the one true God promised by the prophets was nowhere in evidence.

At the most theoretical level, medieval Jews introduced into their view of history the scheme that is central to two major chapters in the book of Daniel. In both chapters 2 and 7 of Daniel, there is reference to a four-part sequence of pre-redemptive empires. Each of these empires was fated to rule for a period of time, with great power and authority. Ultimately, these earthly empires were to be replaced by the true divinely appointed empire, whose reign would last forever. For medieval Jews, the four-part sequence was clear; it involved Babylonia, Persia and Media, Greece, and Rome. The Daniel imagery projected the last – Rome – as the most powerful and cruelest of the four. Medieval Jews understood Rome to be the pagan Roman Empire of antiquity and its subsequent continuations as Christian Rome and the Church. Thus, in this view, the power of medieval Christendom was far from a reflection of messianic redemption. To the contrary, the power of medieval Christendom had been predicted by the book of Daniel and reflected simply the reality of extensive earthly authority. The religious standing of medieval Christendom was no different from that of Babylonia, Persia and Media, and Greece. Just as no one would argue that the power of these first three empires involved anything more than earthly achievement, so too medieval Christendom was an earthly authority only and would eventually be succeeded by the genuinely redemptive phase in human history.[27]

These assaults on the extent and meaning of Christian achievement constituted only half the required response to claims based on contrastive Christian and Jewish fate. The issue of Jewish secondary status, degradation, and sometimes even physical suffering had to be addressed as well, and it was. The traditional explanation for Jewish suffering, widely projected throughout the Bible, focused on the sin-punishment paradigm. Israelite/Jewish sins entailed punishment inflicted by God, who had warned repeatedly against failing to fulfill the demands of the divine-human covenant. This line of explanation for Jewish suffering was of course precisely the approach of early and medieval Christianity, which saw in Jewish circumstances evidence of divine punishment for the sin of Crucifixion. In order to counter the Christian proselytizing thrust, Jewish thinkers had to identify and highlight an authentic and convincing alternative explanation for Jewish suffering.

Jewish thinkers grounded this authentic and convincing alternative in the biblical figure of Abraham and one of the most striking and perplexing episodes of his career. Genesis 22 tells the tale of God's testing Abraham

---

[27] All these Jewish thrusts are discussed in Chazan, *Fashioning Jewish Identity*, chapter 10.

by seemingly demanding the sacrifice of his beloved son Isaac, who had been given him only in very old age. Despite the magnitude of the sacrifice demanded, Abraham hastened to fulfill the divine command. When this willingness was absolutely clear, God negated the order and pronounced bounteous blessings on his faithful servant.

By myself I swear, the Lord declares: Because you have done this and have not withheld your son, your favored one, I will bestow my blessing upon you and make your descendants as numerous as the stars of the heaven and the sands on the seashore. Your descendants shall seize the gates of their foes. All the nations of the earth shall bless themselves by your descendants, because you have obeyed my commandments.[28]

In times of extreme duress, the Jews of medieval western Christendom invoked the imagery of their ancestor Abraham as the model for their behavior and – equally significant – as explanation for their suffering. Thus, in the crusader assaults of 1096 in the Rhineland, the imagery of Abraham is ubiquitous. Let us note but one instance of this imagery. As the assembled crusaders and burghers besieged the bishop's palace in Worms, a Jew named Meshullam ben Isaac stepped forward in the following way.

He called out loudly to all those standing there and to Zipporah his helpmate. "Listen to me, both great and small. This son God gave me. My wife Zipporah bore him in her old age and his name is Isaac. Now I shall offer him up as did our ancestor Abraham with his son Isaac."[29]

Here, Abraham serves as model for immediate behavior and as retrospective explanation for the Jewish suffering of 1096.

Even in more peaceful circumstances, the testing paradigm functioned centrally for the Jews of medieval Christian Europe. Rabbi Meir ben Simon of Narbonne, who has been mentioned repeatedly, felt called upon to deliver a counter-sermon in response to the claims of a Christian preacher who delivered a synagogue address to the Narbonne congregation. It seems clear from the rabbi's response that the Christian preacher highlighted the argument from contrastive fates, for it is on this issue that the Jewish respondent focused. Basing himself on a striking verse in the Song of Songs that distinguishes between the rewards in store for a

---

[28] Genesis 22:16–18.
[29] Chazan, *European Jewry and the First Crusade*, 230.

young woman who behaves like a wall and a young woman who behaves like a door, Meir ben Simon says the following:

"If she be a wall." That is to say, if she stood like a sturdy wall, which is undamaged by stones and likewise she was undamaged and unmoved by idolatry, even though they pressed her continually, "then we will build upon it a silver battlement." That is to say, when the time of redemption comes, they [the heavenly host] will go forth with silver and gold and fine clothing in abundance.

"If she be a door, we will panel it in cedar." That is to say, if she is not strong in her faith and her hands waver and her heart hesitates because of the weight of exile and from a lack of faith, she will not be deemed worthy to go forth with great honor. For cedars are the choicest of trees, but they are much inferior to silver.[30]

According to the rabbi, Jews were being tested by the travails of exile, but continued faith in the Jewish future would result in splendid rewards.

Jews did not restrict themselves to these defensive strategies only. They also went on the offensive. As a result of their place in medieval western Christendom, Jews knew a fair amount about the Gospels and attacked them regularly. Many Jewish polemical works cite Gospel passages and verses and criticize them from diverse perspectives. At the most benign level, Jews alleged that Gospel passages contradict one another, which hardly suggests sacred literature of divine origin. More pointedly, Jews criticized Gospel portrayal of Jesus for projecting him as irrational or immoral. Finally, Jews highlighted purported disparities between the Gospels and contemporary Christian belief and practice. These disparities suggest that medieval Christianity bears no genuine relationship to the Gospels and authentic Christianity.[31]

Additionally, Jewish polemicists attacked Christianity and Christian society for an allegedly low level of rationality and morality, stressing the high standards of Jewish accomplishment in both realms. For Jews, the contrast in rationality and morality was far more significant than the contrast between the material fates of the two communities. Jewish thinkers insistently contrasted the reasonableness of Jewish beliefs with the claimed irrationality of Christian beliefs. Equally or more importantly, they portrayed the decency and morality of the Jewish community

[30] Chazan, *Fashioning Jewish Identity*, 214.
[31] Ibid, chapter 13.

and the Jewish family over against the alleged immorality of the Christian community and family. They projected the Jewish community's higher level of reasonableness and morality as the reason Jews should not consider seriously the Christian alternative. Joining the Christian fold would be – it was claimed – acceding to a lower level of spiritual and moral achievement. If the ultimate objective of religion is actualization of the human potential for rational thinking and ethical behavior, then in the Jewish view Judaism was the only viable alternative, all other contrasts notwithstanding.

Precisely how Jewish leaders conveyed these Jewish polemical defenses and attacks to the Jews of medieval western Christendom is not altogether clear. We must assume that sermons were a constant source of broad education for these Jews and that the rabbis of medieval Europe used their preaching to rebuff Christian pressures and to drive home lessons of Christian inferiority and Jewish superiority.[32] Jews did not have public art to use for educational purposes, as did the Christian majority, but private works of art were used to rebuff Christian claims and to advance Jewish attacks on Christianity and Christian society. Finally, we must also assume that there was much informal conversation among Jews in which these themes were rehearsed and reinforced.

Adequate intellectual response to the diversified thrusts of the Christian missionizing effort was indispensable, but it was by no means sufficient. In addition, Jews had to be regularly reinforced in multiple ways in their sense of the superiority of Judaism and the inferiority of Christianity. Christians regularly encountered the public art that dominated the towns of medieval Europe and projected supportive Christian views.[33] Jews had no such public art available. However, denigration of Christianity permeated every facet of Jewish religious life and every genre of Jewish literature.

The Babylonian Talmud, ensconced at the very center of medieval Jewish religious and intellectual life, was hardly obsessed with Christianity, but it did nonetheless contain a number of damning castigations

---

[32] For a valuable collection of sermons, see Marc Saperstein, ed. and trans., *Jewish Preaching 1200–1800: An Anthology*. For evidence of a sermon preached specifically in response to a Christian sermon, see Robert Chazan, "Confrontation in the Synagogue of Narbonne," 437–57.

[33] Recall the discussion of the importance of public Christian depiction of Judaism and Jews in Chapter 7.

of Christianity and its major figures, especially Jesus and Mary. These castigations – which were not reasoned rejections, but rather explosive condemnations – lay at the heart of the charges leveled by Nicholas Donin at the papal court in 1236 and repeated more fully in the public trial of the Talmud held subsequently in Paris. While many of these powerful passages were expunged from the European Talmud texts, their impact remained.[34] The Talmudic anti-Christian materials were supplemented by an early Jewish counter-history of Christianity, the *Sefer Toldot Yeshu*, which projected Jesus and his family in crudely negative fashion. This text circulated widely in diverse versions, all of which were unified in their broad caricature of the figures held in highest esteem by the Christian world.

When Jews turned to their legal tradition, they found more serious statements on Christianity, which was almost unanimously judged to be polytheistic by the Jewish legal authorities. Here we do not see folkish caricature. The tone of the discussions is serious and thoughtful, and the conclusion is nearly universal. The Jewish religious authorities judged the Christian doctrine of the Trinity to involve recognition of a multiplicity of deities. This conclusion reflected negatively on the Christian tradition, enabled a potent Jewish sense of adherence to the one true God, and thus engendered a strong sense of religious superiority.

The medieval Jewish mystical tradition, with its increasing inroads into Jewish religious sensibilities, was yet another sphere of Jewish intellectual and spiritual life that conveyed the message of Christian inferiority and Jewish superiority. In his wide-ranging analysis of medieval Jewish mystical attitudes toward Christianity and Islam, Elliot R. Wolfson notes the far more extreme mystical condemnation of the former. He concludes: "Christianity is portrayed as the socially abhorrent political force that causes Israel to suffer and that incessantly attempts to lure her onto the path of promiscuity and heresy. Indeed, according to the symbolism embraced by kabbalists of the Zoharic circle, in line with the invectives typical of medieval Jewish texts, Christians are the embodiment of demonic impurity in the world."[35]

---

[34] See the recent study by Peter Schafer, *Jesus in the Talmud*.

[35] Elliot R. Wolfson, *Venturing Beyond*, 136. Note more generally chapter 2 and especially the subsection entitled "Esau/Edom: Demonization of the Other."

Wolfson notes in these observations the broad tendency toward invective in medieval Jewish texts. We have encountered such invective throughout this study. Passages in a wide range of texts regularly designate Christianity, its founding figure, and its *sancta* in harshly derogatory terms, to the point that such locutions become almost standard and anticipated.[36] While it might well be argued that such denigration represents a fairly low level of attack, in fact when constantly invoked in a self-sustaining circle of believers, it has enormous power in inoculating such believers defensively against the pressures of the outside world. The impact of this dismissive language should not be underestimated. For many medieval Jews, the possibility of abandoning the Jewish fold and attaching oneself to the debased beliefs of Christianity became unthinkable.

Jews living in medieval western Christendom were thus exposed on multiple levels to dismissal of Christianity and to the correlative valorization of Judaism. Beyond all this, the Jewish community and family had to act in reality as checks against the blandishments of the dynamic and aggressive Christian environment. The realities of Jewish community and family life are almost impossible to ascertain, but it seems likely that claims of the elevated level of Jewish community and family life were not fabrications. Intellectual arguments for maintaining Jewish identity in the face of the multiple challenges posed by the Christian environment, rejection of Christianity in a range of Jewish intellectual domains, folk traditions that lampooned Christianity, and regular denigration of Christianity as part of the Hebrew lexicon could achieve a great deal, but were certainly not sufficient. Jews had to be convinced of the dignity of their tradition, as reflected most prominently in their communal and familial existence, and it seems that by and large they were.

WHEN WE ABANDON THE SUPERANNUATED NOTION OF MEDIEVAL western Christendom as backward and primitive, we are in a position to appreciate the extent to which this rapidly developing society challenged the identity of its Jewish minority population. The challenge was

---

[36] See Anna Sapir Abulafia, "Invectives against Christianity in the Hebrew Chronicles of the First Crusade," 66–72.

inherent in the dynamism and creativity of the Christian majority and was reinforced by the activist proselytizing of the aggressive Church. Jews took the challenge seriously and developed multiple defenses against it. These Jewish defenses were successful enough to allow the demographic expansion of the Jewish communities of medieval Christian Europe to solidify. While there was steady and occasionally even dramatic defection, the numbers of those leaving the Jewish fold were never sufficient to jeopardize the vibrant growth of the Jewries of medieval western Christendom.

The Jews of medieval Europe saw their majority environment as dynamic and creative and opted to become and remain part of this dynamic and creative milieu. At the same time, these Jews discerned major flaws in medieval Christianity and medieval Christian society, which encouraged them to resist the pressure to amalgamate into the majority and stimulated them to retain their own distinctive Jewish identity.

Epilogue: The Medieval Roots of Modern Jewish Life: Destructive Aftermath and Constructive Legacies

*T*HE VITALIZATION OF WESTERN CHRISTENDOM THAT BEGAN toward the end of the first Christian millennium had, as an unanticipated consequence, development of what was to become eventually the modern world's largest set of Jewish communities. As Christian armies eliminated Muslim enclaves from European soil, Jews long resident in the conquered areas elected to remain under Christian rule. Other Jews, impressed by the newfound dynamism of Latin Christendom, chose to immigrate, strengthening old and small Jewish communities in southern Europe and founding new Jewries in the north. By the year 1500, a considerable Jewish population had emerged in Christian Europe, although Jews had been expelled from the more advanced sectors of western Europe and pushed eastward into the less developed regions of central and eastern Europe.

Jews who opted to stay in areas conquered by Christian armies or who chose to immigrate into western Christendom responded to the lure of economic opportunity. While the economic opportunity was real, the overall circumstances that greeted these Jews were, from many perspectives, daunting. They encountered a Church determined to limit them in multiple ways, political authorities for whom the immigrant Jews represented above all else a useful resource that might be heavily exploited and under certain circumstances jettisoned, and a populace that combined traditional Christian anti-Jewish thinking with normal antipathy toward newcomers. The Jewish experience in this rapidly developing area was both positive and negative. On the one hand, the Jews of medieval Christian Europe flourished demographically, economically, and culturally,

222

in the process contributing in valuable ways to the general maturation of the European economy and system of governance and writing
a new chapter in Jewish history; on the other hand, they suffered from
Church limitations, governmental exploitation, and popular hostility and
violence.

The vitalization of western Christendom did not proceed in linear fashion. There were inevitable fits and starts, periods of enormous progress
and periods of significant regression. Nonetheless, the overall rise of
Christian Europe continued down to the end of the fifteenth century
and beyond. From the sixteenth century through the twentieth century, Christian Europe and its American offshoots came to dominate
ever more decisively on the world scene. Thus, the same appeal to Jews
reasserted itself during the early modern and modern centuries, resulting in the movement of Jews back westward and the resettlement of
areas from which they had earlier been banished, as the barriers to
Jewish settlement in the more westerly areas of Europe slowly dissipated.
As the inhabitants of these areas of Europe began to colonize the New
World, Jews joined in, thereby creating major new centers of Jewish life all
through the Americas. By the early twentieth century, the overwhelming
majority of world Jewry was to be found in the Christian West, in both
Europe and the Americas.

The change that allowed for this westward movement of Jews was the
loosening of the bonds that had linked church and state during the period
1000 through 1500. The Reformation began this process; new patterns of
thought that diminished the hold of traditional religion furthered this
evolution. As Europe became fragmented into a number of Christian religious blocs, the medieval drive toward religious homogeneity weakened
considerably, thereby opening the door to enhanced Jewish settlement.
When altogether new notions of separation of church and state took
hold, impediments to Jewish life grounded in the medieval church-state
nexus diminished more markedly. New notions of the equality of all
members of society removed a second of the liabilities that Jews suffered in Christian Europe during the medieval centuries. Medieval rulers
regularly enticed Jews into their domains, provided them with unique
and supportive protections, exploited their economic successes heavily
through special taxation, and in some instances expelled them as they
became less useful and more unpopular. These tendencies fell by the

wayside as the ideal of equality for all members of society took hold in the modern West, making way in practical terms for the policy of equal treatment under the law.

Jewish exhilaration over the new opportunities in an altered European environment was intense. Many Jews believed that a new epoch in the history of their people had dawned, as the liabilities associated with Jewish life in medieval western Christendom seemed to disappear.[1] Matters turned out to be considerably more complex, however. To be sure, two of the major problems Jews encountered on the medieval scene – the impact of restrictive Church policies and the arbitrary powers of the ruling class – ameliorated. Nonetheless, significant impediments remained. While aspirations for societal homogeneity deriving from the Christian vision weakened, other forms of societal uniformity emerged and fired imaginations. The ideal of a national state in which the traditional identity of Englishmen, Frenchmen, and Germans would be embodied and expressed threatened to make Jews outsiders once again. As the goal of biological uniformity was added as well, Jewish distinctiveness became all the more obvious and utterly inescapable. In addition, traditional Christian ambivalence toward Judaism and Jews, which was intensified as medieval western Christendom encountered a growing Jewish minority, allowed for a wide range of modern views toward Judaism and Jews, many of them pejorative. During the Middle Ages, some of the traditional Christian negativism toward Jews had led to the creation of inflammatory imagery of Jewish malevolence. The efforts of ecclesiastical and secular leadership to dispel this imagery were by and large ineffective. These popular anti-Jewish perceptions of Jewish enmity and harmfulness embedded themselves firmly in European folklore by the end of the Middle Ages, were widely disseminated and believed, and had a profoundly negative impact on modern Jewish life.

The issue to be investigated in this Epilogue is the impact of Jewish life in medieval Latin Christendom upon the Jews of modern Europe. The body of the book has taken issue with the broad sense that the Jewish experience in medieval western Christendom was uniformly negative, the very nadir of exilic Jewish circumstances. While by no means gainsaying

---

[1] Recall the letter of Berr Cerf Berr cited in Chapter 4.

the pernicious aspects of medieval Latin Christendom's treatment of Jews, I have insisted on countervailing positive aspects of Jewish life in medieval Christian Europe as well. The Jewish experience in medieval Europe, I have argued, was much more than a frightful sequence of uninterrupted calamities.

Parallel to the sense of utterly disastrous Jewish experience in medieval Europe is the widely shared notion that the subsequent impact of this experience has been wholly destructive. I shall likewise challenge this latter view. I shall urge that, just as the medieval Jewish experience in Christian Europe was a complex combination of the positive and the negative, so too has the impact of this medieval experience on modern Jewish life involved the beneficial and the baneful.

In the wake of a series of twentieth-century human disasters – two world wars and numerous instances of genocide – many observers have sought to discern the roots of these calamities and have focused their attention on the European Middle Ages, the period during which Europe began its rise to power in the West. We have earlier noted the efforts of R. I. Moore and Dominique Iogna-Prat to analyze the underside of twelfth-century European achievement. Moore harbors no doubt as to the relationship of the twelfth-century persecutory tendencies he has identified and the twentieth-century shortcomings of Western civiliza-tion. In Moore's view, "whether we choose to see the epoch since 1100 as one of progress or decline, to step back a little further is to see that around that time Europe *became* a persecuting society." To this he adds the following provocative observation: "Even if it had not remained one, the reasons for such a change would be worth exploring."[2] For Moore, the deleterious changes that took place in western Christendom during the twelfth century, as it was transformed in his view into a persecuting society, have plagued European and subsequently Western civilization from then until now.

For Jewish history, the twentieth century has been remarkably grim, culminating in the massive losses of the Holocaust. Here too medievalists have sought to locate the roots of the twentieth-century tragedies in the European Middle Ages. In the body of the book, we have noted the

[2] Moore, *Formation of a Persecuting Society*, 5.

analysis of medieval anti-Jewish thinking offered by Gavin I. Langmuir. Langmuir trained as a medievalist, and his research focused on medieval Europe. However, like Moore, Langmuir too was convinced that the medieval tendencies he investigated had ongoing impact on modern life. Langmuir served in the Canadian armed forces during World War II and emerged deeply moved by his awareness of and horror over the Holocaust. He was certain that irrational medieval fear and hatred of Jews laid the foundation for the modern phenomenon of antisemitism and for the Nazi program of destruction of Jews and Jewish life. For Langmuir, modern antisemitism has unmistakable roots in medieval Christian Europe and its views of Jews.

Writing of the massacres of Jews that became more prominent toward the end of the thirteenth century, Langmuir notes:

These massacres were triggered, not by a summons to crusade and the attendant accusation of deicide, but by the new irrational accusations of conspiratorial ritual crucifixion, ritual cannibalism, host desecration, and well-poisoning. . . . These massacres claimed far more victims than the ones connected with the crusades, and the Jews who were killed did not die as martyrs in defense of their Judaic faith; they were the defenseless victims of their killers' delusions. In these attacks we can see, for the first time in European history, a clear parallel to Hitler's delusions and the victims of the camps. Socially significant antisemitism first emerged in medieval Christendom, and it became evermore deeply rooted as the Middle Ages drew to an end.[3]

The Holocaust has had enormous impact on Jews and Jewish thinking. At the same time, it has also resonated sharply in the Christian world, as many Christians have raised the question of the role of traditional Christian antipathy to Judaism and Jews in the emergence of antisemitism and in the Final Solution. Sensitive and distressed Christian thinkers have asserted the destructive role of Christian thinking in general and medieval Christian thinking in particular. Thus, the general tendency toward emphasis on the harmful impact of medieval Christendom and Christianity upon the modern West has been intensified by the soul-searching of Christians in the wake of the Holocaust.[4]

[3] Gavin I. Langmuir, *History, Religion, and Antisemitism*, 305. For more on Langmuir's views, see later sections in this Epilogue.
[4] For more on this tendency, see Chapter 2.

Thus, exploration of the impact of the European Middle Ages on the modern West in general and modern Western Jewish life in particular has been very heavily skewed in negative directions, with an intense focus on the relationship of medieval Europe to Nazism and the Holocaust. In the process, the perception of the medieval Jewish experience as catastrophic has been immeasurably enhanced. Thus, in seeking to reassess the Jewish experience in medieval Europe, I have concluded that it is necessary as well to challenge the emphasis on the wholly deleterious impact of medieval western Christendom on modern Jewish life. Just as the experience itself was an amalgam of difficult circumstances, rich opportunities, and attendant Jewish creativity, so too the legacy left to the Jews of the modern West was similarly complex and multifaceted. Again, I will by no means gloss over the negative – in this case the negative influences bequeathed by the medieval European Jewish experience. Once more, however, I shall direct attention to the countervailing positive aspects of the legacy left by the Jews of medieval Europe to their modern successors.

DESTRUCTIVE AFTERMATH

In our survey of recent thinking about the European Middle Ages, we noted that earlier highly polarized views have given way – in scholarly circles at least – to a more nuanced sense that medieval western Christendom was a rapidly developing and highly creative society. In many ways, the creativity of the European Middle Ages set the stage for Western domination of the modern world. At the same time, a number of important researchers have emphasized the underside of this creativity and have projected the roots of much of the destructiveness of the modern West back into the Christian Middle Ages. This is the case – our survey suggested – for modern Western destructiveness in general and, more specifically, for the harm that the modern West has inflicted on its Jewish population.[5]

The work of R. I. Moore and Dominique Iogna-Prat has focused on the broadly harmful aspects of medieval western Christendom. Moore has argued that the twelfth century in Latin Christendom saw the onset of

[5] See Chapter 3.

persecution directed at a number of out-groups, including prominently –
but by no means exclusively – Jews. Moore attributed this new tendency
toward persecution to structural changes in the political organization
of Latin Christendom. The rise of more effective monarchies, which
involved *inter alia* the creation of a capable bureaucratic class, created –
in Moore's view – the inclination on the part of the new bureaucrats
to bolster their position by emphasizing uniformity and homogeneity,
thereby highlighting elements in society that diverged from the norm.
Moore is explicit in his sense that this destructive tendency, which he
identifies initially in the twelfth century, permeated the rest of the European Middle Ages and has adversely affected the modern West, which has
constituted in Moore's eyes the continuation of the "persecuting society"
of twelfth-century Europe.

Iogna-Prat has focused on much the same period and on the same
discriminatory tendencies, although he locates their roots in the core
religiosity of the European Middle Ages, rather than in political change.
For Iogna-Prat, during the European Middle Ages, beginning in the
eleventh and twelfth centuries, "Christianity had remodeled itself into
Christendom."[6] That is to say that the religious, political, and social
spheres had become one, leading toward a desire for cohesive and shared
identity, with careful specification of factors that separated those who
belonged from those who did not. In this view, the drive toward homogeneity lay in the overarching vision of a Christian society that was to
be internally coherent and consistent, with dissenting elements held at
arm's length or eliminated altogether.

Whatever its genesis, the search for societal uniformity so prominent
during the Middle Ages was maintained in post-medieval Europe as
well. To be sure, the medieval centerpiece of this cohesion – the Roman
Catholic Church – no longer played its previously dominant role. Accelerating religious dissent toward the end of the European Middle Ages
eventuated in the overt and successful challenges of Martin Luther and
others to the hegemony of the Roman Catholic Church. The rise of modern science and the threat to traditional religious thinking it entailed
occasioned an even more complete breakdown of the medieval synthesis. For a dissident group like the Jews, these developments were positive,

---

[6] Iogna-Prat, *Order and Exclusion*, 1.

removing many of the most onerous constraints on the medieval Jewish experience.

However, the ideal of a cohesive and unified society bequeathed by the Middle Ages did not dissipate entirely. Many modern Europeans continued to adhere to the notion of a society unified around religious vision, with the Roman Catholic Church or one of the Protestant alternatives providing the unifying vision. Alternatively, many Europeans committed themselves to a new kind of unity, grounded in national identity rather than religious vision. Englishmen, Frenchmen, and Germans committed themselves to fashioning a national society that would embody the historic identity and ideals of their people. In the process, new potential for exclusion of Jews was created.

Nineteenth-century nationalist thinkers regularly raised the issue of the Jews in their writings and were nearly unanimous in seeing Jews as at least a significant problem. For some, Jewish participation in the new national society was a possibility, contingent upon radical transformation of patterns of Jewish thinking and behavior; for others, Jewish participation was simply unthinkable. A characteristic statement of the former, more optimistic position is that of Theodore Mommsen, a liberal historian and German nationalist, writing in 1880.

The admission into a large nation has its price. The people of Hanover, Hessen, and Schleswig-Holstein are prepared to pay the price, and we all feel that they are giving up a part of themselves. But we make this sacrifice to our common fatherland. The Jews, too, will not be led by another Moses into the Promised Land; whether they sell trousers or write books, it is their duty to do away with their particularities wherever they can do so without offending their consciences. They must make up their minds and tear down all barriers between themselves and their German compatriots.[7]

The previous year, Adolf Stoecker, court chaplain and founder of the Christian Social Workers' Party, expressed a far less optimistic view.

The Jews are and remain a people within a people, a state within a state, a tribe and a foreign race. Sooner or later all immigrants disappear into the people within which they dwell. Not so the Jews. Over against the German essence, they set their unbroken Semitism, against Christianity their stubborn cult of the law or their enmity toward Christians. We cannot judge them. As long as

---

[7] Mendes-Flohr and Reinharz, *The Jew in the Modern World*, 349.

they remain Jews, they cannot change. However, we must protect ourselves from the danger by means of clear understanding.[8]

Jews throughout nineteenth-century Europe attempted to grasp at the more optimistic and encouraging nationalist view and to alter patterns of Jewish living in order to secure a place within the new nation-states. Individual Jews strove to change their behavior and thinking patterns in order to fit smoothly into their surroundings. Jewish schools and religious institutions reconfigured themselves in accord with the dictates of nineteenth-century societal life. Jews constructed their synagogues in consonance with prevailing fashion; Jewish clergymen adopted the garb and demeanor of their Christian counterparts; liturgy was rewritten in order to eliminate problematic passages; Jewish ritual was altered to conform to contemporary European norms. These efforts convinced some in the Christian majority of the Jewish potential for true citizenship; they left many others utterly unmoved. The latter group was certain that the changes were superficial only, that Jews remained a foreign element within society, and that this foreign element presented serious danger to the fragile initiative of molding a new nation-state.

As anthropological science of the nineteenth century began to focus more intensely on the biological foundations of human life, the notion of alternative human races and alternative human racial characteristics established yet another foundation for creating societal cohesion or – to put the matter more negatively – yet another foundation for distancing Jews from modern European civilization. Racial theorizing – like nationalist thinking – tended to focus heavily on the Jews as the most problematic out-group on the European scene, which is surely a destructive legacy of medieval Christian Europe. In the racial survey of European civilization composed by Houston Stewart Chamberlain, the Jews occupy a disproportionately central place, projected as the major challenge – and a potent one at that – to the racial homogeneity and thus the stability and creativity of European civilization.[9] The place of this racial thinking in the mind of Adolf Hitler and the policies of the Nazi regime needs no comment. Once more, the medieval ideal of societal uniformity – reconfigured around a new centerpiece, but with the Jews

[8] Richard S. Levy, ed., *Antisemitism in the Modern World*, 64.
[9] Houston Stewart Chamberlain, *Foundations of the Nineteenth Century*.

again projected as the obviously dissimilar internal element – constituted a destructive legacy of the Christian Middle Ages.

In the immediate wake of World War II and the Holocaust, many observers emphasized the extent to which Nazism was a deviation from Christian principles, a neo-pagan anti-Christian movement. Well-known instances of Christian ecclesiastical leaders opposed to the Nazis – often at the cost of their lives – provided dramatic evidence for this view. Slowly, this early perception has changed, and the extent to which the churches of Germany absorbed much Nazi doctrine has emerged. Already in the 1930s, with the rise of Nazism, the English scholar James Parkes had embarked on an investigation of traditional Christian views of Judaism and Jews and their deleterious impact.[10] The powerful indictments of Jules Isaac and the responses of the Roman Catholic Church in the Second Vatican Council provided important new stimulation for investigating the range of church reactions to Nazism.[11]

A number of scholars have subjected the German churches and their relationship to Nazism to careful scrutiny. These scholars have distinguished among levels of assimilation of Christian and Nazi thinking. Much attention has been accorded to the German Christian movement, which attempted to introduce radical dejudification into Church doctrine and practice, thus attempting to reform, indeed subvert established Church policy.[12] At the same time, it is clear that their more moderate opponents in the Confessing Church absorbed as well much Nazi thinking into their views of Judaism and Jews, without going to the same extremes. Since traditional Christianity was so ambiguous and ambivalent with respect to Judaism and Jews, there was ample opportunity to focus on the negative elements in traditional Church thinking and to

[10] James Parkes, *The Conflict of the Church and the Synagogue*; idem, *The Jew in the Medieval Community*; Robert Andrew Everett, *Christianity without Antisemitism*.

[11] Isaac, a highly respected historian in prewar France, lost his wife and daughter in the Holocaust. Already in 1943, he began work on a remarkable book, *Jesus et Israel*, which he completed in 1946. In it, he enunciated twenty-one propositions that identified the Christian roots of antisemitism and ultimately the Holocaust. He followed this with *Genèse de l'antisémitisme* and *L'Enseignement du mepris*. The last of the three was widely read in the English-speaking world as *The Teaching of Contempt*. On the impact of Jules Isaac on Pope John XXIII and the Second Vatican Council, see Marco Morelli, "Jules Isaac and the Origins of *Nostra Aetate*," 21–28.

[12] For valuable studies of the German Christian movement, see Doris L. Bergen, *Twisted Cross*, and Susannah Heschel, *The Aryan Jesus*.

highlight these negative elements.[13] To conflate the traditional Christian sense of the Jews as mired in physicality, incapable of rising to the level of Christian spirituality, with the racist sense of distinct races with physical, mental, and spiritual characteristics was not all that difficult and was regularly done by large numbers of German Protestants and Catholics.[14]

More dramatically, the innovative folklore about Jews that evolved during the period between 1000 and 1500 took an even heavier toll. In the First Crusade assaults of 1096, some crusaders and their burgher allies attacked Rhineland Jews as the descendants of those Jews in first-century Jerusalem who bore responsibility for the crucifixion of Jesus. Fifty years later, this perception of Jewish enmity evolved from historic malevolence into the alleged hatred of contemporary Jews for all things Christian. Jews purportedly exploited every vehicle at their disposal to bring harm on the Christian faith and Christian folk. Medieval Jews were projected as a constant and profound threat to the Christian societies that housed them.[15]

Langmuir analyzed carefully the anti-Jewish thinking that developed in Christian Europe in the twelfth century. In his view, the analysis showed the continuities between these medieval perceptions and modern antisemitism. Langmuir began his analysis by defining carefully what he believed to be the core of antisemitism.

If antisemitism is defined as chimerical beliefs or fantasies about "Jews," as irrational beliefs that attribute to all those symbolized as "Jews" menacing characteristics or conduct that no Jews have been observed to possess or engage in, then antisemitism first appeared in medieval Europe in the twelfth century.[16]

Langmuir does not mean that antisemitism previously existed and that the preexistent phenomenon made its first European appearance in the twelfth century. Rather, he means that the innovative phenomenon of

---

[13] See Chapter 7.
[14] Among major works, see Gunther Lewy, *The Catholic Church and Nazi Germany*; Uriel Tal, *Christians and Jews in German*, chapter 5; idem, *Religion, Politics, and Ideology in the Third Reich*, essay 6; Robert P. Ericksen, *Theologians under Hitler*; Robert P. Ericksen and Susannah Heschel, eds., *Betrayal: The German Churches and the Holocaust*; David I. Kertzer, *The Popes against the Jews*; Richard Steigmann-Gail, *The Holy Reich: Nazi Conceptions of Christianity*.
[15] See Chapter 8 for details.
[16] Langmuir, *History, Religion, and Antisemitism*, 297.

antisemitism – as he carefully defines it – made its worldwide debut in twelfth-century Europe.

In Langmuir's view, this new phenomenon evolved rapidly and was widely disseminated.

If by "antisemitism" we mean not only its racist manifestation but all instances in which people, because they are labeled Jews, are feared as symbols of subhumanity and hated for threatening characteristics they do not in fact possess, then antisemitism in all but name was widespread in northern Europe by 1350, when many believed that Jews were beings incapable of fully rational thought who conspired to overthrow Christendom, who committed ritual crucifixion, ritual cannibalism, and host profanation, and who caused the Black Death by poisoning wells – even though no one had observed Jews committing any of those crimes.[17]

For Langmuir, what had begun on a small scale in the middle of the twelfth century had evolved into a pan-European phenomenon within two centuries and was fated to play a central role in European fear and persecution of Jews down into the modern centuries.

A close look at some of the classics of modern antisemitism, such as Wilhelm Marr's *The Victory of Jewry over Germanness, The Protocols of the Elders of Zion,* and Adolf Hitler's *Mein Kampf,* shows absorption of many of the medieval allegations we have earlier examined. All three works and many others like them posit an ongoing struggle between Jewry and Germany, France, other nations, or Western society as a whole – a struggle that represents in many ways a continuation of what many medieval Christians saw as an ongoing battle between Judaism and Christianity. In this struggle, many modern Europeans believed that their Jewish contemporaries – like the Jews of medieval Christian Europe – utilized every weapon at their disposal. Again as in the medieval case, Jewish manipulation of the economy looms prominently among the weapons allegedly brandished by Jews. To be sure, new weapons that reflect modern circumstances appear as well. These include purported Jewish manipulation of the institutions of modern democracy and the modern media. New weaponry notwithstanding, the sense of struggle smacks strongly of the medieval sensibilities portrayed in the body of this book.

---

[17] Idem, *Toward a Definition of Antisemitism,* 301–2.

Some scholars have criticized Langmuir for purportedly sketching an inevitable progression from twelfth-century Europe to the gas chambers of the twentieth century, for in effect failing to take notice of the many changes in European civilization from the twelfth to the twentieth century. I am convinced this criticism is spurious, that in fact Langmuir was hardly as unsophisticated and mechanistic as these critics portray him. I think he understood full well the differences in European life from the medieval to the modern. Rather, I believe he was arguing for the creation in the twelfth century of a rich and persuasive folklore about Judaism and Jews, which became part of the fabric of subsequent European civilization. Not everyone in Europe subscribed to this folkloristic imagery, but many did. Under the intense pressures created by relentless change during the nineteenth and twentieth centuries, this negative folklore resurfaced in the struggle to understand and master the rapid and destabilizing processes of change. Thus, the progression from the twelfth century to the twentieth was – for Langmuir – hardly mechanical and inevitable. However, the role of the medieval folklore was – in his view – crucial and must be fully comprehended.

We have focused thus far on the majority population of medieval Europe – on the fostering of an ideal of societal cohesion, on deflection of traditional Church ambivalence with respect to Judaism and Jews in a negative direction, and on the creation and dissemination of destructive imagery of Jews by the European population during the Middle Ages – and have suggested the deleterious impact of these medieval developments on modern Jewish life. Were there baneful influences of the medieval Jewish experience on the Jews themselves? The answer is undoubtedly affirmative, although precisely what these baneful influences were is open to considerable dispute.

Perhaps the simplest negative impact to be noted is the utterly one-sided popular sense held by Jews of this experience in medieval Europe – the broad popular perception with which the body of this book has taken issue. Although Jews and sympathetic non-Jews grudgingly acknowledge the reality of occasional high moments of Jewish cultural and religious creativity, the overall emphasis is upon the negatives – the restrictions, the anti-Jewish violence, and the banishments. While I have acknowledged fully all these negatives, I have insisted on ranging in opposition to them a series of positive developments as well. The reluctance to project a more balanced portrait of medieval Jewish life in Europe may well be counted one of the unfortunate influences of the medieval Jewish experience itself.

The Jewish experience in medieval Europe certainly left modern Jews highly anxious about their circumstances and highly suspicious of their non-Jewish neighbors. Many would deem this a negative legacy of the Jewish experience in medieval western Christendom. Modern Western Jews have absorbed fully the story of recurrent mistreatment at the hands of the political authorities and the more immediately frightening outbreaks of popular violence during the European Middle Ages and as a result have developed a very high level of ongoing anxiety, even when their circumstances have seemed comfortable and placid. To be sure, others would argue strenuously that anxiety and suspicion have been warranted and that modern Jews have been well served by their fears. Indeed, these others would often argue that modern Jews have not sufficiently taken to heart the lessons of medieval Jewish life and that a lack of vigilance has been costly. This debate goes on regularly in contemporary Jewish circles and leaves the sense of a possibly negative and possibly positive internal legacy of Jewish life in medieval Europe.

Considerably less debatable is the modern Jewish absorption of the medieval Jewish stance of intellectual and moral superiority. That medieval stance was necessitated by the intense pressures exerted by medieval Christian society – both implicit and organized – toward conversion of Jews. In the face of these pressures and the realities of Christian dominance, Jews had to erect intellectual and psychological defenses, and they did so quite effectively. The most significant Jewish defense against the realities of Christian numerical, economic, and political superiority was to argue for Jewish spiritual superiority. This meant in effect reversing the standard Christian sense of Jews as biological and physical Israel and Christians as spiritual Israel. In fact – argued medieval Jews – Christians are the thoroughly physical, with their military virtues and political supremacy. Jews are to be sure physically weaker, but they are intellectually and morally far superior to their rough and ready Christian contemporaries.[18] Many modern Jews have embraced these same attitudes, in a setting where they are no longer appropriate, creating yet another negative internal legacy of Jewish life in medieval Latin Christendom.

[18] For full details, see Chapter 9.

The deleterious impact of aspects of medieval Christian Europe upon subsequent Jewish fate cannot be denied. Nonetheless, the deleterious is by no means the whole of the story. A more balanced picture is required, and to the positive elements in that more balanced picture we now proceed.

CONSTRUCTIVE LEGACIES

While much scholarly and even more popular attention has focused on the residual negative impacts of medieval western Christendom on modern Jewish life, very little attention has been paid to the positive influences of Jewish life in medieval western Christendom on Jewish experience in the modern West. The circumstances established for Jewish existence in medieval Christian Europe were extremely difficult. At the same time, difficulties notwithstanding, the Jewish population of medieval western Christendom grew steadily. By the end of our period in 1500, Jewish population in Christian Europe – miniscule in the year 1000 – was approaching parity with the heretofore dominant Jewish population of the Muslim sphere, and it subsequently outstripped the Jewish population of the Muslim world decisively. This population growth was in and of itself a positive legacy for modern Jewish life – both in terms simply of the large number of descendants of the Jews of medieval western Christendom and of the fact that these descendants were part of the dynamic Christian West. Moreover, the combination of difficult circumstances and demographic growth suggests at very least that the Jews of medieval western Christendom developed successful strategies for coping with their constricting environment. These coping mechanisms – generally insufficiently acknowledged –prepared Jews very well for their subsequent successes in the modern West.

Utilizing the analysis in Part II of this book, we shall focus on eight areas of Jewish achievement in medieval western Christendom that have benefited Jewish life in the modern West:

- demographic growth, which eventuated in the largest Jewry in the world;
- transfer of the center of gravity in Jewish population from the Islamic sphere, which was in a process of decline, to the Christian sphere, which came to dominate the West;

- readiness for residential relocation, in the service of improvement of circumstances;
- attraction to urban centers;
- capacity for economic innovation and risk-taking;
- shift toward business and finance, which made literacy and numeracy key elements in economic success;
- a well-developed communal structure that buttressed Jewish life on the corporate and individual levels;
- experience as a beleaguered minority inured to extensive pressure for abandonment of Jewish identity and equipped with the capacity to resist such pressures.

While not regularly recognized, these achievements prepared Jews well for their encounter with the opportunities and challenges of modernity.

Demographic growth. In the year 1000, the demographic center of worldwide Jewry lay in the Muslim sphere, with the Jewish population of medieval western Christendom miniscule in comparison. From 1000 to 1500, this ratio began to shift strikingly. The Jewish population of medieval Europe moved steadily toward parity with the Jewish population of the Islamic world. Subsequent to 1500, the Jews of western Christendom became the majority element in worldwide Jewry.

This steady and accelerating growth of Jewish population in medieval Europe is well known, but its implications have not been sufficiently stressed. In the body of the book, this reality has been highlighted recurrently as an indication that Jewish experience in medieval Latin Christendom cannot have been as bleak as often portrayed. Jews living with the hatred and persecution often attributed to Jewish life in medieval western Christendom either would have been destroyed by the hostility and oppression or would have at least pulled up stakes and sought greater security elsewhere. Likewise, this same reality must be acknowledged as an important and positive legacy of Jewish life in medieval Christian Europe to the Jews of the modern West. The augmented Jewish population that eventuated from the Jews of medieval Latin Christendom has immeasurably enriched modern Jewish life in the West.

Population numbers are extremely important for any human community. Larger populations provide a robust foundation for societal life and the potential for creativity in a wide spectrum of human endeavor, ranging from the basic and material through the cultural and spiritual. Thus, the demographic strength of the Jewish communities of medieval Christian Europe in and of itself constitutes a major achievement and a positive legacy for Jewish life in the modern West.[19]

Shift in the center of gravity from the Islamic to the Christian sphere. The growth of the Jewish population of medieval western Christendom resulted from a major transition in power and creativity in the West. In the year 1000, the Islamic sphere outstripped the Christian sphere in every conceivable way – population, military power, economic achievement, technological sophistication, and cultural creativity. The vitalization of Latin Christendom in the late tenth and on into the eleventh and twelfth centuries began to alter that balance, and the maturation of western Christendom in multiple ways, coupled with the decline in the Muslim world, served as the backdrop to the growth of Jewish population in western Christendom, difficulties encountered by these Jews notwithstanding.

Indeed, despite all the difficulties the Jews of medieval western Christendom encountered, they regularly chose to remain in the Christian sphere, except where there were almost no options for doing so. As barriers to Jewish life in the western areas of medieval Christian Europe multiplied toward the end of the thirteenth century and as banishments from England and France took place, these European Jews did not opt to abandon western Christendom. While we are not privy to their calculations, it seems likely that they continued to recognize the burgeoning power of Latin Christendom and chose to remain within this difficult but dynamic environment. Only at the end of the fifteenth century, when the Jews who had been expelled from Aragon, Castile, and Portugal found few refuges open to them in the southern sectors of Christian Europe, did large numbers seek haven back in the Muslim world. As the Christian sphere came to dominate increasingly the global scene, Jewish presence in this area set the stage for Jewish enjoyment of – and suffering from – the most vibrant developments of modernity.

Readiness for residential relocation. As early modern and modern Jews and non-Jews have assessed the Jewish experience in medieval Christian

---

[19] Recall Baron's early and continuing emphasis on Jewish population growth, noted in Chapter 4.

Europe, there has been heavy emphasis on forced dislocation in the form of governmental banishments. An initial wave of expulsions began toward the end of the thirteenth century and continued into the early fourteenth century. The two major banishments of this period were from England and royal France, with a number of lesser expulsions as well.[20] The second major wave of expulsions took place toward the end of the fifteenth century and on into the sixteenth century, with the major event the banishment from Aragon and Castile, again with smaller expulsions across both southern and northern Europe.[21] The deleterious impact of these expulsions was of course considerable.

At the same time, voluntary population movement was a parallel aspect of Jewish life in medieval western Christendom. While less dramatic than the forced dislocations, in fact overall more Jews moved during our period voluntarily than forcibly. The very inception of northern European Jewry – a new set of Jewish settlements destined to grow at a steady and then remarkable rate – was the result of the willingness of Mediterranean Jews during the eleventh and twelfth centuries to abandon preexistent settlement patterns and venture forth into uncharted areas. The Jews of northern Europe maintained this readiness for movement over the ensuing centuries. The Jews of northern France struck out westward into England; the Jews of the Germanic lands were prepared to move eastward into Poland and Hungary.

In addition, within all these areas Jews – facing significant economic limitations – were willing to take risks and relocate in search of economic opportunities, fanning out from larger urban enclaves into smaller towns and regularly creating new Jewish settlements. Willingness to relocate was a major feature of Jewish life in medieval Christian Europe, and the capacity to make necessary adjustments to the difficult circumstances of medieval Jewish life served these Jews well. This was an important cast of mind bequeathed by these medieval Jews to their modern descendants.

Subsequent to 1500, the descendants of the Jews of medieval western Christendom showed continued capacity to assess circumstances and to risk the challenges of relocation. During the sixteenth century, new opportunities beckoned in the under-populated areas of southern

---

[20] See Chapter 5.
[21] Ibid., and Israel, *European Jewry in the Age of Mercantilism*, chapter 1.

Poland, and Jews took advantage of these opportunities. More importantly yet, changes in central and western Europe attendant upon the Reformation opened new opportunities for Jewish settlement in areas (especially northern European areas) from which Jews had earlier been banished. Late-sixteenth- and seventeenth-century Jews were quick to seize upon these opportunities and to create new and rapidly growing Jewish enclaves all across central and western Europe.[22]

Toward the middle of the nineteenth century, dramatic new opportunities in the Western Hemisphere – especially in the United States – and the availability of relatively inexpensive oceanic transportation set in motion a vast population shift of Jews. There were, to be sure, negative developments that influenced the desire to move, but the decisive factor in this vast relocation was the perception of economic opportunity and the willingness to take the risks of moving in search of these opportunities. In both these regards, the nineteenth-century Jews were – probably unknowingly – following in the footsteps of their medieval ancestors.

The latter decades of the twentieth century and the onset of the twenty-first century have been witness to enhanced population movement that is part of the larger phenomenon of globalization. In a significant and unacknowledged manner, the Jews of medieval Christian Europe and their descendants in the modern West early on recognized the benefits of residential mobility. This has enabled the Jews of the modern West to take maximal advantage of the opportunities offered on the ever-shifting international scene. Residential relocation is risky and frightening. The Jews of medieval western Christendom and their descendants have been willing to take the risks and overcome the anxieties and have profited considerably thereby.

Capacity for economic innovation and risk-taking. Prior to their experience in medieval western Christendom, Jews involved themselves in a diversified range of economic activities. As Jews settled in the rapidly developing northern areas of medieval western Christendom, their economic options became increasingly restricted. We have noted the invitation to Speyer that projects the Jewish newcomers as traders and the subsequent twelfth- and thirteenth-century legislation that focuses on Jewish moneylenders. Jews in medieval Christian Europe seem to have

[22] Ibid.

become accustomed to economic limitations and, as a result, to have learned to evaluate the general economy and locate lacunae that they could usefully fill and from which they might handsomely profit. For much of the period between 1000 and 1500, the Jewish specialty was moneylending, which was both important to the general economy and highly unpopular.[23]

Living on the economic margins always entails elements of risk. In a general way, living on the economic margins works well in a dynamically expanding society and economy; moribund societies are inimical to such risky economic postures. Overall, medieval Christian Europe was by and large a dynamically expanding society, which was advantageous to the marginal economic activities of the Jews. At the same time, risky business entails a significant level of failure, and Jews suffered from the inevitable reality of occasional failure. Finally, living on the economic margins is almost never popular. Since the populace at large tends to fear and loathe change, those who seem to benefit from changing circumstances and especially changing economic circumstances have been almost universally despised. Such was the case for the Jews of medieval western Christendom. There, the combination of living on the economic margins, the traditional negative imagery of Jews, and a normally negative stance toward the money trade combined to create powerful anti-Jewish mythology. Nonetheless, assessing and filling economic needs was a key achievement of the Jews of medieval western Christendom and another major legacy bequeathed to their successors.

During the early modern centuries, change in political structures and the economy created new opportunities for Jews. We have just now noted significant demographic movement during this period, which was regularly related to new economic opportunities. The Jews of Poland, for example, discerned new options as estate managers for absentee Polish landlords. These options lay at the heart of the Jewish movement into the Ukraine. In central and western Europe, the more rapidly changing environment offered a multitude of new possibilities, which Jews quickly exploited. In the nineteenth and twentieth centuries, Jews were fully aware of dynamic change in the economy and were again attracted to the innovative. Generally encountering obstacles in the well-established

---

[23] See Chapter 6.

sectors of the economy, Jews gravitated to the new, the risky, and the profitable – at least for those whose guesses proved correct. Once again, this gravitation to the innovative proved regularly unpopular, encountering the hostility that is the norm for those embracing and sponsoring change.

The twentieth and twenty-first centuries have seen no diminution in economic innovation and no lessening of Jewish attraction to it. As the economies and technologies of the West have created new outlets of all kinds and economic opportunities have continued to multiply, Jews – often continuing to encounter difficulty in penetrating old and established sectors of the economy – have found plentiful openings in the new and marginal, generally with very great success. Entire new sectors of the economy have often been viewed as "dominated" by Jews. While Jews have never had the numbers to dominate new sectors of the economy, they have achieved considerable prominence in a number of new fields.[24] To a significant extent, this is a continuation of patterns created in medieval western Christendom, as Jews sought to overcome the limitations imposed upon them.

Attraction to urban centers. During the first half of the Middle Ages, Jewish population, centered in old sectors of Jewish settlement, was widely diffused. While Jews by and large abandoned agriculture and the countryside, they continued to occupy themselves in a range of economic activities and to live in the largest and smallest of urban environments. The Jews attracted northward into the newly developing sectors of Europe tended to cluster initially in the larger urban centers, where business opportunities were fullest. With the passage of time, as Jewish economic life failed to diversify, economic necessity drove Jews into smaller urban enclaves. The propensity for urban enclaves, especially larger ones, is regularly manifest among the descendants of the Jews of medieval Christian Europe.

As new opportunities emerged in sixteenth- and seventeenth-century central and western Europe, Jews attracted in that direction largely made their way to major urban centers. When the French Revolution abolished

---

[24] For a striking example of such Jewish prominence, note the entertainment field and popular culture, which are always in search of what is new. See especially Neal Gabler, *An Empire of Their Own.* Note more broadly Stephen J. Whitfield, *In Search of American Jewish Culture* and Andrew R. Heinze, *Jews and the American Soul.*

the prevailing restrictions on Jewish settlement, the rapid emergence of a large Jewish population in the capital city of Paris was striking. Indeed, Paris has remained home to the largest segment of French Jewry from then until now. Likewise, as European Jews made their way westward in massive numbers to the United States, their settlement pattern shows the same propensity toward residence in large cities, initially along the eastern seaboard. Jewish residential patterns in the United States continue to show a preference for large urban centers down to the present.

The tendency toward settlement in major urban centers has had a number of salutary effects on modern Jewish life. The obvious factor in the Jewish choice of such urban centers has been the economic opportunity they have offered, and modern Western Jews – like their ancestors in medieval Christian Europe – have benefited from these economic opportunities. Likewise, concentration in major urban areas has meant a disproportionate Jewish visibility and voice in societal issues. Jews in medieval western Christendom were disproportionately in the public eye – both for good and ill, and the same has been true for their descendants as well. Finally, major urban centers tend to be the locus for economic and cultural creativity and innovation, and once more both medieval and modern Jews have enjoyed the challenge and stimulation of this creativity and innovation.

Shift toward business, which made literacy and numeracy key elements in economic success. As the Jews of medieval Christian Europe gravitated increasingly to the business sector, the traditionally positive Jewish orientation to literacy was powerfully reinforced. Traditional Jewish religious praxis emphasizes direct engagement with authoritative and classical tests, meaning that literacy – at least for Jewish males – has regularly been a religious requirement. When business needs were joined to the basic requirements of Jewish religious faith, literacy became a yet more central feature of Jewish life. The Jewish business orientation in medieval western Christendom added numeracy to literacy. Jews involved in business and especially in the money trade had to develop quantitative skills and obviously did so.

There is considerable evidence of the ways in which medieval Jews acquired literacy, but almost no evidence for the acquisition of numeracy. When we reach the modern period, educational opportunities for Jews changed dramatically. One of the offshoots of the separation of church and state was diminution of the power of the Church over education at all levels. The new secular schooling settings opened vast new horizons for Jewish acquisition of literacy and numeracy. One of the most striking features of nineteenth- and twentieth-century Jewish life has been exploitation of these new schooling settings. The most dramatic index of this fruitful exploitation has been Jewish enrollment in the universities of both Europe and the Americas. Evidence indicates that Jews in these two areas have regularly been enrolled in universities at many times the level of the rest of the population.[25] This reflects full Jewish awareness of the importance of education for economic success. In this awareness, modern Jews have been in the forefront of what is by now universal acknowledgment of the benefits of education. These Jewish behaviors follow lines set out for modern Jews by their forebears in medieval western Christendom.

A well-developed communal structure. In the face of the challenges encountered in medieval western Christendom, a key element in successful Jewish coping with difficult circumstances was the creation of an effective communal structure. This structure provided a wide range of services to its Jewish constituents: maintaining relations with the authorities of church and state and – to the limited extent possible – with the majority populace; affording necessary internal social services for the indigent, the elderly, the ill, and the wayfaring; creating and maintaining the institutions of religious life and education required by the communities. The Jews of medieval Europe seem to have accomplished all this quite impressively. Jewish sources focus recurrently on the successes of their communal structure, often advancing these successes as arguments for the superiority of the Jewish religious faith underlying the communal system. Judaism – it was argued – emphasizes concern and care for all elements in the population and backs up the religious commitment

---

[25] On Jews in European universities, see Keith H. Pickus, *Constructing Modern Identities*, and Harriet Freidenreich, *Female, Jewish, and Educated*. For the United States, see the Pew Forum on Religion and Public Life and its recent U.S. Religious Landscape Survey. The survey findings on comparative demographics (see http://religions.pewforum.org/comparisons#) show the percentage of Americans in general who complete college at 16% and who complete graduate school at 11%. For Jews, the parallel percentages are 24% and 35%. Thus, Jewish completion of graduate school is more than three times the rate of the population at large, again indicating disproportionate Jewish utilization of the higher education system.

with community institutions that provide requisite concern and care for all.

Separation of church and state and the creation of new-style polities posed serious problems for this Jewish communal structure. No longer buttressed by the support of the non-Jewish authorities, Jewish communal agencies now had to be reconstructed on a purely voluntary basis. The question of course was whether this potentially problematic transition could be achieved. The answer is clearly in the affirmative. Modern Jews in Europe and the Americas have been successful in erecting a new and sophisticated Jewish organizational network grounded entirely in voluntarism. Jews have recognized the importance of this network to Jewish survival and have been prepared to pay the price for creation of necessary institutional frameworks. This suggests that the Jewish institutional structures established by the Jews of medieval Christian Europe provided a solid foundation for Jewish institutional life in the modern West.

Experience as a spiritually beleaguered minority. The Jews of medieval western Christendom have often been portrayed as profoundly challenged on the material plane, but utterly secure in their spiritual lives. This assessment is grounded in a traditional sense – both Jewish and Christian – of Jewish spiritual life lived out on a different plane from the rest of the world (for Jews, this is a virtue; for Christians, this is a liability). In fact, however, this assessment is inappropriate for the Jews of medieval western Christendom. Living in the midst of a militarily, economically, politically, *and* spiritually vibrant society, these Jews faced both covert and overt challenges to Jewish identity. Jews could by no means remain oblivious to the achievements of medieval Christian Europe. These achievements confronted them at every turn. Indeed, precisely these achievements convinced the Jews of the southern areas of Europe to remain in place and to transfer their allegiance to the new Christian rulers of territories heretofore ruled by Muslims. More strikingly yet, these achievements convinced adventuresome Jews to move northward into territories in which Jews had never permanently settled. Finally, these achievements persuaded Jews displaced from their homes to stay in medieval Christian Europe instead of seeking refuge elsewhere.

The covert challenge of living in a dynamic and creative majority milieu was fairly quickly supplemented by the Church's accelerating commitment to aggressive missionizing among non-Christians, with a considerable focus on proselytizing among Jews. The powerful Roman Church committed considerable resources to this missionizing effort, thus confronting Jews directly and regularly with arguments for the advantages of Christianity and the shortcomings of Judaism. These efforts on occasion bore results across medieval Christian Europe. Nonetheless, maintenance of Jewish identity was overall quite successful. In the long term, conversion out of the Jewish fold, while a reality, did not adversely affect the Jewish population of medieval western Christendom.

Jewish successes took place at many levels. Most readily identifiable are the intellectual responses. The Jews of medieval western Christendom created a rich and effective polemical literature, which defended against the Christian thrusts and aggressively attacked the Christian alternative. These intellectual responses penetrated deeply into the medieval Jewish psyche and retained their impact on modern Jews as well. We recall, for example, the extent to which much of Heinrich Graetz's thinking absorbed the defensive lines sketched out by his medieval forebears.[26]

Less readily identifiable are the emotional resources called upon and/or created by the medieval Jews in their response to the Christian challenge. While it was important to argue the superiority of life in the Jewish community and to claim that Jews treated one another with great respect and benevolence, it was even more important to build the kind of community that made such claims plausible. Jewish life – again despite all its difficulties – had to be perceived as more dignified and more spiritually elevated than life in majority Christian society. Precisely how medieval Jews achieved this can no longer be reconstructed, but it is clear that they did so. For without such convictions, Jews could not have survived the pressures they confronted. Once again, these medieval successes – in this case no longer amenable to historical reconstruction – played a role of utmost significance during the period between 1000 and 1500 and left an enduring legacy for the succeeding centuries.

As was true for Jewish communal organization, maintenance of Jewish identity required major transition from the medieval period into modernity. Enlightenment thinking profoundly challenged the God-centered view of human affairs and placed humanity firmly at the center of all

---

[26] See Chapter 4.

matters intellectual and spiritual. Medieval Jews could ultimately reassure themselves that their God was the one true God and that their revelation was the one true revelation. These claims, however, resonated far less effectively among modern Jews.

Here, the medieval Jews already pointed the way to a more humanistic alternative. While they continued to believe the truth of their God and their revelation, the exigencies of the medieval Christian assault on Jewish identity and the role of rational considerations in that assault moved the Jews of medieval Christian Europe to advance rational counterarguments. They examined closely key Christian doctrines, such as Incarnation and the Trinity, and argued that these doctrines violated the canons of reason. They scrutinized the lavishness of Church architecture, the Church's valorization of physical images, and the role of saints in Christian religious praxis and argued for the intellectual and moral superiority of more austere Jewish ritual. For the Jews of medieval Latin Christendom, Judaism was obviously the simpler and more rational faith and indeed the more ethically grounded faith as well. As modern Jews faced the challenge of maintaining their identity as a minority community in a dynamic modern environment, these medieval arguments continued to move modern Jews, as they had moved their medieval predecessors.

CONCLUDING REMARKS

Looking back at the influences exerted by the medieval experience of Jews in Christian Europe, we can discern a variety of such influences. The simplest, most direct, and most incontrovertible involve sheer physical change. The growing Jewish population of Christian Europe and the shift in the balance of world Jewish population from the Muslim sphere to Christian Europe are realities with which there can be no serious argument. These momentous changes, which took place between 1000 and 1500, did much to shape Jewish experience during the modern period. As a result of developments during the second half of the Middle Ages, large numbers of Jews were positioned to take advantage of the opportunities provided by the modern West. To be sure, these Jews were also positioned to suffer from some of the most destructive tendencies of modern Western life.

The creation of negative stereotypes about Jews and their impact on modern Jewish fate is somewhat less tangible, but likewise seems readily convincing. While these stereotypes were grounded in traditional Christian thinking and Church teaching, they increasingly assumed the status of widely acknowledged empirical truth. Thus, the Church efforts to combat these pernicious views produced limited results, since many Europeans "knew for a fact" the truth of the anti-Jewish allegations.[27] While the pressures that afflicted modern European societies differed markedly from those of the Middle Ages, the modern pressures – like the medieval pressures – bore the potential for activating imagery of Jewish malevolence and harmfulness. Faced with the horrific disaster of the Black Death in the middle of the fourteenth century, many medieval Europeans fell back upon the mythology of Jewish malevolence and power to explain their dire circumstances. Confronted with threatening and little understood innovations during the nineteenth and twentieth centuries, many modern Europeans did much the same thing, invoking long-held views about the dangers their Jewish contemporaries posed.

The kind of impact that may arouse the most suspicion is the recurrent suggestion that modern Jews absorbed from their medieval predecessors a set of attitudes and outlooks created under the difficult circumstances of medieval Europe and that continuation of these attitudes and outlooks served the Jews of modern Europe well. The notion of such continuity, extending over a number of centuries, may strike many readers as forced or illusory. Yet much recent research in both history and the social sciences has focused on precisely this notion of fundamental outlooks shared by human communities over extended periods of time.

Historians – especially in France – have for some time now focused on attitudes (*mentalités*) that have developed over long historical stretches (*la longue durée*). To be sure, defining *mentalités* has proven no easy matter, even for those historians deeply committed to their study. Following are some reflections by one of the leading figures in this field, Michel Volvelle.

Attempts have been made, over the past twenty years, to provide a definition of "mentality." Yet I know of no better definition than the one offered by Robert Mandrou when he was asked about this very point, defining it as a

[27] See Chapter 8.

history of "visions of the world." This definition is attractive and satisfies my own tastes, and yet it is undeniably vague. . . . We have progressed from a history of mentalities, which in its beginnings essentially stuck to the level of culture or of clear thought . . . to a history of attitudes, forms of behaviour and unconscious representations. This is precisely what is registered in the trends of new research – childhood, the mother, the family, love, sexuality and death.[28]

Students of mentalities have joined themselves regularly to yet another tendency especially prominent in recent French historical research, the focus on *la longue durée*, the extended time frame. Let us again cite Volvelle.

It is clear, if we pass from the history of cultures or of clear thought to the new field of history of mentalities, which deals with the domain of attitudes, behaviour and what some scholars call "the collective unconscious" (Philippe Aries), that the longest time frame is undeniably necessary. There are no struggles nor even, strictly speaking, sudden changes or events in the history of the family, of attitudes to childhood, collective sociability or death, to list almost haphazardly the new fields which have been opened.[29]

For historians of mentalities, the persistence of fundamental attitudes and behavior patterns argued in this Epilogue would make perfect sense.

Social scientists as well have come to emphasize these ingrained habits of mind. Sociologists in a wide range of fields have begun to highlight the importance of social legacies. This range of fields includes transnational studies, investigation of immigrant patterns, codes of honor, and even patterns of body care and health. In a recent popular work devoted to the factors in success on the American scene, Malcolm Gladwell has drawn heavily from the available sociological research and has argued strongly for the positive influence of a variety of legacies on members of diverse contemporary American subcommunities. Some of Gladwell's language seems strikingly close to that of the historians of mentalities, although his starting point is radically different.

The culture we belong to and the legacies passed on by our forebears shape the patterns of our achievement in ways we cannot begin to imagine. It's not enough to ask what successful people are like, in other words. It is only

[28] Michel Volvelle, *Ideologies and Mentalities*, 5.
[29] Ibid., 135.

by asking where they are *from* that we can unravel the logic behind who succeeds and who doesn't.[30]

Indeed, one of the chapters in Gladwell's book – "The Three Lessons of Joe Flom" – focuses heavily on American Jews, in a way that reflects much of the argument of this Epilogue. Characteristic are the following observations.

Jewish immigrants like the Floms and the Borgenichts and the Janklows were not like the other immigrants who came to America in the nineteenth and early twentieth centuries. The Irish and the Italians were peasants, tenant farmers from the impoverished countryside of Europe. Not so the Jews. For centuries in Europe, they had been forbidden to own land, so they had clustered in cities and towns, taking up urban trades and professions. Seventy percent of the East European Jews who came through Ellis Island had some kind of occupational skills.[31]

The argument of this Epilogue is that the circumstances and predispositions described by Gladwell much predate the nineteenth century and Jewish arrival in America. Indeed, Gladwell himself points to the legacy of many centuries of European Jewish life, during which the restrictions imposed on Jewish economic activity resulted in the mastery of urban trades and professions, a mastery that – he urges – lies at the root of much Jewish success in the new American environment.[32]

The experience of Jews in medieval western Christendom was surely difficult and projected destructive residues onto the modern West. To leave the matter at this, however, is to do a disservice to these Jews and likewise to the larger environment that hosted them. The thinkers of the Enlightenment painted medieval western Christendom in the most dismal of colors. Views have slowly moderated, however, and there is widespread recognition that simplistic evaluation of a complex medieval society is no longer appropriate. Medieval western Christendom was at

[30] Malcolm Gladwell, *Outliers: The Story of Success*, 19.
[31] Ibid., 142.
[32] Unwavering American Jewish support for liberalism and the Democratic Party, despite the dramatically improving economic circumstances of the American Jewish community that should seemingly have turned Jews in a conservative direction, has been carefully documented by social scientists and stridently decried by recent neo-conservatives. For our purposes, it serves as striking reinforcement for the historians' focus on *la longue durée*, for Gladwell's emphasis on legacy, and for the arguments of this Epilogue.

one and the same time a creative and destructive civilization; it has left a legacy to the modern world that is both extremely positive and extremely negative.

Parallel maturation in views of the Jews of medieval western Christendom has not yet taken place to the same degree. Overall, the Jewish experience in medieval Christian Europe continues to be presented from an almost wholly negative perspective, both in terms of the experience itself and in terms of its impact on Jewish life in the modern West. While much that has proven destructive and harmful on the modern Jewish scene has undoubtedly emanated from medieval Christian Europe, the positive legacies should not be overlooked. To do so is to distort the realities of medieval Christian Europe in general and – perhaps more pointedly – to obscure the creativity of its Jewish minority in particular.

Despite all its shortcomings vis-à-vis Jews and Jewish life, medieval western Christendom offered enough advantage to maintain the loyalty of its Jews, who opted regularly to remain in this difficult but dynamic environment and thus slowly build the world's largest Jewish population. These Jews developed coping mechanisms that enabled them to survive and to overcome the liabilities of their circumstances. Subsequently, many of these coping mechanisms have proven valuable and effective for their descendants on the modern scene as well. Continuing to face challenges as a minority community in a dynamic and creative majority ambiance, modern Jews have drawn upon the rich legacy of their ancestors, activating many of the coping strategies that enabled these ancestors to overcome similar and sometimes yet more difficult obstacles. Awareness and acknowledgment of these Jewish successes provide a far more balanced picture of the legacy of medieval western Christendom and its Jews to the modern West and its Jews.

Bibliography

Aberth, John. *The Black Death: The Great Mortality of 1348–1350: A Brief History with Documents.* Boston: Bedford/St. Martin's, 2005.

Agus, Irving A., ed. and trans. *Urban Civilization in Pre-Crusade Europe.* 2 vols. New York: Yeshiva University Press, 1968.

Alfonsi, Petrus. *Dialogue against the Jews.* Trans. Irven M. Resnick. Washington, D.C.: Catholic University of America Press, 2006. *The Fathers of the Church: Medieval Continuation.*

Augustine. *Concerning the City of God against the Pagans.* Trans. John O'Meara. New York: Penguin, 1972.

————. "In Answer to the Jews." Trans. Sister Marie Ligouri. In *Saint Augustine: Treatises on Marriage and Other Subjects*, 387–414. Ed. Roy J. Deferrari. Washington, D.C.: Catholic University of America Press, 1955. *The Fathers of the Church: A New Translation.*

Baer, Fritz, ed. *Die Juden im christlichen Spanien.* Rev. ed. 2 vols. Farnborough: Gregg International, 1970.

Baer, Seligman, ed. *Seder Avodat Yisrael.* Rev. ed. Jerusalem: Schocken, 1937.

Chazan, Robert, ed. and trans. *Church, State, and Jew in the Middle Ages.* New York: Behrman House, 1980.

Chamberlain, Houston Stewart. *Foundations of the Nineteenth Century.* Trans. John Lees. London: John Lane, 1913.

Diderot, Denis and Jean d'Alembert. *Encyclopédie ou dictionnaire raisonné des sciences, des arts et des métiers.* 17 vols. Div. locs.: div. pubs., 1761–65.

Dinur, Ben Zion, ed. *Yisrael ba-Golah (Israel in Diaspora).* Rev. ed. 2 vols. Tel Aviv: Dvir, 1958–72.

————, ed. *Yisrael be-Arzo (Israel in Its Land).* Tel Aviv: Dvir, 1938.

Eidelberg, Shlomo, trans. *The Jews and the Crusaders.* Madison: University of Wisconsin Press, 1977.

Eusebius. *The History of the Church.* Trans. G. A. Williamson and rev. Andrew Louth. London: Penguin Books, 1989.

Gesta Francorum et Aliorum Hierosolimitanorum. Ed. and trans. Rosalind Hill. Oxford: Clarendon Press, 1962. *Oxford Medieval Texts.*

Goldschmidt, E. D. *The Passover Haggadah: Its Sources and History* (Hebrew). Jerusalem: Mossad Bialik, 1960.

Grayzel, Solomon, ed. and trans. *The Church and the Jews in the XIIIth Century*. 2 vols. Philadelphia and New York: Dropsie College and Jewish Theological Seminary, 1933–89.

Habermann, Abraham, ed. *Sefer Gezerot Ashkenaz ve-Zarfat*. Jerusalem: Tarshish, 1945.

ha-kohen, Joseph. *Sefer Emek ha-Bakha (The Vale of Tears) with the Chronicle of the Anonymous Corrector*. Ed. Karin Almbladh. Uppsala: Acta universitatis upsaliensis, 1981.

Herman of Cologne. *Hermannus quondam Judaeus: Opusculum de conversione sua*. Ed. Gerlinde Niemeyer. Weimer: H. Bohlaus, 1963. *MGH Quellen zur Geistesgeschichte des Mittelalters*.

Horrox, Rosemary, ed. and trans. *The Black Death*. Manchester: Manchester University Press, 1994.

ibn Verga, Solomon. *Shevet Yehudah*. Ed. Azriel Shohet, Jerusalem: Mossad Bialik, 1947.

Kupfer, Ephraim. "Towards the History of the Family of R. Moses b. Yom Tov, the Notable of London" (Hebrew). *Tarbiz* 40 (1971):385–87.

Levy, Richard S., ed. *Antisemitism in the Modern World: An Anthology of Texts*. Lexington: D. C. Heath, 1991.

Mendes-Flohr, Paul and Jehuda Reinharz, eds. *The Jew in the Modern World: A Documentary History*. 2nd ed. New York: Cambridge University Press, 1995.

Rigord. *Histoire de Philippe Auguste*. Ed. Elisabeth Carpentier et al. Paris: CNRS Editions, 2006.

Saperstein, Marc, ed. and trans. *Jewish Preaching 1200–1800: An Anthology*. New Haven: Yale University Press, 1989.

Stillman, Norman A. *The Jews of Arab Lands: A History and Source Book*. Philadelphia: Jewish Publication Society, 1979.

Transactions of the Parisian Sanhedrin. Trans. M. Diogene Tama. London: Charles Taylor, 1807.

Usque, Solomon. *Consolation for the Tribulations of Israel*. Trans. Martin A. Cohen. Philadelphia: Jewish Publication Society, 1965.

William of Chartres. "De vita et miraculis sancti Ludovici." In *Recueil des historiens des Gaules et de la France*, 20:27–41. Ed. Martin Bouquet et al. 24 vols. Paris: Imprimerie nationale, 1737–1904.

SECONDARY WORKS

Abulafia, Anna Sapir. "Invectives against Christianity in the Hebrew Chronicles of the First Crusade." In *Crusade and Settlement: Papers Read at the First Conference of the Society for the Study of the Crusades and the Latin East Presented to R. C. Smail*, ed. Peter W. Edbury, 66–72. Cardiff: Cardiff University Press, 1985.

Abulafia, David. "The King and the Jews – the Jews in the Ruler's Service." In *The Jews of Europe in the Middle Ages (Tenth to Fifteenth Centuries)*, ed. Christophe Cluse, 43–54. Turnhout: Brepols, 2004.

Ashtor, Eliyahu. *The Jews of Moslem Spain*. Trans. Aaron Klein and Jenny Machlowitz Klein. 3 vols. Philadelphia: Jewish Publication Society, 1973–84.

Assis, Yom Tov. *Jewish Economy in the Medieval Crown of Aragon 1213–1327*. Leiden: E. J. Brill, 1997.

Bachrach, Bernard S. *Early Medieval Jewish Policy in Western Europe*. Minneapolis: University of Minnesota Press, 1977.

Baer, Yitzhak. *A History of the Jews in Christian Spain*. Trans. Louis Schoffman et al. 2 vols. Philadelphia: Jewish Publication Society, 1961–66.

Baldwin, John W. *The Government of Philip Augustus: Foundations of French Royal Power in the Middle Ages*. Berkeley: University of California Press, 1986.

Baron, Salo. "Medieval Nationalism and Jewish Serfdom." In *Studies and Essays in Honor of Abraham A. Neuman*, ed. Meir Ben-Horin et al., 17–48. Leiden: E. J. Brill, 1962.

————. *A Social and Religious History of the Jews*. Rev. ed. 18 vols. New York: Columbia University Press, 1952–83.

————. *The Jewish Community*. 3 vols. New York: Columbia University Press, 1937.

————. *A Social and Religious History of the Jews*. 3 vols. New York: Columbia University Press, 1937.

————. "Ghetto and Emancipation: Shall We Revise the Traditional View?" *The Menorah Journal* 14 (1928):515–26.

Baumgarten, Elisheva. *Mothers and Children: Jewish Family Life in Medieval Europe*. Princeton: Princeton University Press, 2004.

Behrend, Nora. *At the Gates of Christendom: Jews, Muslims, and "Pagans" in Medieval Hungary, c. 1100–c. 1300*. Cambridge: Cambridge University Press, 2001.

Beinart, Haim. *The Expulsion of the Jews from Spain*. Trans. Jeffrey M. Green. Oxford: Littman Library of Jewish Civilization, 2002.

Ben Sasson, Haim Hillel. *A History of the Jewish People*. Cambridge, Mass.: Harvard University Press, 1976.

Benson, Robert L. and Giles Constable, eds. *Renaissance and Renewal in the Twelfth Century*. Cambridge, Mass.: Harvard University Press, 1982.

Bergen, Doris L. *Twisted Cross: The German Christian Movement in the Third Reich*. Chapel Hill: University of North Carolina Press, 1996.

Bickerman, Elias J. "The Historical Foundations of Postbiblical Judaism." In *The Jews: Their History Culture, and Religion*, 3rd ed., 2 vols., ed. Louis Finkelstein, 70–114. Philadelphia: Jewish Publication Society, 1966.

Bisson, Thomas N. *The Crisis of the Twelfth Century: Power, Lordship and the Origins of European Government*. Princeton: Princeton University Press, 2009.

Brooke, Christopher. *Europe in the Central Middle Ages 962–1154*. Harlow: Longman, 1964. A General History of Europe.

Chazan, Robert. "'Let Not a Residue nor a Remnant Escape': Millenarian Enthusiasm in the First Crusade." *Speculum* 84 (2009):289–313.

————. *The Jews of Medieval Western Christendom*. Cambridge: Cambridge University Press, 2006.

————. *Fashioning Jewish Identity in Medieval Western Christendom*. Cambridge: Cambridge University Press, 2004.

_____. *Medieval Stereotypes and Modern Antisemitism*. Berkeley: University of California Press, 1997.

_____. *Barcelona and Beyond: The Disputation of 1263 and Its Aftermath*. Berkeley: University of California Press, 1992.

_____. *Daggers of Faith: Thirteenth Century Christian Missionizing and the Jewish Response*. Berkeley: University of California Press, 1989.

_____. *European Jewry and the First Crusade*. Berkeley: University of California Press, 1987.

_____. "Emperor Frederick I, the Third Crusade, and the Jews." *Viator*, 8 (1977):83–93.

_____. "Confrontation in the Synagogue of Narbonne: A Christian Sermon and the Jewish Response." *Harvard Theological Review*, LXVII (1974): 437–57.

_____. "Anti-Usury Efforts in Thirteenth-Century Narbonne and the Jewish Response." *Proceedings of the American Academy for Jewish Research*, 41–42 (1973–74):45–67.

_____. *Medieval Jewry in Northern France*. Baltimore: Johns Hopkins University Press, 1973.

_____. "The Blois Incident of 1171: A Study in Inter-Communal Organization." *Proceedings of the American Academy for Jewish Research* 36 (1968):13–31.

Cohen, Jeremy. *Living Letters of the Law: Ideas of the Jew in Medieval Christianity*. Berkeley: University of California Press, 1999.

Constable, Giles. *The Reformation of the Twelfth Century*. Cambridge: Cambridge University Press, 1996.

Dobson, R. B. *The Jews of York and the Massacre of 1190*. York: University of York, 1974.

Elukin, Jonathan. *Living Together, Living Apart: Rethinking Jewish-Christian Relations in the Middle Ages*. Princeton: Princeton University Press, 2007.

Emery, Richard. *The Jews of Perpignan in the Thirteenth Century*. New York: Columbia University Press, 1959.

Engel, David. "Crisis and Lachrymosity: On Salo Baron, Neobaronianism, and the Study of Modern European Jewish History." *Jewish History* 20 (2006):243–64.

Ericksen, Robert P. *Theologians under Hitler: Gerhard Kittel, Paul Althaus, and Emanuel Hirsch*. New Haven: Yale University Press, 1987.

Ericksen, Robert P. and Susannah Heschel, eds. *Betrayal: The German Churches and the Holocaust*. Minneapolis: Augsburg-Fortress Press, 1999.

Everett, Robert Andrew. *Christianity without Antisemitism: James Parkes and the Jewish-Christian Encounter*. Oxford: Pergamon Press, 1993.

Fredriksen, Paula. *Augustine and the Jews: A Christian Defense of Jews and Judaism*. New York: Doubleday, 2008.

Freidenreich, Harriet. *Female, Jewish, and Educated: The Lives of Central European University Women*. Bloomington: Indiana University Press, 2002.

Funkenstein, Amos. "Collective Memory and Historical Consciousness." *History and Memory* 1 (1989):5–26.

Gabler, Neal. *An Empire of Their Own: How the Jews Invented Hollywood*. New York: Anchor Books, 1989.

Gager, John. *Reinventing Paul*. New York: Oxford University Press, 2000.

Gladwell, Malcolm. *Outliers: The Story of Success*. New York: Little, Brown and Company, 2008.

Goitein, S. D. *A Mediterranean Society*. 6 vols. Berkeley: University of California Press, 1967–93.

Goldin, Simha. *The Ways of Jewish Martyrdom*. Trans. Yigal Levin and ed. C. Michael Copeland. Turnhout: Brepols, 2008. *Cursor Mundi*.

Graetz, Heinrich. *The Structure of Jewish History and Other Essays*. Trans. Ismar Schorsch. New York: Jewish Theological Seminary, 1975.

———. *History of the Jews*. 5 vols. Philadelphia: Jewish Publication Society of America, 1891–5.

Grenholm, Cristina and Daniel Patte, eds. *Reading Israel in Romans: Legitimacy and Plausibility of Divergent Interpretations*. Harrisburg: Trinity Press International, 2000.

Grossman, Avraham. *The Early Sages of Ashkenaz: Their Lives, Leadership, and Works (900–1096)* (Hebrew). Jerusalem: Magnes Press, 1988.

Haskins, Charles Homer. *The Renaissance of the Twelfth Century*. Cambridge, Mass.: Harvard University Press, 1927.

Haverkamp, Eva. "Martyrs in Rivalry: The 1096 Martyrs and the Thebean Legion." *Jewish History* 23 (2009):319–342.

Hay, Denys. *Europe in the Fourteenth and Fifteenth Centuries*. 2nd ed. Harlow: Longman, 1989. *A General History of Europe*.

Heinze, Andrew R. *Jews and the American Soul*. Princeton: Princeton University Press, 2004.

Heschel, Susannah. *The Aryan Jesus: Christian Theologians and the Bible in Nazi Germany*. Princeton: Princeton University Press, 2008.

Horowitz, Elliot. *Reckless Rites: Purim and the Legacy of Jewish Violence*. Princeton: Princeton University Press, 2006.

———. "The Jews and the Cross in the Middle Ages: Towards a Reappraisal." In *Philosemitism, Antisemitism and 'the Jews,'* ed. Tony Kushner and Nadia Valman, 114–31. Aldershot: Ashgate, 2004.

Iogna-Prat, Dominique. *Order and Exclusion: Cluny and Christendom Face Heresy, Judaism, and Islam, 1000–1150*. Trans. Graham Robert Edwards. Ithaca: Cornell University Press, 2002.

Isaac, Jules. *The Teaching of Contempt*. Trans. Helen Weaver. New York: Holt, Rinehart and Winston, 1964.

———. *Genèse de l'antisémitisme*. Paris: Calmann-Levy, 1956.

———. *Jesus et Israel*. Paris: Fasquelle, 1946.

Israel, Jonathan I. *European Jewry in the Age of Mercantilism 1550–1750*. 3rd ed. Oxford: Littman Library of Jewish Civilization, 1998.

Jordan, William Chester. *Europe in the High Middle Ages*. London: Penguin Books, 2002.

———. *The French Monarchy and the Jews*. Philadelphia: University of Pennsylvania Press, 1989.

Katz, Jacob. *Out of the Ghetto*. Cambridge, Mass.: Harvard University Press, 1973.

———. *Exclusiveness and Tolerance: Jewish-Gentile Relations in Medieval and Modern Times*. Oxford: Oxford University Press, 1961.

Kedar, Benjamin Z. *Crusade and Mission: European Approaches toward the Muslims.* Princeton: Princeton University Press, 1984.

Kelly, John. *The Great Mortality.* New York: HarperCollins, 2005.

Kertzer, David I. *The Popes against the Jews: The Vatican's Role in the Rise of Modern Anti-Semitism.* New York: Alfred. A. Knopf, 2001.

Kohn, Roger. *Les Juifs de la France du Nord dans la seconde moitié du XIV siècle.* Louvain: Peeters, 1988.

Langmuir, Gavin I. *History, Religion, and Antisemitism.* Berkeley: University of California Press, 1990.

———. *Toward a Definition of Antisemitism.* Berkeley: University of California Press, 1990.

———. "Thomas of Monmouth: Detector of Ritual Murder." *Speculum* 59 (1984):822–46.

———. "'Judei Nostri' and the Beginning of Capetian Legislation." *Traditio* 16 (1960): 203–69.

Lasker, Daniel J. *Jewish Philosophical Polemics against Christianity in the Middle Ages.* 2nd ed. Oxford: Littman Library of Jewish Civilization, 2007.

Levin, Chaviva. "Jewish Conversion to Christianity in Medieval Northern Europe Encountered and Imagined, 1000–1300." Unpublished doctoral dissertation. New York University, 2006.

Lewy, Gunther. *The Catholic Church and Nazi Germany.* New York: McGraw-Hill, 1964.

Marcus, Ivan G. *Rituals of Childhood: Jewish Acculturation in Medieval Europe.* New Haven: Yale University Press, 1996.

Merback, Mitchell B., ed. *Beyond the Yellow Badge: Anti-Judaism and Antisemitism in Medieval and Early Modern Visual Culture.* Leiden: Brill, 2008.

Meyerson, Mark D. *A Jewish Renaissance in Fifteenth-Century Spain.* Princeton: Princeton University Press, 2004.

———. *Jews in an Iberian Kingdom: Society, Economy, and Politics in Morvedre, 1248–1391.* Leiden: Brill, 2004.

Moore, R. I. *Formation of a Persecuting Society.* 2nd edition. Oxford: Blackwell, 2007.

Morelli, Marco. "Jules Isaac and the Origins of Nostra Aetate." In *Nostra Aetate: Origins, Promulgation, Impact on Jewish Catholic Relations,* ed. Neville Lamdan and Alberto Melloni, 21–28. Berlin: Lit Verlag, 2007.

Muller, Jorg R. "Erez gezerah – 'Land of Persecution:' Pogroms against the Jews in the regnum Teutonicum from c. 1280 to 1350." In *The Jews of Europe in the Middle Ages (Tenth to Fifteenth Centuries),* ed. Christoph Cluse, 245–60. Turnhout: Brepols, 2004.

Mundill, Robin. *England's Jewish Solution: Experiment and Expulsion, 1262–1290.* Cambridge: Cambridge University Press, 1998.

Mundy, John H. *Europe in the High Middle Ages 1150–1309.* Harlow: Longman, 1973. *A General History of Europe.*

Myers, David N. *Re-Inventing the Jewish Past: European Jewish Intellectuals and the Zionist Return to History.* New York: Oxford University Press, 1995.

Nirenberg, David. *Communities of Violence: Persecution of Minorities in the Middle Ages.* Princeton: Princeton University Press, 1996.

Parkes, James. *The Jew in the Medieval Community*. London: Soncino, 1938.

————. *The Conflict of the Church and the Synagogue*. London: Soncino, 1934.

Pickus, Keith H. *Constructing Modern Identities: Jewish University Students in German 1815–1914*. Detroit: Wayne State University Press, 1999.

Richardson, H. G. *The English Jewry under Angevin Kings*. London: Methuen, 1960.

Riley-Smith, Jonathan. *The Crusades, Christianity, and Islam*. New York: Columbia University Press, 2008.

Roth, Cecil. *A History of the Jews in England*. 3rd ed. Oxford: Oxford University Press, 1964.

Rubin, Miri. *Gentile Tales: The Narrative Assault on Late Medieval Jews*. New Haven: Yale University Press, 1999.

Schafer, Peter. *Jesus in the Talmud*. Princeton: Princeton University Press, 2007.

Schmitt, Jean-Claude. *La Conversion d'Hermann le Juif: Autobiographie, histoire et fiction*. Paris: Edition du Seuil, 2003.

Scholem, Gershom G. *Sabbatai Sevi, the Mystical Messiah, 1626–1676*. Princeton: Princeton University Press, 1973.

Schur, Yechiel Y. *Care for the Dead in Medieval Ashkenaz*. Unpublished doctoral dissertation. New York University, 2008.

Shatzmiller, Joseph. *Shylock Reconsidered: Jews, Moneylending, and Medieval Society*. Berkeley: University of California Press, 1990.

Shepkaru, Shmuel. *Jewish Martyrs in the Pagan and Christian Worlds*. New York: Cambridge University Press, 2005.

Sorkin, David. *The Transformation of German Jewry, 1780–1840*. New York: Oxford University Press, 1987.

Southern, R. W. *The Making of the Middle Ages*. New Haven: Yale University Press, 1953.

Stacey, Robert C. "The Conversion of Jews to Christianity in Thirteenth-Century England." *Speculum* 67 (1992):263–83.

————. *Politics, Policy, and Finance under Henry III: 1216–1245*. Oxford: Oxford University Press, 1987.

Steigmann-Gail, Richard. *The Holy Reich: Nazi Conceptions of Christianity, 1919–1945*. Cambridge: Cambridge University Press, 2003.

Stendahl, Krister. *Final Account: Paul's Letter to the Romans*. Cambridge: University Lutheran Press, 1993.

Tal, Uriel. *Religion, Politics, and Ideology in the Third Reich: Selected Essays*. London: Routledge, 2004.

————. *Christians and Jews in Germany: Religion, Politics, and Ideology in the Second Reich, 1870–1914*. Ithaca: Cornell University Press, 1975.

Toch, Michael. "Economic Activities of German Jews in the Middle Ages." In *Wirtschaftsgeschichte der mittelalterlichen Juden*, ed. Michael Toch, 181–210. Munich: R. Oldenbourg Verlag, 2008.

————, ed. *Wirtschaftsgeschichte der mittelalterlichen Juden*. Munich: R. Oldenbourg Verlag, 2008.

————. "The Formation of a Diaspora: The Settlement of Jews in the Medieval German Reich." *Aschkenaz* 7 (1997):55–78.

Todeschini, Giacomo. "Christian Perceptions of Jewish Economic Activity in the Middle Ages." In *Wirtschaftsgeschichte der mittelalterlichen Juden,* ed. Michael Toch, 1–16. Munich: R. Oldenbourg Verlag, 2008.

Tolan, John. *Petrus Alfonsi and His Medieval Readers.* Gainesville: University of Florida Press, 1993.

Volvelle, Michel. *Ideologies and Mentalities.* Trans. Eamon O'Flaherty. Chicago: University of Chicago Press, 1990.

Weinryb, Bernard D. *The Jews of Poland: A Social and Economic History of the Jewish Community in Poland from 1100 to 1800.* Philadelphia: Jewish Publication Society, 1973.

Whitfield, Stephen J. *In Search of American Jewish Culture.* Hanover: Brandeis University Press, 1999.

Wills, Garry. *What Paul Meant.* New York: Penguin Books, 2006.

Wolfson, Elliot R. *Venturing Beyond: Law & Morality in Kabbalistic Mysticism.* Oxford: Oxford University Press, 2006.

Yerushalmi, Yosef Hayim. "A Jewish Classic in the Portuguese Language." In *Consolação às tribulações de Israel,* 1:15–123. 2 vols. Lisbon: Fundacao Calouste Gulbenkian, 1989.

——. *Zakhor: Jewish History and Jewish Memory.* Seattle: University of Washington Press, 1982.

Yuval, Israel J. *Two Nations in Your Womb: Perceptions of Jews and Christians in Late Antiquity and the Middle Ages.* Trans. Barbara Harshav and Jonathan Chipman. Berkeley: University of California Press, 2006.

Ziegler, Philip. *The Black Death.* London: William Collins, 1969.

Index